CONSUMED BY WAR

CONSUMED BY WAR

European Conflict in the 20th Century

Richard C. Hall

THE UNIVERSITY PRESS OF KENTUCKY

Scholarly publisher for the Commonwealth,
serving Bellarmine University, Berea College, Centre
College of Kentucky, Eastern Kentucky University,
The Filson Historical Society, Georgetown College,
Kentucky Historical Society, Kentucky State University,
Morehead State University, Murray State University,
Northern Kentucky University, Transylvania University,
University of Kentucky, University of Louisville,
and Western Kentucky University.
All rights reserved.

Editorial and Sales Offices: The University Press of Kentucky
663 South Limestone Street, Lexington, Kentucky 40508-4008
www.kentuckypress.com

14 13 12 11 10   5 4 3 2 1

Maps by Dick Gilbreath

Library of Congress Cataloging-in-Publication Data

Hall, Richard C. (Richard Cooper), 1950–
    Consumed by war : European conflict in the 20th century / Richard C.
Hall.
        p.   cm.
    Includes bibliographical references and index.
    ISBN 978-0-8131-2558-9 (hardcover : alk. paper)
    1. Europe—History, Military—20th century. 2. War—History—20th
century 3. Politics and war—Europe—History—20th century. I. Title.
    D431.H35 2010
    355.02094'0904—dc22
                                            2009031485

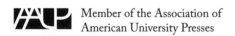 Member of the Association of
American University Presses

For Audrey

CONTENTS

MAPS

ACKNOWLEDGMENTS

This work has its origins in the graduate courses offered by Carole Rogel and Williamson Murray at Ohio State University. It developed over the next twenty years as I offered versions of this material in courses I taught at the University of Nebraska–Lincoln and at Minnesota State University. At these great institutions I was able to explore some of the ideas expressed herein in the classroom. I also benefited from the critiques of colleagues such as Erwin Griesehaber and Paul and Loretta Burns. At Georgia Southwestern I received a reduction in my course load through the efforts of David Garrison, allowing me to work on this study. The manuscript benefited from the criticism of a number of reviewers. The comments of Malcolm Muir were especially helpful. Finally, the patience and support of my wife, Audrey, are the firm foundation for all my endeavors.

Chapter 1

BALKAN WARS, 1878–1914

The Great Powers system dominated European politics since at least the Treaty of Westphalia in 1648. The most politically and militarily powerful countries of Europe maintained a loose mandate to regulate international affairs. This regulation usually depended on the upholding of a balance of power among the major countries so that no one country or coalition became overwhelmingly dominant in Europe. During the nineteenth century these powers included Austria, France, Great Britain, Prussia, and Russia. In 1861 a newly united Italy joined them. In 1866 the Austrians and Prussians fought over which of them would unify Germany. Five years later, after the German states fought a war against France, Germany united around an industrialized Prussia.

The rise of German economic and political power determined Europe's parameters at the beginning of the twentieth century. The defeat of France by the German states in the Franco-German War of 1870–1871 and the subsequent unification of Germany altered the relatively loose oversight of the Great Powers in Europe. It replaced the dominant power in the west with one in middle of the continent. Chancellor Otto von Bismarck (1815–1898) sought to maintain the new German Reich's hegemony through the establishment of an alliance system.

France was hostile to a united Germany because of the loss of its paramount position in Europe. Also, over Bismarck's objections, the German emperor, Kaiser Wilhelm I (1797–1888), and the German military demanded the annexation of the two eastern French provinces of Alsace and Lorraine. To preserve German power, Bismarck attempted to create an alliance with Austria-Hungary and Russia. Both of these large, conservative empires shared Bismarck's conservative perspectives, and both were willing to accept German leadership in European affairs. Great Britain, safe on its island guarded by the Royal Navy, secure in its industrial economy, and maintaining a global empire, did not seek continental commitments.

Nevertheless, Bismarck failed to establish a firm conservative eastern European alliance system for Germany. Events in southeastern Europe provoked disagreements between Austria and Russia. That area, called the Balkans (after the Turkish word for the central Bulgarian mountain range), became a zone of conflict in the late nineteenth century. The importation of a European nationalist ethos into the European provinces of the Ottoman Empire aroused a strong desire among the peoples living there to emulate their western European neighbors. They perceived that with the attainment of nationalist states, the means of economic and political development would follow.

In 1876 nationalist uprisings in the Ottoman province of Bosnia-Hercegovina incited Montenegrin and Serbian intervention and Russian interest. The Montenegrins wanted to annex neighboring Hercegovina, while the Serbs sought to unite with Bosnia. Russian volunteers went to Serbia to fight against the Ottomans but achieved little success, and Serbia had to acknowledge defeat in 1877. In 1878 the Bulgarians also rose up against Ottoman rule, and overt Russian intervention in the Bulgarian revolt resulted in the Russo-Turkish War. The Treaty of San Stefano of 3 March 1878 established a large Bulgaria, which Austria-Hungary and Great Britain opposed. Bismarck brokered a settlement at Berlin that stabilized the Balkans temporarily. In July 1878 the Congress of Berlin divided the large Russian-sponsored Bulgaria into three parts: the principality of Bulgaria, nominally subject to the Ottoman Empire; the autonomous Ottoman province of Eastern Rumelia; and Macedonia, restored to direct Ottoman rule.

Seven years later, in 1885, a new Balkan crisis occurred when the Bulgarian principality annexed Eastern Rumelia against the wishes of its Russian patron. In response to the growth of neighboring Bulgaria, Serbia invaded it. Austria then intervened to save its Serbian clients when a Bulgarian counterattack threatened to overrun Serbia. This turn of events, in which both Austria and Russia were thwarted in their Balkan policies, caused another breakdown in relations between them. Once again a diplomatic arrangement among the three eastern emperors collapsed.

Even before this second Austro-Russian disagreement over the Balkans, Bismarck had sought a more stable alliance arrangement to preserve German supremacy in Europe. In 1882 he organized the Triple Alliance consisting of Germany, Austria-Hungary, and Italy. The next year this alliance, through the efforts of Austria-Hungary, added a relationship with Romania. Bismarck had chosen Austria over Russia to prevent the Habsburgs from reviving the idea of a Greater Germany based on the unification of Austria and Germany under their control.

Two years after the Bulgarian crisis of 1885, Bismarck concluded the Reinsurance Treaty with Russia to prevent issues in the Balkans from becoming a further source of tension among the Great Powers. This agreement promised benevolent neutrality if Germany or Russia went to war with a third power, unless either of them initiated a war against Austria or France. It also recognized Russia's special interests in the Balkans, especially in Bulgaria. Bismarck intended this arrangement to prevent a problem in the Balkans from leading to war among the Great Powers. It was also meant to prevent a Franco-Russian alliance. This treaty effectively checked the Austro-Russian rivalry over the Balkans. Unfortunately, it lasted only three years. Before the Reinsurance Treaty could be renewed, the new German kaiser, Wilhelm II (1859–1941), forced Bismarck to retire in 1890. His successors as chancellor declined to renew the Reinsurance Treaty.[1]

The Russians made some efforts to restore the arrangement with Germany. When this proved impossible, they recognized their vulnerability in Balkan issues and turned to France. In 1894 republican France and tsarist Russia concluded an entente, making them allies. Germany now had potential enemies on both its western and eastern frontiers.

The formation of a second Great Powers alliance left Great Britain as the only unattached Great Power. In 1898 the British and Germans undertook preliminary talks about an arrangement, without result. After that, British and German relations cooled largely due to the construction of a German navy. The British perceived the development of German naval power as a threat to their security. To gain access to the high seas, any German warship would have to pass the British coast, either through the English Channel to the south or around Scotland to the north.

In 1904 the British took two steps to counter the perceived threat of a German navy. They began construction of a technically superior class

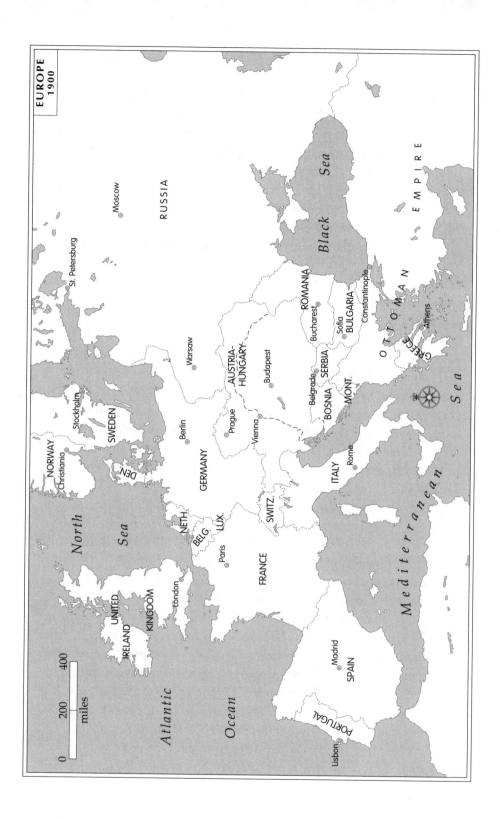

EUROPE
1900

RUSSIA

Moscow

St. Petersburg

NORWAY
SWEDEN
Christiania
Stockholm

DEN.

North Sea

Atlantic Ocean

UNITED KINGDOM
IRELAND
London

NETH.
BELG.
LUX.

Paris

FRANCE

GERMANY
Berlin
Warsaw

Prague
AUSTRIA-HUNGARY
Vienna
Budapest

SWITZ.

ITALY
Rome

SPAIN
Madrid

PORTUGAL
Lisbon

Mediterranean Sea

Black Sea

ROMANIA
Bucharest

SERBIA
Belgrade
BOSNIA
MONT.
BULGARIA
Sofia

Constantinople

OTTOMAN EMPIRE

GREECE
Athens

miles
0 200 400

of warships, the *Dreadnought* battleships. With ten twelve-inch guns and turbine engines, these ships were more powerful and swifter than any other battleship afloat. About the same time, the British also reached a diplomatic arrangement with France. This agreement did not yet extend to Russia. Only in 1907, after the British had overcome difficulties with Russia arising from the Russo-Japanese War and disputes over Persia, Afghanistan, and Tibet, did the Triple Entente consisting of Britain, France, and Russia coalesce.[2] For the first time since the Congress of Vienna in 1815, the Great Powers of Europe had divided into two alliance systems.

These systems were by no means absolute. In 1905 Kaiser Wilhelm II lured his cousin, Tsar Nicholas II (1868–1918), into an arrangement after a meeting between the two at the Finnish port of Björkö. This treaty was essentially a defensive alliance between Germany and Russia, and it would have corrected Wilhelm's mistake in allowing the Reinsurance Treaty to lapse. After the tsar's return to St. Petersburg, however, his ministers persuaded Nicholas that any such understanding with Germany was inconsistent with Russia's obligations to France. A subsequent agreement demonstrated the flexibility of the Great Powers arrangements. In 1909, with the Racconigi agreement, Italy and Russia came to an understanding about Balkan issues, the straits question, and Italian interests in North Africa. This accord cut directly across alliance lines and demonstrated that Italy and Russia had no major divisive issues.

Despite the seething resentments between France and Germany, the naval rivalry between Britain and Germany, and the various colonial disputes as the Great Powers attempted to impose European control over the globe, no general war broke out necessitating the activation of alliance obligations. The Great Powers always managed to settle such disputes among themselves. Prior to their entente, the British and French resolved their dispute over the control of Sudan resulting from the Fashoda incident in 1896. In the first Moroccan crisis in 1905–1906 and again in the second Moroccan crisis in 1911, they managed to resolve disputes arising from control of Morocco and other African territories without recourse to armed hostilities. In 1907, prior to their entente, the British and Russians settled issues arising from areas of influence and control of Persia, Afghanistan, and Tibet. As late as the summer of 1914, the British and Germans were close to reaching an agreement to divide the African colonies of Portugal if the Lisbon government wanted to sell them or demonstrated an inability to manage them. Only the outbreak of war prevented the signing of this Anglo-German colonial agreement.

Great Powers oversight was not always possible in the case of European and especially Balkan problems. The situation there was too complex to be completely contained within the Great Powers system. Essentially, there were three dimensions to the Balkan problem. The first was the question of the Ottoman Empire. Although a Great Power itself until the end of the seventeenth century, the Ottoman Empire had seriously declined since that time. The Ottomans had failed to maintain economic, military, and political pace with the rest of Europe. As a result, relative Ottoman power declined, and the Ottomans' control of their southeastern European possessions weakened.

The resulting power vacuum attracted the attention of the other Great Powers, leading to the second problem. In particular, Austria and Russia sought to realize imperialistic goals at the expense of the fading power of the Ottoman Empire. The Austrians had vague ambitions of extending their rule into the western part of the Balkan Peninsula, perhaps even as far as the Aegean port of Salonika. The Habsburg Empire had struggled to accommodate the nationalist demands of at least eleven distinct groups—Croats, Czechs, Germans, Hungarians, Italians, Poles, Romanians, Serbs, Slovenes, Slovaks, and Ukrainians—within its frontiers. The *Ausgleich* (Compromise) of 1867, coming in the aftermath of defeat in the Austro-Prussian War of 1866, bestowed wide political authority on the Hungarian elite and transformed the Habsburg Empire into Austria-Hungary. This arrangement satisfied only the Hungarians. With the possibility of domination in Italy and Germany gone after 1866, the dual monarchy sought to distract the nationalities and eliminate the appeal of nationalism growing outside its frontiers (especially south Slavic nationalism) by advancing into the Balkans.

The Russians had a more specific agenda in southeastern Europe. They posed as the champion of the Orthodox peoples there, which included the Bulgarians, Greeks, Montenegrins, Romanians, and Serbs. Among these peoples the Russians sought to emphasize their cultural and in some cases linguistic affinities. The Russians also sought to control the strategic straits region between the Black Sea and the Aegean Sea. All Russian ports on the Baltic Sea and the Barents Sea froze over in winter, and Vladivostok on the western Pacific was too remote to be useful. Only through the Black

Sea and its choke point at Constantinople could the Russians maintain year-round maritime commerce. Control of Constantinople would also give the Russians possession of the ancient Byzantine capital, thus reinforcing Russia's attempt to lead the Orthodox peoples of Europe.

A third issue complicating the situation in the Balkans was the strong nationalist inclinations of the mainly Orthodox peoples living there. At the beginning of the nineteenth century, only the Montenegrins on their remote Black Mountain enjoyed any kind of political autonomy. First the Serbs and then the Greeks succeeded in establishing national states, but without the geographic expectations their nationalist ideologies demanded. By 1859 a Romanian state emerged. The success of Italian unification in 1861 and German unification ten years later greatly increased the hopes of eastern European peoples that they too could achieve national liberation and unification and replicate Germany's economic and political achievements. After the Russo-Turkish War and the Congress of Berlin in 1878, an autonomous Bulgaria appeared. None of these Balkan states was satisfied with its geopolitical situation. All sought expansion at the expense of their neighbors.

The crux of Bulgarian, Greek, Ottoman, and Serbian rivalry at the beginning of the twentieth century was the ethnically mixed Ottoman province of Macedonia. Armed bands of Albanians, Bulgarians, Greeks, Serbs, and Turks roamed Macedonia and neighboring Kosovo, fighting against the Ottoman authorities and against one another. This chaotic situation established a precedent for the kind of complex all-against-all fighting that would occur in Russia during the civil war of 1918–1921, eastern Poland, and western Ukraine, and especially in Yugoslavia during the Second World War and Bosnia in 1992–1995 during the collapse of Yugoslavia. In all these cases, most of the burdens of war in terms of lives and material would fall on the local civilian populations.

In 1903 an uprising by Bulgarian-sponsored bands in Macedonia resulted in much bloodshed. The brutal Ottoman response was a temporary setback for the Bulgarian cause in Macedonia. The Mürzteg agreement between Austria-Hungary and Russia limited the consequences of the Macedonian uprising to Macedonia. With Hungarian issues distracting the dual monarchy and the growing dispute with Japan concerning Russia, neither Great Power wanted to become involved in a conflict in southeastern Europe.

The Great Powers had limited success in maintaining clients in the region. An 1883 treaty oriented Romanian foreign policy toward Austria-Hungary. The Romanians had a Hohenzollern king, Carol I (1839–1914), and concerns about their Russian neighbors. Until 1903 the Serbs more or less enjoyed the protection of the Viennese government. That year, however, dissident Serbian army officers murdered King Alexander Obrenović (1876–1903) and his Bohemian-born Queen Draga (1861–1903). The pro-Russian Peter Karageorgević (1844–1921) replaced the murdered Alexander. Three years later Serbia became embroiled in an economic dispute with Austria-Hungary, the so-called Pig War, when the Austrians refused to allow Serbian livestock into their country for more than a year.

Since obtaining autonomy in 1878, Bulgaria wavered in and out of Russian favor. In 1902 the Bulgarians concluded a military agreement with Russia, but the presence of Austrian-born Prince Ferdinand on the Bulgarian throne continued to make relations with Russia problematic. The ruler of tiny Montenegro, Prince Nikola Petrović-Njegoš (1841–1921), accepted support from Austria, Italy, and Russia. This support did not buy loyalty, however. The Balkan countries all cultivated economic, military, and political relationships with the Great Powers, and the existence of two competitive alliance systems enabled the Balkan countries to maneuver between them. The purpose of these relationships and these maneuvers was to forward Balkan nationalist agendas.

The first major Balkan crisis of the twentieth century began in 1908. In July a group of reform-minded Ottoman officers and officials known as the Committee of Union and Progress—more popularly called the Young Turks—seized power in Constantinople and announced a program of modernization of the Ottoman Empire. They understood that only by modernizing could the empire survive the predations of its neighbors. The Young Turks' coup marked the beginning of the Long War.

The potential revival of the "sick man of Europe" caused the Austrians and Russians to act. At a conference in Buchlau, Austria, on 15 September 1908, the Austro-Hungarian foreign minister Alois Aehrenthal (1854–1912) met with the Russian foreign minister Aleksander Izvolski (1856–1919) to discuss mutual action in response to the events in Constantinople. There Izvolski agreed to accept Austro-Hungarian annexation of Bosnia-Hercegovina. The Austrians had occupied these

Ottoman provinces since 1878, managing them as a Balkan Habsburg colony. In return, Aehrenthal promised to support a revision of the straits convention that limited Russian access to the Mediterranean Sea through the Black Sea. The Russians wanted easier passage through the Ottoman-controlled straits for economic as well as strategic reasons.

Before Izvolski could secure the other Great Powers' agreement to greater Russian access through the straits, Aehrenthal announced the Austrian annexation of Bosnia-Hercegovina. As a gesture of compensation to Serbia and Montenegro, the Austrian army withdrew from the Sandjak of Novi Pazar, a narrow strip of land separating Serbia from Montenegro. The Austrian army had occupied the Sandjak in 1878 to prevent a union between the two Serbian states and to position itself to move farther into the Balkans toward Salonika. At the same time, after some coordination with Vienna, the Bulgarians declared complete independence from the Ottoman Empire, and Prince Ferdinand, the Bulgarian monarch, assumed the medieval Bulgarian title of tsar.

These actions provoked outrage in St. Petersburg and in the Serbian capital of Belgrade. The ensuing imbroglio became known as the Bosnian Crisis. The Austrians had achieved an advantage in the Balkans unmatched by the Russians. Also, Bosnia, an area of Serbian nationalist *desirada,* had come under direct Austrian rule. Germany's strong show of support for Austria and a lack of enthusiasm among the other Great Powers for an enhanced Russian presence in the eastern Mediterranean Sea forced the Russians and Serbs to back down from any consideration of the use of force in the Bosnian Crisis.[3]

Despite the success in Bosnia-Hercegovina in 1908, the Austro-Hungarian government perceived its international situation to be deteriorating in the face of growing Serbian nationalism. The Germans feared that their main ally was in danger of some kind of collapse. France entertained similar concerns about tsarist Russia, which had undergone military defeat and domestic revolution a mere three years earlier. The vulnerabilities of both Austria and Russia hinged on the Balkans.

Like the Great Powers, the Balkan peoples responded to the Young Turks' coup. The first to react were the Albanians, who had played an important role in the Ottoman Empire for a long time, providing soldiers and administrators for the Ottoman sultans. Only at the end of the nineteenth century did a small Albanian intelligentsia begin to promote the concept of an Albanian national identity. By the turn of the century this sense had grown, and many Albanians perceived the Ottomanization policies of the Young Turks as a threat to their newly realized national existence. In 1910 the Albanians rose in revolt against the Ottomans.

The Bulgarians, Greeks, Montenegrins, and Serbs also reacted against the Young Turks. They sought a means of coordinated action before a strengthened Ottoman Empire could obstruct the achievement of their nationalist agendas. Up until the time of the Bosnian Crisis, the greatest obstacle to any united Balkan action against the Ottomans had been conflicting Bulgarian, Greek, and Serbian claims to the Ottoman province of Macedonia. After their setback in the Bosnian Crisis, the Russians attempted to restore their position in the Balkans by encouraging the formation of an anti-Austrian arrangement between Bulgaria and Serbia. To facilitate the formation of this Balkan alliance, the Russian tsar agreed to guarantee a solution to the Macedonian question if and when it came into play. Based on the assurances of the Russians, the Sofia and Belgrade governments formed a Balkan League in March 1912. That summer both Bulgaria and Serbia made individual arrangements with Greece and Montenegro. This Balkan alliance hastened to act against the Ottoman Empire while it was still embroiled in a war against Italy in North Africa. The Balkan League, encouraged by Russia to serve as a bulwark against further Austro-Hungarian expansion into the Balkans, instead turned completely around to confront the Ottoman Empire.

King Nikola of Montenegro, who had assumed the title *king* in 1910 in emulation of Tsar Ferdinand of Bulgaria, initiated the First Balkan War on 8 October 1912. Before the other allies could join in, the Ottomans declared war on the Balkan alliance on 17 October. The Ottomans were confident that their army, recently upgraded with the help of German advisers, would quickly prevail against their Balkan adversaries.

The main theater of the ensuing conflict was Thrace, owing to the fact that the bulk of the Ottoman army in Europe was positioned in front of its capital at Constantinople. While one Bulgarian army blocked and besieged the major Ottoman fortress at Adrianople (Edirne), two others achieved major victories against the Ottomans at Kirk Kilisse and Buni Hisar/Lule Burgas. The battle of Buni Hisar/Lule Burgas ranged across central Thrace. In terms of the number of participants and casualties, this

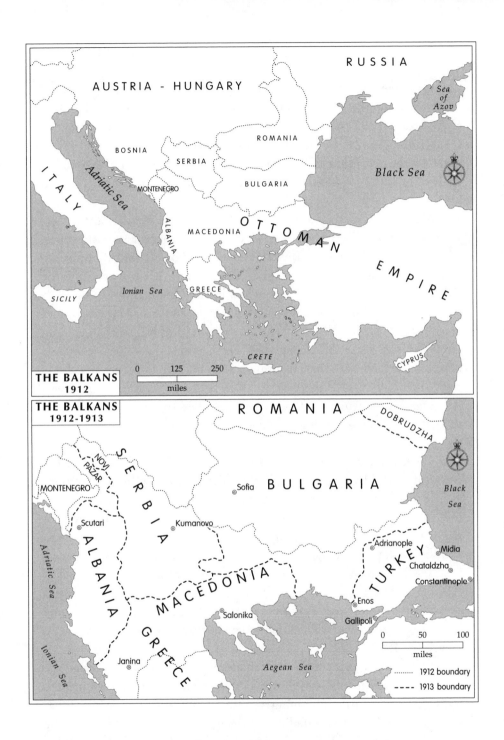

THE BALKANS
1912

RUSSIA

AUSTRIA - HUNGARY

BOSNIA

SERBIA

ROMANIA

MONTENEGRO

BULGARIA

ALBANIA

MACEDONIA

Adriatic Sea

ITALY

O T T O M A N

E M P I R E

Black Sea

Sea
of
Azov

SICILY

Ionian Sea

GREECE

CRETE

CYPRUS

0   125   250

miles

THE BALKANS
1912-1913

ROMANIA

DOBRUDZHA

NOVI
PAZAR

SERBIA

BULGARIA

Sofia

Black
Sea

MONTENEGRO

Scutari

Kumanovo

ALBANIA

Adriatic Sea

MACEDONIA

Adrianople

Midia

Chataldzha

TURKEY

Constantinople

Salonika

Enos

Janina

GREECE

Gallipoli

Ionian Sea

Aegean Sea

0   50   100

miles

.... 1912 boundary

- - - - 1913 boundary

was the largest battle in Europe between the Franco-German War of 1870–1871 and the First World War. The defeated Ottomans fell back to Chataldzha, their last line of defense, about twenty-five miles in front of Constantinople. The Bulgarians slowly pursued them. The attack undertaken by the exhausted and epidemic-ridden Bulgarians on 17 November against the Ottoman positions at Chataldzha failed, and both sides settled into a period of trench warfare.

Meanwhile, in the western part of the Balkan Peninsula, the Serbian army broke the western Ottoman army at Kumanovo in northern Macedonia on 23 October. The Serbs then advanced against diminishing Ottoman resistance into Macedonia, Kosovo, and Albania, reaching the Adriatic coast in December. In the south, the Greek army advanced in two directions. One column moved through southern Macedonia and entered Salonika on 8 November, one day ahead of a Bulgarian column moving south toward the same goal. Farther west, another Greek force besieged the town of Janina (Ioannina). Montenegrin forces advanced into the Sandjak of Novi Pazar and attacked Scutari (Shkodër) in northern Albania. All the while the Greek navy patrolled the Aegean in a largely successful attempt to prevent the Ottomans from transferring troops from Anatolia to Europe as reinforcements.

The Ottomans signed an armistice with Bulgaria, Montenegro, and Serbia at Chataldzha on 3 December. However, Greek military operations against the Ottoman Empire continued, unaffected by the armistice. At the time of the armistice, Ottoman Europe was limited to the three besieged towns of Adrianople, Janina, and Scutari; the Gallipoli Peninsula; and the small part of eastern Thrace behind the Chataldzha lines.

The Balkan Wars also produced a new European nation. Parts of Albania had been in revolt against the Ottomans since 1910. As a result of the Ottoman collapse, a group of Albanian notables, with Austrian and Italian support, declared Albanian independence at Valona (Vlorë) on 28 November 1912.

The rapid victories of the Balkan alliance surprised and alarmed the Great Powers. The Austro-Hungarian government was determined to prevent the Serbs from obtaining a foothold on the Adriatic. To emphasize this, the Austrians mobilized their army in December 1912, and a serious crisis ensued. While delegations from the Balkan allies attempted to negotiate a final peace with the Ottomans in London, a conference of

Great Powers ambassadors was also meeting in London to ensure that the interests of the powers would prevail in any Balkan settlement and to defuse the Albanian crisis. Led by Austria-Hungary and Italy, they recognized Albania's independence on 12 December. Somewhat later, the Serbs reluctantly acceded to the Great Powers' demand that Serbian troops evacuate northern Albania.

A coup on 23 January 1913 established a Young Turks government in Constantinople. The Young Turks had been out of power at the beginning of the Balkan War, and this new government was determined to continue the war, mainly to retain Adrianople. After the new Ottoman government denounced the armistice on 30 January, hostilities recommenced, to the detriment of the Ottomans. Janina fell to the Greeks on 6 March, and the Bulgarians took Adrianople on 26 March 1913.

The siege of Scutari, however, incurred international complications. The Austrians demanded that this largely Albanian-inhabited town become part of the new Albanian state. Because of this demand, Serbian forces aiding the Montenegrin effort withdrew. The Montenegrins persisted in the siege, however, and succeeded in taking the town on 22 April. This caused outrage among the Austrians and Italians. The Austrians threatened war if the Montenegrins did not abandon their prize, and they secured the support of the Great Powers for this enterprise. A flotilla consisting of warships from all the powers except Russia appeared off the Adriatic coast of Montenegro and forced the Montenegrins to withdraw less than two weeks later, on 5 May.[4] The Scutari crisis represented the second time in four months that the Austrians had threatened war over a Balkan issue.

Meanwhile, peace negotiations resulted in the preliminary Treaty of London, signed on 30 May 1913, between the Balkan allies and the Ottoman Empire. Under the terms of this treaty, the Ottoman Empire in Europe receded to only a narrow band of territory in eastern Thrace defined by a straight line drawn from the Aegean port of Enos to the Black Sea port of Midya. This treaty conformed to the demands of the London ambassadors' conference.

During the First Balkan War, while the Bulgarians contended with the major portion of the Ottoman army in Thrace, the Serbs occupied most of Macedonia. Austrian prohibitions prevented the Serbs from realizing their ambition to obtain an Adriatic port in northern Albania, so as compensation, the Serbs sought to strengthen their hold on Macedonia. The Greeks never agreed to any settlement with Bulgaria over Macedonia and indicated that they would retain the Macedonian areas they occupied. The Bulgarians, who had fought the Ottomans in Thrace for Macedonia, were determined to retain this area as well as acquire those parts of Macedonia promised to them by the March 1912 treaty with Serbia. Hostilities among the allies over the Macedonian question escalated throughout the spring of 1913, from exchanges of notes to actual shooting between Bulgarian and Greek troops in southern Macedonia. Russian attempts at mediation between Bulgaria and Serbia were feeble and fruitless.

On the night of 29–30 June 1913 Bulgarian soldiers began local attacks against Serbian positions in southeastern Macedonia. These attacks soon exploded into a general war. Both the Bulgarians and their erstwhile Greek and Serb allies welcomed a war to resolve their dispute over Macedonia. Greek and Serbian counterattacks soon pushed the Bulgarians back past their pre-1912 frontiers. Then, just as the Bulgarian army began to recover and stabilize the situation on the western and southwestern frontiers, Romanian and Ottoman armies invaded the country. The Romanians pursued their self-assigned role as "gendarme of the Balkans." In particular, they wanted to obtain the rich agricultural territory of southern Dobrudzha to broaden their Black Sea coast and balance Bulgarian gains elsewhere in the Balkans. The Ottomans wanted to recover Adrianople. The Bulgarian army, already heavily engaged in the west against the Greeks and Serbs, was unable to resist the Romanians and Ottomans.

Under these circumstances, with every neighboring country actively hostile, Bulgaria had to sue for peace. Under the Treaty of Bucharest, signed on 10 August, Bulgaria lost most of Macedonia to Greece and Serbia and southern Dobrudzha to Romania. The Treaty of Constantinople, signed on 30 September 1913, ended Bulgaria's brief control of Adrianople and restored Ottoman rule in eastern Thrace.

The Balkan Wars resulted in huge military casualties. The Bulgarians lost around 65,000 men, the Greeks 9,500, the Montenegrins 3,000, and the Serbs at least 36,000. The Ottomans lost as many as 125,000.[5] In addition, tens of thousands of civilians died from diseases and other causes. Deliberate atrocities occurred throughout every theater of war, especially in Kosovo. In military terms, the Balkan Wars were the precursor of the First World War. Mass mobilization, large turning movements, and trench warfare all occurred during this conflict. New weapons such as airplanes and rapid-fire artillery were utilized. Yet few lessons from the Balkan Wars enlightened the European military establishments that would soon find themselves engaged in conflict. One reason was the brief interval between the end of the Balkan Wars and the beginning of the First World War. Another reason was that the Balkan states did not welcome foreigners who wanted to observe their operations. Many of those military attachés who did examine the Balkan Wars ignored the tactical lessons that might have had import for the conduct of the First World War. Instead, they focused on issues that tended to confirm preconceived doctrines.

The Balkan Wars initiated a period of conflict in Europe that would end only in 1921. The Great Powers struggled to manage this conflict. The Serbs' ambitions in northern Albania and the Adriatic coast and the Montenegrins' in Scutari caused some tension among the Great Powers, particularly between Austria-Hungary, which supported Albania, and Russia, which supported Montenegro and Serbia. The powers themselves coped with these tensions at the London ambassadors' conference.[6] They even cooperated to eject the Montenegrins from Scutari.

One important consequence of the Balkan Wars was the alienation of Bulgaria from Russia. Up until 1913, Bulgaria had been Russia's most important connection in the Balkan region. Bulgaria's proximity to Constantinople, especially after the gains in eastern Thrace during the First Balkan War, afforded Russia a valuable position from which to pressure this vital area. The failure of Russian diplomacy to mediate the dispute over the disposition of Macedonia led to Bulgaria's catastrophic defeat in the Second Balkan War. Even as the Bulgarian catastrophe transpired, a new pro-Austrian government in Sofia headed by Vasil Radoslavov (1854–1929) followed the familial inclinations of Tsar Ferdinand and turned away from Russia and toward the Triple Alliance for redress. This left Serbia as Russia's only ally in the Balkans. When Austro-Hungarian chastisement threatened Serbia in July 1914, the Russians had to act to protect Serbia or else lose the Balkans completely.

The ambitions of the Montenegrins and Serbs in Albania greatly increased Austro-Hungarian antipathy toward these two south Slavic states. The Viennese government was determined that Serb power should not increase in the Balkans. On two separate occasions, in December 1912 and again in April 1913, the Austro-Hungarians came into conflict with the Serbs and Montenegrins over Albanian issues. Another Austro-Serbian conflict over Albania occurred in the fall of 1913. Serbian troops remained active in northern Albania after the treaties of London and Bucharest in order to confront those Albanians who opposed the Serbian occupation of Kosovo and to maintain Serbian claims to northern Albania and an outlet on the Adriatic. On 17 October 1913 the Austrians issued an ultimatum, demanding that the Serbs withdraw from northern Albania.[7] The Serbs acquiesced. For the third time in a year, the Austro-Hungarian government threatened military action against Serbia over the Albanian issue. Only the collective restraint of the Great Powers and the Serbs' apparent compliance with Austrian demands prevented the outbreak of war in the autumn of 1913. At this point, any Balkan issue could provide an excuse for an Austro-Serbian war.

The issue that eventually ignited a European war occurred not in northern Albania but in Bosnia. Just as the Great Powers could not control their putative Balkan client states, the Balkan states could not control the strong nationalist ambitions of the groups within their own countries. Fighting continued in the Balkans after the Treaty of Bucharest. Throughout 1913 and 1914 Albanians in Kosovo continued to resist the imposition of Serbian rule. The Internal Macedonian Revolutionary Organization resisted Serbian control of Macedonia. Although some factions of this organization enjoyed the support of the Sofia government, they by no means accepted its control. Bulgaria provided material aid, recruits, and sanctuary for the insurgents.

The situation was similar in Serbia. Some of the officers who had murdered King Alexander Obrenović in 1903 formed a secret society called Unity or Death in 1911. Popularly known as the Black Hand, this society advocated a program of nationalist expansion directed against the Habsburgs and Ottomans. Essentially, this organization operated outside the control of the Serbian government. Elements in the Black Hand made contact with a number of disaffected Serbian youths in Bosnia and provided them with weapons. One of these young men, Gavrilo Princep (1894–1918), had been born into a poor Serbian peasant family in Obljaj, Bosnia. Princep, together with six other young men, traveled to the Bosnian capital of Sarajevo in May 1914 with the intention of perpetrating a terrorist act during the announced visit of Grand Duke Francis Ferdinand

(1863–1914), heir to the throne of Austria-Hungary. Princep shot Francis Ferdinand and his morganatic consort Sophie Chotek (1868–1914) in Sarajevo on 28 June 1914 with a pistol bearing the marks of a Serbian military arsenal.

Austro-Hungarian authorities immediately arrested Princep and made the inference that he had acted on Serbian orders. After almost a month of dithering, they decided to engage in a punitive war against the Serbs. On 23 July the Austrians delivered an ultimatum in Belgrade, demanding extensive rights of intervention in Serbia. The Serbian government called on St. Petersburg for support, which placed the Russians in a quandary. The loss of the Russo-Japanese War in 1905 had stymied Russian expansion in Asia. When the Bulgarians turned to the Triple Alliance to redress their losses in the Balkan Wars, the Russians lost a valuable strategic ally. If Austria occupied and contained Serbia, Russia could be excluded from the Balkans altogether. The St. Petersburg government decided to support the Serbs.[8] Although they accepted many Austrian demands, the Serbs would not allow Austrian investigators into their country, and on 28 July 1914 the Austrians declared war on Serbia.

At this point, the solidarity of the Great Powers on Balkan issues collapsed. Attempts by the British foreign minister, Sir Edward Grey (1862–1933), to arrange a Great Powers conference to resolve these issues proved futile.[9] The Germans intended to uphold the Triple Alliance, and the French adhered to the Triple Entente. Failure to do so in both cases could have resulted in loss of the alliance partner and collapse of the alliance itself. The British hesitated but ultimately fulfilled their commitment to the entente. When it became apparent that war was imminent, the Italians and Romanians chose not to honor their commitment to the Triple Alliance and adopted a neutral position. Both decided to await the course of events before making any commitment.

Conflict in twentieth-century Europe began with the nationalist urges of the peoples of southeastern Europe. The Great Powers system, which had managed to limit nineteenth-century European wars in terms of duration and location, was unable to restrain the nationalist passions erupting in southeastern Europe. These conflicts among the Great Powers continued into the twentieth century. Those taking place beyond the confines of Europe—in Sudan, Morocco, Persia, and elsewhere—were managed within the context of the system. Those originating in Europe, and especially those in southeastern Europe, proved to be unmanageable. The Balkan Wars of 1912–1913 initiated a war that would sweep most of the continent within two years and last beyond 1918. In a larger sense, the conflict that began in 1912 would endure in one form or another throughout the twentieth century. That century would begin with conflict in southeastern Europe and end with conflict in southeastern Europe. The cause of these problems would be the same: uncontrolled, untoward nationalism.

Chapter 2

WESTERN FRONT

The Great Powers had anticipated the outbreak of general war in Europe for some time. They drafted their male citizens and drilled their armies year after year to be ready when war came. All the Great Powers based their military strength to some degree on their industrial prowess. None of them, however, recognized the extent to which industrial technology had altered the battlefield. Modern, mass-produced weapons, including machine guns and rapid-firing artillery, would give generals tactical abilities far beyond their strategic capacities. New weapons such as gas, flamethrowers, airplanes, and tanks would increase the horrors and casualties of combat. As yet, there was no clear idea how to best utilize these weapons.

Given the geography of the Great Powers alliance system, two arenas of combat were obvious. One was in northwestern Europe in the area between France and Germany. The Low Countries—Belgium, Luxembourg, and the Netherlands—were included in this arena because of the limited geographic possibility for maneuver in northeastern Europe. Because of its relatively small size, limited topographic variation, and well-developed transportation infrastructure, this western arena offered the better opportunity for decisive action. The other obvious arena was the much larger and much less developed eastern plain, stretching from the sandy shores of the Baltic Sea to the snow-covered heights of the Carpathian Mountains. The opportunities for decisive action here were considerably fewer.

In western Europe, all armies benefited from industrial economies, homogeneous populations, and literate recruits. The strongest European army was that of Germany, which had almost 900,000 men and was supported by an excellent system of reserves. This army could rely on the formidable German industrial and technical infrastructure. Although

Germany had been united only since 1871, its forces were homogeneous and literate. Germany also had a technologically accomplished navy whose relatively recent nascence left it unhampered by obsolete equipment.

France possessed an army of more than 900,000 men, but this number was slightly misleading. Colonial obligations thinned the ranks of the French army in Europe. The French possessed a fine artillery arm, especially with their 75mm field gun. Like the Germans, the French had a solid industrial base and a well-educated population.

Alone among the Great Powers, Great Britain did not rely on conscription to fill its army's ranks. The British had a well-trained and well-equipped professional army of around 235,000 men, but the extensive British Empire required the presence of many of these soldiers on other continents. The experience of the Boer War in South Africa in 1899–1902 had provided the British army with seasoned officers and noncommissioned officers. This was of immense importance in maintaining a professional army. Britain's main military force was not the army, however, but the Royal Navy. The Royal Navy was the largest in the world and the pride of Great Britain.

The Belgian army was small, underfunded, and hampered to a degree by the binational Flemish (Dutch) and Walloon (French) nature of the country itself. Its determined but antiquated army consisted of picturesque units of soldiers in leather hats and machine guns in dogcarts. Unlike that of the Great Powers, the Belgian strategy was defensive. It relied on a series of forts, with the major one at Liège, to provide security against an invasion from the east. In the summer of 1914 the Belgian army had 117,000 men but little modern equipment.

These armies perceived offensive action as the means to achieve victory, so all the great European armies trained for the attack. They relied on cavalry and élan to carry the day. Recent experience in the Boer War, the Russo-Japanese War, and especially the Balkan Wars, where the effects of concentrated firepower had proved devastating to attacking forces, made little impression on the main European armies. All anticipated that the campaign would be short, victorious, and glorious.

Each of the Great Powers had developed plans for the deployment of its forces in case of war. These had already caused some problems. The Russian General Staff failed to envision a war against only Austria, so when they began to array their forces, they mobilized against Germany as well. This alarmed the Germans and led to their decision to implement their own war plans.

The French planned an offensive directly into German-held Alsace and Lorraine. They planned to vent their fury against the Germans in a raging advance, anticipating that élan would impart the decisive advantage to their efforts. In 1914 they were on the seventeenth iteration of their offensive plan. Thus, this was known as Plan XVII.

As a consequence of the Franco-Russian entente of 1894, the German General Staff under the direction of General Alfred von Schlieffen (1833–1913) had to confront the tremendous problem of enemies on both the western and eastern frontiers. Concentrated, the German army could defeat either enemy, but divided, it risked defeat. Therefore, General von Schlieffen decided to deal with the enemy forces one at a time. Huge distances, illiterate soldiers, and a problematic transportation system portended a slow Russian mobilization. The German General Staff calculated that the Russians would need six weeks to move their armies into position for an attack. The Russians' poor performance in 1904 when mobilizing for the war against Japan only reinforced the Germans' perceptions. This calculation gave the Germans six weeks to attack France and destroy the French armies. They did not want to risk a direct confrontation with the French in Alsace-Lorraine, which could cause their armies to lose time. Instead, they planned to attack France in the north by wheeling around through neutral Belgium, Luxembourg, and the Maastricht appendix of the Netherlands; sweep around Paris; and press up against the rear if the French armies attacked into Alsace and Lorraine. After crushing the French against the frontier, the Germans could take advantage of the excellent German railroad system and arrive in time to meet the oncoming Russians. Helmut von Moltke (1848–1916), who succeeded von Schlieffen as chief of staff in 1905, modified this plan slightly, limiting the German sweep to Belgium and Luxembourg. The Netherlands could remain neutral and function as a commercial outlet, or breathing tube, for Germany. At the same time, von Moltke strengthened the left wing of the German attack. The Schlieffen Plan held some promise of a rapid and decisive German victory on both fronts, but it also guaranteed that Britain would enter the war. Great Britain could not tolerate the German presence in general and the German naval presence in particular immediately across the English Channel.

Upon the German declaration of war, the French implemented Plan XVII, which concentrated their army into three groups. The ensuing clashes with the Germans are often referred to as the Battle of the Frontiers. They attacked into Alsace, into Lorraine, and finally into the Ardennes region of Luxembourg and southeastern Belgium. The offensive into Alsace made little headway. The attack into Lorraine enjoyed initial success, and the French army entered Mulhouse. The French commander, General Joseph Joffre (1852–1931), maintained his focus on Lorraine, despite ominous reports of the progress of German forces into Belgium. German counterattacks in Lorraine demonstrated the effectiveness of machine-gun fire against the highly motivated advancing French infantry. On 22 August Joffre tried again by ordering a northeasterly attack into the Ardennes. It too failed. By 24 August the French offensive into Lorraine was finished. The French armies were almost back to their starting positions in France. These positions along the border with German-held Alsace-Lorraine remained static throughout the remainder of the war. The French offensive had failed. In the Battle of the Frontiers, the French army had suffered a tremendous defeat, with losses as high as 300,000. In this initial French defeat, however, was the genesis of a far more important French victory on the river Marne. The French armies' failure to maintain a sustained presence in Alsace-Lorraine providentially left them in a position to turn to meet the oncoming Germans in the north.

Upon Germany's decision for war, von Moltke implemented the Schlieffen Plan.[1] On 1 August German armies entered Luxembourg and occupied the entire country by the next day. The main elements of the German army invaded Belgium three days later, on 4 August. The British declared war on Germany that same day and prepared to send troops to the continent. The British government was not prepared to allow the German military, and especially its naval power, to establish itself across the English Channel. Belgian forces stoutly resisted the German invasion but only managed to slow it; ultimately, they could not contain it. The Germans quickly advanced to the major Belgian defensive positions around Liège. They imposed a harsh regimen on the Belgian civilian population, even executing hostages. After suffering high casualties, the Germans used heavy howitzers to reduce the fortresses around Liège. The city itself fell on 7 August, and the last fortress on 16 August. The Belgian army then retreated in a northwesterly direction toward Antwerp so as not to be cut off and pinned against the Dutch frontier by the German advance.

The Germans then proceeded with the Schlieffen Plan, turning to the south and entering French territory. The Belgian fortresses around Namur fell on 25 August. Meanwhile, on 20 August, the right wing of the German advance entered Brussels. Resolute Belgian resistance slowed the Schlieffen Plan by two or three days. The actions of the Belgian army, like those of the Bulgarian and Serbian armies during the Balkan Wars, demonstrated that the smaller European countries could field impressive and determined military forces. The Belgian resistance surprised the nervous Germans, who responded by committing atrocities against the civilian populations in eastern Belgium and northeastern France. They destroyed many buildings, including the famous library at Louvain, and executed more than 6,000 civilians they suspected of armed opposition, despite the lack of any substantial proof. These German actions prefigured similar outrages in the next war.

As the Germans advanced into France, the French armies and the British Expeditionary Force, which had arrived at the front on 22 August, fell back before them. By the end of August the Germans, weary from marching under the hot summer sun, began to slow down. As they moved farther from their command and supply bases, the Germans experienced increasing communications and logistics problems. Also, contrary to German expectations, two Russian armies invaded East Prussia. In response, on 25 August von Moltke ordered two army corps and a cavalry division from the German right wing to the east to strengthen German defenses.

The six oncoming German armies had little contact with one another. When a gap appeared between the Germans' First and Second Armies, General Alexander von Kluck (1846–1934) attempted to close it. Von Kluck, commander of the German First Army, ordered it to turn to the east, north of Paris, instead of moving around the city, as set out in the plan. He thus presented a vulnerable flank to the French defenders in Paris.

The result of these circumstances was the first great encounter in western Europe: the Battle of the Marne. On 5 September General Joffre ordered the French and the British Expeditionary Force to undertake a counterattack against the flank of the German First Army at the Marne

River north of Paris.[2] By 9 September this counterattack forced the German Second Army and then von Kluck's First Army to retreat. They fell back in good order to the Aisne River. The German advance was stopped, and Paris was saved. The Battle of the Marne was the greatest military engagement in western Europe since the nearby Battle of Waterloo ninety-nine years before. The French victory on the Marne meant the defeat of the Schlieffen Plan. The Battle of the Marne left both victor and vanquished with no clear concept of how to proceed, however. Both the German and the French operational plans had failed, and neither the French nor the German General Staff had prepared alternative strategies.

After the German retreat to the Aisne River, both sides extended their fronts in a northwesterly direction to the English Channel. In a series of engagements, the British and French on one side and the Germans on the other side tried to outflank and envelop each other in the fall of 1914. These actions became known as the "Race to the Sea." Fighting developed along the Aisne River and in Picardy. Farther east the Germans advanced near Verdun and took St. Michel.

As the battle arena extended across northern France, the Germans decided to eliminate the Belgian and British forces in Antwerp to prevent them from attacking the German left flank and also to end Antwerp's use as a port of disembarkation for British troops and supplies. The Germans brought up heavy artillery to pound the fortifications around the city. The siege began on 28 September, and the defenders had little hope of holding out for long. Antwerp fell to the Germans on 10 October, but not before most of the Belgian army as well as most of the British marines had escaped. The Belgians, under the command of King Albert, then positioned themselves in the southwestern corner of their country. After flooding the area southeast of Nieuport, they remained in position from Nieuport to Ypres, maintaining an active presence and defending their country until the end of the war.

The final action of the Race to the Sea and of the year 1914 on the western front occurred around the town of Ypres. From 13 October to 22 November, intense fighting occurred around this northwestern Belgian town as the Germans attempted to gain control of the Belgian and French channel ports and turn the entente's flank. British and French forces succeeded in holding a salient around Ypres in the face of strong German attacks. The Belgian, British, French, and German armies all sustained heavy casualties at Ypres. So high were the losses among young recruits in the newly trained German units that the Germans referred to the battles around Ypres as *kindermord,* the murder of innocents. The Ypres salient remained a focus of fighting on the western front for much of the rest of the war.

By the end of 1914 the armies on the western front had settled into opposing networks of trenches. These field fortifications extended from the English Channel near the Belgian city of Nieuport into northern France through the Champagne region, around the ancient fortress city of Verdun, along the Franco-German border in Lorraine, through the Vosges Mountains slightly into German territory in southern Alsace, to the Swiss frontier. Elaborate networks of supply, communication, and even rest and recreation trenches often extended far behind the front lines. Life for the soldiers in these positions was cold in the winter, hot in the summer, smelly, wet, and generally miserable.[3] Insects feasted on both living and dead during the summer, and rats were a constant presence. Smells emanating from putrefying corpses and from the consequences of humans living in such close quarters imposed a stultifying oppression on the front lines. The often flooded trenches located in the low-lying areas of Flanders were especially terrible for the soldiers stationed there. A no-man's-land stretching from a hundred yards to more than two miles wide separated the opposing trench lines. Various sizes of artillery and mortars located to the rear of the trenches added tremendous destructive power to the machine guns situated at close intervals in the front lines. The German positions were, from the first, more sophisticated than those of the French and British. Labyrinthine trench systems extended several miles behind the front lines. Narrow-gauge railroads delivered men and supplies to the trench systems.

The division of their army between the western and eastern fronts forced the Germans to adopt a conservative defensive strategy overall. They could not allow an enemy breakthrough on either front. The French, however, could not accept the trench positions as permanent, because that would mean they acquiesced to the presence of German invaders on French soil. Despite the failure of their offensive strategy in August 1914, the French continued to attack their enemy.

The trenches on the western front represented the failure of both sides' offensive plans in 1914. Neither possessed the tactical and technical ability to cross in force the no-man's-land between the trench networks. This was not immediately apparent, however, especially to the French. In 1915 both sides attempted to end the stalemate and achieve a decisive result with large offensives intended to smash through the trench networks and break out into the weakly held areas in the rear.

The static nature of the war on the western front limited the consequences for the Belgian and French civilian populations who lived near the battlefields.[4] Whereas the no-man's-land and the areas around the trench networks suffered total devastation, rear regions often remained untouched by fighting. In their march through Belgium and northern France, the Germans destroyed many buildings both during the fighting and as reprisal for alleged resistance, most notably the great library in the Belgian city of Louvain. Also, fearing a repeat of the situation in 1870 during the Franco-German War—when French irregulars, or franc-tireurs, had harassed German soldiers—the German army behaved harshly toward civilian populations. It acted against real and imagined opposition, taking and even shooting civilian hostages.

The extended front also limited the ability of both sides to act against the other. Neither side possessed the resources to operate along the entire length of the western front, so throughout the war, they could undertake actions only along specific lengths of the front. These actions sometimes became major battles. Supplementary attacks often took place further down the lines to divert the enemy's attention and draw off reserves and resources. In the other sections of the front, artillery and mortar barrages, sniping, and occasional raids from the other side provided horrid relief from the otherwise stultifying boredom.

Offensives continued on the western front through much of 1915. The attackers usually signaled their intentions with several days of heavy artillery bombardment of enemy positions. The French launched an offensive in Champagne on 20 December 1914. This effort lasted into March, with little result except for heavy casualties. At 94,000, French losses were twice those of the Germans.

On Christmas Eve 1914, at some locations along the western front, soldiers from both sides spontaneously declared an armistice and celebrated the holiday together, exchanging gifts and even playing soccer. Official discouragement from high-ranking officers and rising casualty rates prevented such a Christmas celebration from occurring again.

The British undertook an offensive at Neuve Chappelle in Artois in March 1915 and achieved some local successes. Based on these successes, the British commander, General Sir John French (1852–1925), hoped to send his cavalry into the German rear, where it would disrupt German command, logistics, and signals. But before the British could deploy their horsemen, the infantry attacks ran out of energy and gradually ceased. The British never succeeded in breaking through the German positions. The attempt to utilize the cavalry demonstrated the British command's inability to adjust to the new strategic and tactical situation imposed by the stalemate in the trenches.

The Germans initiated an offensive of their own on the western front at Ypres on 22 April. The resulting Second Battle of Ypres was intended to divert the entente's attention from the movement of German forces from the western front to the east to deal with the Austro-Hungarian emergency there. At Ypres the Germans employed chlorine gas for the first time on the western front.[5] They had already used it against the Russians at Bolimov near Warsaw in the east, but with little effect. The cold of the east had condensed the gas at ground level, where it remained harmless. At Ypres the gas had a great initial impact and caused heavy casualties among the French North African troops opposite the Germans. A gap of almost five miles opened in the French lines. But because of the previous lack of success against the Russians, the Germans did not anticipate the gas's effectiveness and failed to have reserves ready to exploit the gap in the French lines. By the time the Germans attempted to break through, the French had rushed reinforcements into the lines and restored their positions. After this initial German use of poison gas, both sides utilized it. Although it greatly increased the horrors of the fronts, it failed to provide a decisive advantage. It did not help the Germans, who were unable to eliminate the Ypres salient in their 1915 attacks. They did succeed, however, in maintaining their positions in the west while dealing with the Austro-Hungarian problem in the east.

In May 1915 the French tried to overrun the German lines in Artois. The attack was intended in part to take pressure off the failing Russians. Despite British support farther up the line, this French effort ended the same month it began. The entente attacks achieved only heavy British and French casualties. In September of that year they attempted again to break the German lines in Champagne and undertook yet another offensive in

Artois. Farther up the lines, the British launched supplemental attacks at Loos. The British and French hoped to take advantage of the weakened German forces on the western front. Over the summer the Germans had continued to transfer many soldiers to the east to press the Russians after the breakthrough at Gorlice-Tarnow. Following their established pattern, the French gained a few square miles of territory but sustained heavy casualties. They were unable to proceed beyond the first or second German lines of defense. All these operations ended as defensive victories for the Germans. The German defensive strategy proved successful in containing the attacks and eroding the strength of the British and French.

By the end of the year both sides on the western front were becoming weary. Neither had achieved a great victory to sustain morale at the front and inspire enthusiasm at home. Both sides had lost more than 200,000 men, with little result. Although the Germans had achieved defensive successes in most of the 1915 western front battles, they could not win the war that way. They lacked the material and human resources to endure indefinitely against the entente forces, which had access to greater amounts of material and manpower.

The defeats the Germans inflicted on the Russians, beginning with the breakthrough at Gorlice-Tarnow in the summer of 1915 and the subsequent occupation of much of Congress Poland (the part of Poland assigned to Russia by the Congress of Berlin) and Lithuania, brought stability and security to the eastern front. At this point General Erich von Falkenhayn (1861–1922), who had replaced the ailing von Moltke as chief of the German General Staff in September 1914, was reluctant to advance into the endless space of defeated Russia while the western front remained active. Though susceptible to a German advance, Russia still raised the specter of a Napoleonic scenario in the German high command.

From 6 to 8 December 1915 representatives from the British, French, Italian, and Russian staffs met at General Joffre's headquarters in Chantilly, France, to formulate a common strategy against the Central Powers.[6] There the entente agreed to undertake simultaneous attacks on the western, eastern, and Italian fronts beginning in February 1916. Before they could implement this coordinated strategy, however, the Germans began their own offensive.

At the beginning of 1916 von Falkenhayn decided to utilize the German reserve to achieve a decisive result on the western front.[7] He intended to apply a new strategy to this end. Instead of launching attacks across no-man's-land to break through the trench lines and advance to the enemy's rear, von Falkenhayn wanted to erode French strength by attrition. This strategy involved sharp attacks on enemy positions, withdrawals, and counterattacks. In this way von Falkenhayn hoped to bleed the French army to death. The location he chose to implement this strategy was the salient of Verdun, where French positions protruded into the German lines. This medieval fortress city had been the location of the 843 treaty that had divided the Carolingian Empire among the grandsons of Charlemagne into France, Germany, and, between them, Lotharingia, or Lorraine. It had also served as the bastion guarding the northeastern French frontier up to modern times. Layers of forts protected the city. Von Falkenhayn knew that the French would be reluctant to withdraw from Verdun even in the face of heavy German attacks. This determination to defend the Verdun salient would enable the Germans to kill the French in their trenches.

After a delay caused by bad weather, which deprived them of the element of surprise, the Germans began attacking Verdun on 21 February 1916. Four days later the Germans easily captured one of the most important French defensive positions, Fort Douaumont. The French had failed to place an appropriate garrison in the fort. At this point, General Henri-Philippe Pétain (1856–1951) received orders to lead the French forces in Verdun, and he inspired the defenders to greater effort.[8] Nevertheless, the Germans succeeded in taking Fort Vaux, another important defensive position, on 7 June. A series of bloody attacks and counterattacks ensued. Heavy artillery bombardments were a constant factor. The Germans inflicted huge casualties on the French but sustained heavy losses themselves.

By the end of June, however, the German efforts began to wane. They were distracted by the dramatic success of the Brusilov offensive in the east—a Russian advance that threatened to bring about the collapse of the Austro-Hungarian army. At the beginning of July another distraction appeared much closer to Verdun when the new British commander, General Sir Douglas Haig (1861–1928), opened his long-anticipated offensive along the Somme River in French Flanders. After the Somme offensive began, the Germans around Verdun assumed defensive positions. The grim and bloody fighting continued through the remainder of 1916. The

French gradually pushed the Germans out of the areas they had occupied around Verdun. By 24 October the French recaptured Fort Douaumont, and on 2 November they took Fort Vaux. These French successes restored the salient of Verdun. Von Falkenhayn's plan had almost succeeded in bleeding the French army to death, however. The French sustained around 350,000 casualties. But the German losses were also very high, almost matching the French totals. Among these was von Falkenhayn himself. The heroes of the eastern front, General Paul von Hindenburg (1847–1934) and General Erich Ludendorff (1865–1937), replaced him in command of the German army. On the other side of the trenches, Joffre also became a casualty of Verdun. The French government eased him out of command in December 1916, and General Robert Nivelle (1856–1924) replaced him. Even though the French army had held Verdun, the cost in lives had made Pétain a modern Pyrrhus.[9]

Meanwhile, on 1 July the British and French began their attacks on the Somme. General Haig intended to break through the German lines with his "New Army," the result of an intensive recruitment effort. The British still eschewed conscription but encouraged enlistment with a variety of incentives. For instance, they allowed group enlistments in "pals" regiments. In these units, football clubs, schoolboys, factory workers, and other groups could train and serve with their friends. This New Army, its name evocative of Oliver Cromwell's New Model Army in the English Civil War, was committed to the summer offensive. After a seven-day bombardment so intense that it rattled windows in London seventy-five miles away, Haig ordered his troops forward on 1 July along a twenty-mile front.[10] The British command was confident that the bombardment had eliminated the defenders' capacity to resist. Some British officers kicked soccer balls in the direction of the German lines, and a Scottish officer played the bagpipes. But when the British troops advanced toward the German lines, German soldiers emerged from their bunkers, manned their machine guns, and slaughtered the British. On the first day of the Somme battle, more than 19,000 British soldiers died. Despite such horrendous losses, Haig pressed on with the attacks. French forces nearby achieved some local successes. Haig ordered additional attacks on the night of 13–14 July and again on 20 July. Another major British attack occurred on 15 September. On this occasion, the British employed a new

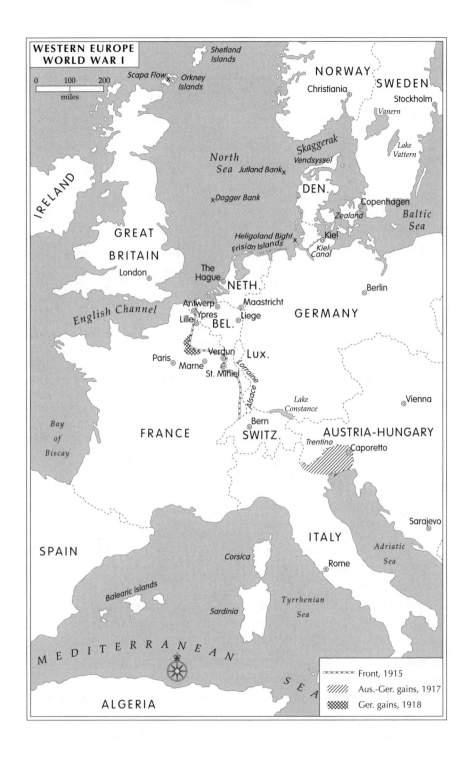

WESTERN EUROPE
WORLD WAR I

0   100   200
miles

Shetland
Islands

NORWAY   SWEDEN

Scapa Flow ×   Orkney   Christiania
                Islands   Stockholm

                                                  Vanern

IRELAND

North   Skaggerak
Sea   Jutland Bank× Vendsyssel   Lake
                                            Vattern
       ×Dogger Bank
                            DEN.

GREAT   Copenhagen   Baltic
BRITAIN   Zealand   Sea

                    Heligoland Bight×   Kiel
London   The Frisian Islands   Kiel
                Hague   Canal
                        NETH.   Berlin

           English Channel Antwerp Maastricht
                        Ypres Liege   GERMANY
                    Lille BEL.
                                Verdun LUX.
           Paris   Vienna
                    Marne St. Mihiel
Bay   Lake
of   Constance
Biscay   FRANCE   Bern
                            SWITZ. AUSTRIA-HUNGARY
                                    Trentino   Caporetto

                                                 Sarajevo

SPAIN   ITALY   Adriatic
                        Corsica   Sea
                                    Rome
                Balearic Islands
                        Sardinia   Tyrrhenian
                                    Sea

        M E D I T E R R A N E A N

                                    S E A
ALGERIA

                            ⌗⌗⌗⌗⌗ Front, 1915
                            ////   Aus.-Ger. gains, 1917
                            ⊠⊠⊠   Ger. gains, 1918

weapon—the tank. Although forty-nine of these mechanical fortresses were in operation at the beginning of the attack, only nine remained functional throughout the engagement. Though this first use of the tank was not auspicious, the British had introduced a weapon that had the potential to alter the battlefield.

The western front was the most critical arena of the First World War. A German victory on the western front would ensure German success on the eastern fronts. The defeat of France on the western front would not only eliminate Germany's main continental enemy but also remove British troops from continental Europe and deprive the entente of the material wealth of the British Empire and the United States. German success in the east, however, was no guarantee of victory in the west. The material resources of Russia and eastern Europe were widely dispersed over a large land area that lacked a viable transportation structure.

The failure of the Schlieffen Plan left the Germans without a clear strategic goal. After their initial advances in 1914, for the most part, they remained on the defensive in the west. The demands of the eastern front required them to manage their manpower carefully. They could not spread their forces too thinly on either the western or the eastern front. A serious breakthrough in either east or west could mean the end of the German military effort. Only at Ypres in 1915 and at Verdun in 1916 did they undertake major offensive efforts in the west. Neither was successful.

The British and French remained consistently on the offensive. They sought to eject the Germans from French soil, remove them from proximity to Britain in Belgium and northern France, and regain French sources of raw materials taken by the Germans at the beginning of the war. Using heavy artillery barrages followed by mass attacks on specific points in the German defenses, they intended to punch holes in the German positions, which they could then exploit with cavalry to advance to the rear. These offensive efforts consistently failed, with heavy casualties on every occasion. The huge losses of men and material did not warrant the small adjustments in the line achieved by the entente's efforts.

The attempts by both sides to introduce new, technically sophisticated weapons onto the battlefield offered little tactical advantage and little chance of breaking the stalemate. The flamethrowers, poison gas, and tanks that appeared on the western front only increased the suffering of the soldiers fighting there.

By the end of 1916 both sides were becoming weary of the death and destruction on the western front. Huge losses had failed to bestow any military advantage to either the entente or the Germans. The end of the war appeared no closer than it had a year ago. The ongoing stalemate on the western front was particularly ominous for the Germans. They had expended much of their manpower reserves in the attrition battles of 1916. At the same time, the British sea blockade cut them off from global sources of food and raw materials. In 1917 important events away from the western front broke the stalemate and provided both sides with the opportunity to win the war.

Chapter 3

EASTERN FRONTS

The eastern campaigns during the first phase of the First World War were much more complex and fluid than those in the west. The main focus of the eastern fighting was the vast border region between Germany and Austria-Hungary on one side and Russia on the other. A multitude of peoples lived in this region, including Byelorussians, Germans, Jews, Lithuanians, Poles, and Ukrainians. This area was much more topologically varied than the arena in western Europe. It also lacked the modern infrastructure of the west, including dense networks of roads and railroads and urban areas in close proximity to one another. Moreover, because of the Serbian role in initiating the conflict, more than one eastern arena would draw the military resources of both alliance systems. Several secondary arenas in northeastern Italy, the southeastern corner of Thrace at Gallipoli, Macedonia, and Romania added to the complexity of the conflict. These lesser arenas dispersed the military and material resources of both sides.

The Russians had the largest army in Europe, with more than 1,350,000 men on active duty. This size, however, was not necessarily a source of strength. A feeble railroad system bound the vast country together. As many as three-fourths of the soldiers were illiterate, and a significant proportion belonged to the numerous non-Russian nationalities living in the empire. These men often had an imperfect understanding of the Russian language and limited sympathy for Russian goals. Nevertheless, the Russian army was the only Great Power European army with the experience of fighting a modern war. The war against Japan in 1904–1905 might have provided the Russians with valuable information about the nature of modern warfare, but their chaotic and corrupt staff system impeded the utilization of these experiences to reform the Russian army.

Austria-Hungary had an army of about 450,000 men, and it reflected the ethnic complexity of the country. German was the language of command. Every soldier was required to know eighty words of German, and officers had to learn the language of their units. Obviously, the national diversity of the Austro-Hungarian army was an obstacle to efficiency. Loyalty to state objectives also became an issue, especially if Austria-Hungary opposed countries where conationals lived across the frontier, such as Italy, Romania, or Serbia. But Czechs and Ukrainians were also tempted by the idea of Pan-Slavic solidarity with Russia, and even Poles were not expected to completely submit their national interests to the purposes of the Habsburg state.

Italy had an army of 345,000 soldiers. This army was hampered by illiteracy and regionalism, and its leadership did not always reflect ability and merit. Also, Italy's industrial base was weak and lacked the requisite raw materials, especially metallic ores, to maintain production. Italy's North African venture in 1911–1912 had exhausted much of its military capacity. In 1914 the Italian army had not recovered from the conquest of Libya.

The Serbian army had been at war since October 1912. Its soldiers were experienced and tough, but the duration and intensity of the Balkan conflicts had eroded its strength and exhausted its material resources. The civilian population was also weary from two years of continuous warfare. The closely allied Montenegrin army was little more than a national militia, and it had not met great success in the Balkan Wars. The élan of its soldiers did not compensate for their lack of training and a modern military infrastructure.

Hard fighting in the Balkan Wars had decimated the ranks of the Bulgarian army and exhausted its material support. Nevertheless, the frustrations of the Balkan Wars had hardened Bulgarian veterans and increased their determination to rectify the perceived injustices in the Treaty of Bucharest.

Like its Bulgarian and Serbian counterparts, the Romanian army had large numbers of peasant recruits, but its officer corps was weak. Also, since its participation in the Russo-Turkish War of 1877–1878, the Romanian army's only experience consisted of the suppression of the great Romanian peasant revolt of 1907 and the virtually unopposed invasion of Bulgaria in 1913.

The Ottoman army also had large numbers of tough peasant soldiers in its ranks. The efforts of the Young Turks to modernize the Ottoman army had not had time to prove successful, and the effects of German training had not been obvious during the Balkan Wars. After its poor showing in the Balkan Wars, the Germans had increased their efforts to reform the Ottoman army. In November 1913 Kaiser Wilhelm sent General Otto Liman von Sanders (1855–1929) to Constantinople to accelerate the training of the Ottomans in the aftermath of their defeats in the First Balkan War. This undertaking caused a diplomatic imbroglio with Russia. The St. Petersburg government perceived no advantage in a revived Ottoman Empire supported by the kaiser's Germany. This dispute provided the Germans with an opportunity to demonstrate their domination of Europe. Despite Russian objections, Liman von Sanders remained in the Ottoman Empire. Nevertheless, the military ability of the Ottoman army remained problematic at the outbreak of war.

Russian Front

The Russians intended to use their numerical superiority to conduct simultaneous offensives against both Austria and Germany. The initial absence of German offensive preparations in the east led the Russians to contemplate a major attack on Austria-Hungary. However, French alarm at the preponderance of German power coming their way led the Russian command to direct two armies to East Prussia.

With the outbreak of war, Austrian and Russian offensive actions produced a complex series of battles in East Prussia and Poland. In the north, two Russian armies were hastily mobilized and moved to the German border, where they advanced into German territory to cut East Prussia from the main body of Germany. The Russian First Army under General Pavel Rennenkampf (1854–1918) crossed into East Prussia from the east. At the East Prussian villages of Stallupönen on 17 August and Grumbinnen three days later, Rennenkampf achieved victories over inferior German forces. He failed, however, to pursue his success. At the same time, the Russian Second Army under General Alexander Samsonov (1859–1914) advanced into East Prussia from the south. This situation disconcerted the local German commander. The Russians had acted in half the time anticipated by the Schlieffen Plan. With the main force of the German army marching through Belgium, the German high command sent retired general Paul von Hindenburg to take command of the German Eighth Army and stabilize the situation in East Prussia. Erich Ludendorff, instrumental in the recent German success at Liège, met him on a train at Hanover to serve as his chief of staff. This established the partnership that led Germany through the final three years of the war. Using interior lines of transportation, especially railroads, the Germans moved most of their available forces to confront the advancing Russian Second Army. Only a thin German screen remained in front of the Russian First Army. Because of the speed of its deployment, logistical problems plagued the Second Army and hampered its advance. Beginning on 27 August, the Germans struck at the Russian flanks and surrounded much of the invading force.[1] Perceiving no escape, General Samsonov shot himself two days later. The Germans destroyed the Russian Second Army, inflicting more than 11,000 casualties. Recalling the victory of the Polish-Lithuanian army over the Teutonic knights in nearby Tannenberg in 1410, Hindenburg and Ludendorff sought to signify the reversal of this eastern European military success against the Germans by naming their victory over the Russians Tannenberg. Later, in the middle of September, the German Eighth Army drove the Russian First Army, which had failed to come to the aid of its comrades farther south, out of German territory in the Battle of the Masurian Lakes. Although the Russians suffered two major defeats, the rapidity of their invasion of East Prussia had disrupted the calculations of the Schlieffen Plan. To address this unexpected situation, von Moltke detached five divisions from the western advance and sent them east. Ironically, the German victory occurred before the arrival of these troops. The Russians were an important factor in the French victory on the Marne.

Meanwhile, in Austrian Galicia and Russian Poland, opposing armies advanced against each other. On the Austrian General Staff, General Franz Conrad von Hötzendorf (1852–1925) developed a complex plan to deal with Austria's complicated geographic situation, with potential enemies in both the north and the south. The plan divided the Austro-Hungarian forces into three groups: one group (Minimal Group Balkan) was to defend the Balkan frontier against Serbia, one group (A Staffel) was to defend the Galician frontier against Russia, and one mobile group (B Staffel) was to provide an offensive capacity for either front.

Implementation of this plan depended on the timely functioning of the railroads. But because of the separate Austrian and Hungarian railroad systems and the linguistic complexities of Austria-Hungary, the plan was problematic from the start.

Even before the first combat, Conrad bungled the implementation of his war plans. He carried out plan B against Serbia before learning of Russia's declaration of war. When the news of war with Russia reached the Austrian General Staff, it reversed itself and its forces. Troops destined for the Balkan front received orders to turn around and go to the Russian front, using the chaotic dual railroad systems. As a result, when Austro-Hungarian troops reached their assigned locations in Galicia or in Croatia and Bosnia on 23 August, they were confused, exhausted, and in no condition to undertake their offensives.

Rather than advancing due north from Austrian Galicia into Russian Poland, where they might pinch off the Russians or pin them against Germans in East Prussia, three Austrian armies advanced in a northeasterly direction into Poland. Von Moltke had encouraged this Austrian attack, expecting it to draw a Russian response and facilitate the implementation of the Schlieffen Plan in the west. At the same time, four Russian armies advanced toward Galicia from the east. The Austrians and Russians collided in eastern Galicia. Initially, the Austrians enjoyed some success against the Russians around Krasnik on 23–25 August. At the Battle of Komorow, however, which began on 26 August in Poland, the Russians routed the Austrian Third Army. The other Russian forces achieved success all along the line against the Austrians. The Russians then moved westward and advanced along a wide front into eastern Galicia. There, in the Battle of Lemberg (L'vov, L'viv, or Lwow), they seized the fourth largest city in the Habsburg Empire and pushed the Austrian armies behind the San River. In these engagements the Austrians lost almost one-third of their combat effectiveness. Only the fortress of Przemyśl, with a garrison of 120,000, held out behind the Russian lines. The Russians reached Przemyśl on 24 September but lacked the heavy guns to invest it. An Austro-Hungarian counteroffensive drove the Russians back and relieved the fortress on 11 October. Less than a month later, however, on 6 November, the Russians returned and surrounded the fortress. Although they got the better of the Austro-Hungarians in the back-and-forth fighting in Galicia, the Russians failed to take full advantage of their victory. Their logistical system could not support an offensive so distant from their home bases, and most of the Russian commanders lacked the initiative to pursue the offensive. The Austrians incurred heavy casualties, as high as 350,000, including many senior and veteran noncommissioned officers and officers infused with the Habsburg spirit. The Austro-Hungarian army never completely recovered from the defeat in east Galicia. This was the beginning of the end of the Habsburg Empire.

The Austro-Hungarian defeat forced the German high command to recognize the impending danger in the east. The Russian armies in Galicia had reached the Carpathians. From there they were in a position to threaten the industrial regions of Silesia within Germany. After their successes in East Prussia, von Hindenburg and Ludendorff decided to undertake an offensive in Poland to take the pressure off their fading Austrian allies. In October 1914 German forces advanced toward the Russian fortresses around Warsaw. By November the Germans had reached Lodz, but the Russians held on to the city. During intense fighting from 16 to 25 November, the Russians managed to rally and threatened to entrap a significant German force. The northern wing of a German attempt to envelop Lodz was itself surrounded by significant Russian forces. General Rennenkampf, who had bungled the invasion of East Prussia, failed to spring the trap, and the Germans managed to escape in a muddy, muddled retreat. This incident emphasized to the Germans the danger of advancing too far into the primitive vastness of the Russian Empire. Nevertheless, the Russians considered their position at Lodz exposed. They evacuated the city on 6 December and withdrew to the Bzura and Ravka rivers. At the same time, the Austro-Hungarian army regained some composure and managed to push the Russians to the northeast. This effort improved Austrian morale, but it failed to restore the Austrian strategic position. Przemyśl remained under siege, and on 22 March 1915 it surrendered to the Russians. They gained almost 120,000 Austro-Hungarian prisoners of war, including nine generals.

Before the Russians could redeploy their soldiers freed by Przemyśl's surrender, the Germans struck in Galicia. Having obtained some success against the Russians in the Second Battle of the Masurian Lakes in February 1915, the Germans sought to bolster their fading Austro-Hungarian allies by a major offensive in the east. They transferred troops from the west to participate in this major effort against the Russians. On

2 May the Eleventh German Army and the Fourth Austro-Hungarian Army, heavily outnumbering the opposing Russian Third Army, launched an offensive between the Galician towns of Gorlice and Tarnow. The surprised Russians had constructed only rudimentary defensive positions, and the Austro-German force soon overwhelmed them. German forces reached the San River on 16 May. The Austrians regained Przemyśl for the final time on 3 June, and by 22 June, Austro-Hungarian forces retook Lemberg. The Russians continued retrograde movements throughout the summer in what they called the "Great Retreat." Warsaw fell on 5 August. By September 1915 the Russians had withdrawn from all of Congress Poland and Galicia. In the north, following up on the success of Gorlice-Tarnow, the Germans advanced to the Dvina River almost all the way to Riga. This was the single greatest Russian defeat of the First World War.[2] The tsar sacked his uncle, Grand Duke Nicholas (1856–1929), as commander in chief of the Russian military and took the job himself. This left governmental affairs in St. Petersburg in the incapable hands of German-born Tsarina Alexandra (1872–1918) and her dubious adviser, a Siberian monk known as Rasputin (1872–1916). The Central Powers' emergency in the east was over for the time being. After the first year of fighting, the Russians' initial offensive into East Prussia had failed, and they had lost Poland. Only against the Austrians had they achieved significant success.

Over the winter of 1915–1916 the Russian army recovered somewhat. Russian industry began to produce weapons and ammunition. Recruits and war materials restored the Russian army's offensive capabilities. On 18 March 1916 it opened an offensive at Lake Naroch, east of Vilnius in northeastern Belarus. The Russians, seeking to divert the Germans from Verdun, enjoyed great numerical superiority. Nevertheless, the Germans inflicted as many as 100,000 casualties on the attackers. By the end of April the Germans had returned to the positions they held before the onset of the Russian attacks.

A much more successful Russian effort began on 4 June 1916. Undertaken in part to relieve the French at Verdun, this new Russian effort, planned and led by General Alexei A. Brusilov (1853–1926), unleashed heavy artillery barrages followed by infantry attacks against the surprised Austro-Hungarians at several locations.[3] Originally, these attacks were to be feints for stronger efforts against the Germans farther north. But the entire Austrian front in Volhynia and Galicia collapsed in the face of Brusilov's well-planned offensive. By 12 June, a little over a week after the offensive began, the Russians had broken through on the Germans and four Austro-Hungarian armies. The Russians overran the Austrian province of Bukovina and advanced to the Carpathians to threaten Lemberg again.[4] They captured more than 350,000 Austro-Hungarian soldiers. The German allies rushed reinforcements from the west to shore up the failing Austro-Hungarians, and German and Austrian units combined right down to the company level. By July the Russians had run out of energy. In September 1916 the Germans and Austrians pushed the Russians back to their lines of departure. The Brusilov offensive led to the end of the old Habsburg and Romanov armies. Only a major infusion of German support maintained the Austro-Hungarian army, which, after the summer of 1916, was under the complete control of the Germans. This was also the last major effort of the tsarist army. Within six months, with its paladins dead on the battlefields of eastern Poland or in German or Austrian prison camps, the tsarist monarchy itself collapsed.

Ottoman Empire

The victories of the Balkan allies in 1912–1913 almost completely expelled the Ottomans from Europe. After the 1913 Peace of Constantinople, they clung only to eastern Thrace, the scene of Bulgarian victories in 1912 and 1913. The Liman von Sanders mission helped maintain German influence in the Ottoman army after the Balkan Wars. Nevertheless, when the First World War broke out, the Ottomans hesitated to become involved so soon after the defeats of 1912–1913. Initially, they declared neutrality. Soon after the war began, the British navy confiscated two warships under construction for the Ottoman navy. The German navy immediately offered two German warships in the Mediterranean, the *Goeben* and the *Breslau,* as replacements. The outbreak of war had left these two German ships in peril. After being chased by the British Mediterranean squadron, the two ships arrived in Constantinople and ostensibly entered the service of the Ottoman navy. These two warships, still under German command, attacked Russian ports in the Black Sea at the end of October. These attacks clinched the deal. The Russians declared war on 4 November, and the Ottomans joined the Central Powers. As a result, fighting began on the southeastern fringes of Europe.

One such area was along the remote Ottoman-Russian frontier, where Anatolia meets the Caucasus land bridge between the Black and Caspian seas. The Ottomans undertook an offensive in horrific winter conditions in eastern Anatolia. At the Battle of Sarikamis in December 1914 and January 1915, the Russians inflicted a severe defeat on the Ottomans. Nearly the entire Ottoman force was wiped out by the Russians and the weather.

Since the end of the nineteenth century, the Ottoman government had perceived a threat in the rise of nationalism among the Christian Armenian population of eastern Anatolia. After the Ottoman defeat at Sarikamis, pro-Russian Armenian bands occasionally attacked Ottoman units in eastern Anatolia, and some Armenians joined the Russian army. In response, the Ottoman government ordered the deportation of the civilian Armenian population of eastern Anatolia in 1915. Carried out haphazardly and brutally, this deportation caused the deaths of as many as a million Armenians. These "Armenian massacres" set a grim precedent of ethnic cleansing that Adolf Hitler would later note and emulate. Such ethnic cleansing had occurred earlier during the Balkan Wars and would happen again during European conflicts throughout the twentieth century.

Little military activity occurred on the Anatolian front in 1915. The defeats resulting in the "Great Retreat" in Poland preoccupied the Russian command. The struggle at Gallipoli and the Armenian problem consumed most of the Ottomans' military and material resources. After a year of relative inactivity, however, fighting revived in eastern Anatolia. At the beginning of January 1916, a Russian army, seeking to divert the Ottomans from a British force mired in Mesopotamia, began an offensive. After some terrible winter fighting, the Russians took the fortress of Ezerum on 15 February. Aided by a landing of Russian troops on the Black Sea south of Batum, the offensive moved westward. On 18 April 1916 Russian forces entered the ancient Black Sea port of Trebizond (Trabzon), but they were unable to proceed farther westward due to logistical problems.

At the western end of the Ottoman Empire, a much more visible and vital struggle occurred in 1915. The accession of the Ottoman Empire to the Central Powers alliance had increased Russia's relative isolation from Britain and France. Only a treacherous route through the Arctic Ocean to the White Sea, unavailable in the winter, or the long passage to the Pacific port of Vladivostok made Russia accessible to the other Entente Powers. The British and French governments sought to redress this problem through the Ottoman Empire. In an effort to establish a viable year-round supply route to Russia, a combined British and French fleet planned to force the Dardanelles, the passage between the Aegean Sea and the Sea of Marmara, and then the Bosporus, linking the Sea of Marmara to the Black Sea. The British in particular perceived the Ottoman Empire as a relatively easy target of opportunity. The Ottomans, after all, had recently suffered stunning defeats at the hands of the Balkan alliance. The Ottoman capital of Constantinople astride the Bosporus was an obvious objective. Bombardments of the outer forts of the Dardanelles, begun on 19 February 1915, failed to have the desired effect. From 3 to 18 March the flotilla attempted to force the Dardanelles, but a combination of fire from the forts and floating mines forced it to withdraw. A notable loss was the French battleship *Bouvet*, which struck a mine on 18 March and sank with 640 crewmen. The British battleships *Irresistible* and *Ocean* were also lost in this engagement.

In the face of this naval failure, the entente commanders decided to seize the Gallipoli Peninsula to silence the forts on the European side of the straits. The entente spurned a Greek offer of assistance because of concerns that Greek ambitions conflicted with those of Russia. British, Australian, and New Zealand troops landed at Gallipoli on 25 April, while a diversionary French force landed on the Asian side of the Dardanelles.[5] The prior naval activity had made the entente's intentions obvious to the Ottoman defenders, and neither the invaders on the Asian shore nor those on the Gallipoli Peninsula made much headway. The French soon withdrew from Asia. The Ottomans on Gallipoli occupied the heights and poured fire down on the mainly Australian and New Zealand troops on the beaches. On 6–7 August the entente landed additional soldiers at Suvla Bay about seven miles northeast of the initial position in an effort to outflank the Ottomans. This effort also stalemated. On 8 December the British began to withdraw their forces. This process continued until 9 January, when the British navy evacuated the remaining entente forces.

The Ottoman victory at the Dardanelles and Gallipoli infused their forces with confidence. One Ottoman division commander at Gallipoli, Mustafa Kemal (1881–1938), later known as Atatürk, gained considerable status from this success. The victory had come at considerable cost, however, with the Ottomans sustaining as many as 300,000 casualties.

The entente's failure to force the passage to the Black Sea meant the continued isolation of Russia. Although an influx of entente supplies might not have prevented the Russian defeat on the eastern front and the descent into revolution and chaos, the material strengthening of the Russian army might have enabled it to persevere until American entry into the war finally broke the deadlock.

Italy

Although a member of the Triple Alliance since 1882, Italy rejected its obligations to Austria-Hungary and Germany in the summer of 1914. On 3 August the Italians announced a policy of neutrality, ostensibly because the Austrians had failed to consult them before declaring war on Serbia. In fact, for some time the Italians had perceived their main national aspirations to be in Austrian territory, especially in Trentino (South Tyrol) and Istria. The ensuing stalemate in the west increased the potential value of Italian participation for both sides. Bargaining between the warring powers for Italian favors ensued. The Central Powers offered Tunis, Corsica, and Nice. Under German pressure, the Austrians even offered Trentino in March 1915 after their reverses in Galicia. The Entente Powers were in a much better position to offer the Italians Austrian territory. The Pact of London, reached on 26 April 1915, promised the Italians not only Trentino and Istria but also much of Dalmatia, the Albanian port of Valona, and a protectorate over the rest of Albania in return for participation in the war on the side of the entente. On 23 May Italy declared war on Austria-Hungary. Formal war between Italy and Germany did not begin until 28 June 1916. Acknowledgment of Italy's annexation plans provided an incentive for Austro-Hungarian soldiers from the regions coveted by the Italians to fight with an ardor not always found on other fronts.

The topography of the battlefield did not favor the Italians. The rugged mountainous terrain, often bare rock karst, along the border with Austria forced them to attack uphill against the fire of the Austrian defenders. Two main fronts developed along the frontier of northeastern

Italy. The Trentino front to the north was extremely mountainous. The Isonzo front to the east was only slightly less so. The extreme topography of the Trentino front limited the ability of both the Austrian defenders and the Italian attackers to concentrate men and material. At the beginning of the war the Italians were able to seize three Austrian salients but could proceed no further.

Most of the Austro-Italian fighting occurred on the Isonzo front. The Italians quickly advanced to the Isonzo River in Austria in an effort take the provincial town of Gorizia and reach the important Adriatic port of Trieste. During four campaigns in 1915 they could advance no further. Both sides suffered enormous casualties in these battles. By the end of 1915 the Isonzo front had stalemated, like most others during this conflict. Among the Italian soldiers fighting on this front was a thirty-two-year-old former schoolteacher named Benito Mussolini (1882–1945). He reached the rank of corporal before being wounded and discharged in 1917. A fifth Isonzo offensive began in March 1916, with similar results. It ended because of events farther west.

In May 1916 Austro-Hungarian chief of staff Conrad von Hötzendorf launched an offensive from Trentino in an effort to cut off the Italian army fighting on the Isonzo front. The Austrians undertook this effort against the wishes of their German allies, who were engaged in heavy fighting at Verdun and wanted the use of the Austrians' Škoda heavy artillery there. After some initial success, this offensive stalled. The Brusilov offensive then forced the Austro-Hungarians to divert units from Italy to the Russian front and wind down their offensive in Trentino. Over the remainder of 1916 the Italians renewed their efforts on the Isonzo front. Five more offensives took place, with few results. The Italians finally succeeded in taking Gorizia on 8 August 1916 in the Sixth Battle of the Isonzo, but for the most part, they stopped there. The stalemate that had come to characterize the western front had seeped into the Italian front.

Southeastern Europe

While large Austrian, German, and Russia armies confronted one another on the eastern front, a complicated campaign developed in southeastern Europe. The original intent of Austrian war preparations had been a punitive invasion of Serbia. Although the Russians' entrance into the war prevented the Austrians from directing the preponderance of their forces against the Serbs, they still sought to inflict retribution. Bombardment of the Serbian capital Belgrade from across the Danube and from Austrian monitors in the Danube began on the day Austria declared war, 28 July. An invasion of Serbia began on 11 August when the Austro-Hungarians under General Oskar Potiorek (1853–1933) initiated an attack from the north and west, intending to nip off the northwestern corner of Serbia. One Austrian force crossed the Sava River to move on Sabac, one crossed the Drina to advance toward the Jadar Valley, and a third advanced across the upper Drina Valley. The Austrian forces amounted to more than 250,000 men. Nevertheless, the slightly outnumbered Serbs under Vojvoda Radomir Putnik (1847–1917) repulsed the invaders at the Battle of Cer Mountain. This was the first entente victory of the First World War. By 25 August the defeated Austrians were completely out of Serbia. Ironically, the victorious Putnik had been vacationing in Austria at the outbreak of war, and the Austrians had gallantly permitted him to return to his command.

Although Serbian forces had not recovered from the losses of the Balkan Wars, let alone the casualties incurred at Cer Mountain, Putnik mounted a counterattack. One group crossed the Sava River into Srem; another advanced into Bosnia, taking Višegrad and almost reaching Sarajevo. At the same time, Montenegrin soldiers moved into Hercegovina and northern Albania (Montenegro had allied with Serbia on 3 August 1914). In June 1915 they reentered Scutari, the northern Albanian town the Great Powers had forced them to leave two years earlier. None of these efforts met with much success. The Serbs lacked sufficient ammunition to hold on to enemy territory and had to withdraw. The failure of most Bosnians to welcome the Serbian and Montenegrin invasion was a disappointment to Serbian nationalists.

A second Austrian invasion of Serbia began on 8 October, but Serbian defenders repulsed the attempt to cross the Drina from Bosnia. A more substantial Austrian effort, the third of the war, began on 10 November. Crossing the Sava River west of Belgrade, the Austrians advanced to the east. On 2 December they took the Serbian capital and then advanced to the south toward Niš. This triumph was short-lived. A Serbian counterattack on the Kolubara River routed the invaders, and by 15 December

EASTERN EUROPE
WORLD WAR I

SWEDEN

Petrograd

Baltic Sea

Moscow

R U S S I A

Minsk

GERMANY

Tannenberg

Warsaw

Brest
Litovsk

Kursk

Kiev

Kharkov

Tsaritsyn

Gorlice

Przemysl

Rostov

Budapest

AUSTRIA-HUNGARY

Iaşi

Black   Sea

ROMANIA

Cer

Belgrade

Bucharest

Niš

SERBIA

Sofia

MONT.

BULGARIA

Constantinople

Dobro
Pole

ALB.

Gallipoli

Salonika

GREECE

OTTOMAN EMPIRE

Athens

0   150   300
miles

.... International boundary

- - - - Eastern front-November, 1914

— - — Eastern front-November, 1916

••••••••• Armistice line-December, 1918

the Serbs had returned to their capital.[6] The losses incurred during the repulse of the Austrians and the typhus epidemic ravaging their country prevented any pursuit of the Austrians.

At the beginning of 1915 the conflict in the Balkans shifted from the military to the diplomatic arena. Both the Central Powers and the Entente Powers focused their efforts on Bulgaria. The entry of the Ottoman Empire into the war on the side of the Central Powers in November 1914 made the position of Bulgaria critical for both sides. If it were allied to the Entente Powers, Bulgaria could facilitate an attack on the Ottoman capital of Constantinople, as well as the opening of a water route to Russia through the straits and the Black Sea. If tied to the Central Powers, Bulgaria could solidify the land connection from central Europe to the Ottoman Empire. Bulgaria's price for joining the war was Macedonia—a prize that had been denied it in the diplomatic settlement of the Congress of Berlin in 1878 and again by military defeat in the Balkan Wars. The Bulgarians negotiated with both sides throughout the spring and summer of 1915. The advantage lay with the Central Powers because Serbia, the Entente Powers' ally, held Macedonia. Efforts to persuade the Serbs to cede all or part of Macedonia to the Bulgarians in return for areas of Austria-Hungary were unsuccessful; the Serbs refused to part with it. Gaining the support of Bulgaria was particularly critical for the entente's efforts at Gallipoli, because Bulgarian participation might well have doomed Constantinople. Bulgarian armies had come within twenty-five miles of the ancient imperial city during the First Balkan War. The Central Powers, however, promised the Bulgarians all of Macedonia. All they had to do was take it. Bulgaria accordingly signed a series of military and economic agreements with the Central Powers in September 1915.

The next month, on 5 October, one Austro-Hungarian and one German army under the overall command of Field Marshal August von Mackensen (1849–1945) invaded Serbia from the north. On 12 October two Bulgarian armies invaded Serbia from the east, one army moving toward Niš and the other toward Skopje. These attacks overwhelmed the already exhausted Serbs. Belgrade fell on 10 October to the invaders from the north, and Niš fell to the Bulgarians on 5 November. On 13 January 1916 Austro-Hungarian forces seized the remote Montenegrin capital Cetinje. The Serbian army, accompanied by civilians and 20,000 Austro-Hungarian prisoners of war, retreated to the west across the northern Albanian mountains. After heavy losses to the weather, disease, and hostile Albanians, the survivors reached the Adriatic at Durazzo (Durrës) and at San Giovanna di Medua.[7] With the aid of the entente and the unenthusiastic support of the Italians, they eventually found shelter on the Greek island of Corfu.

Even before the invasion of Serbia, British and French troops had disembarked at the Greek port of Salonika at the invitation of Greek prime minister Eleutherios Venizelos (1864–1936) in an effort to support their beleaguered Balkan ally. A 1913 treaty obligated the Greeks to help the Serbs, and the British and French attempted to move up the Vardar valley to render assistance.[8] Only a small French force moving north reached the Serbs before the oncoming Bulgarians cut them off and forced the entente units back down the valley and across the Greek frontier. The Bulgarians wanted to pursue these soldiers back to Salonika, force them back on their ships, and, in so doing, acquire the port for the newly conquered Macedonia and eliminate Macedonia as a battlefield. However, because of the pro-German sentiments of Greek King Constantine (1868–1923), the brother-in-law of the German kaiser, the Germans refused to allow their Bulgarian allies to cross the Greek frontier.

Meanwhile, King Constantine withdrew his support from Prime Minister Venizelos, who then resigned. No entente offers, including the island of Cyprus, persuaded the king and his advisers to abandon neutrality. As a result, the British and French found themselves ensconced in Salonika, with Greece as an increasingly reluctant host and the armies of the Central Powers just a short distance away at the northern Greek frontier. The entente forces established positions extending from Salonika to the northern Greek frontier, and when the Italian, Russian, and Serbian contingents in Corfu had recovered from their ordeal, they joined the British and French in the Salonika encampment. Across the Greek border, Austrian, Bulgarian, German, and Ottoman forces kept the entente bottled up in Salonika.

In the spring of 1916 the Germans finally consented to repeated Bulgarian requests for an invasion of Greece. The pro-German commander of Fort Rupel, a Greek installation that guarded the northern border, surrendered to the Bulgarians on 26 May 1916. Later that summer Bulgarian and German units defeated an entente offensive at Lake Doiran. Bulgarian troops then moved into eastern Macedonia, taking Seres on

19 September and Drama and the port of Kavala on 18 September. In the autumn the entente forces, now supplemented by Italians, Russians, and the revived Serbian survivors of the retreat across Albania, pushed Bulgarian and German forces west of Salonika to the north, reaching Bitola (Monastir) on 19 November before logistical difficulties, the arrival of winter, and stiffening Bulgarian resistance forced them to halt. Before this offensive ended, the entente forces in Salonika established a connection with the Italians in southern Albania. This exchange of territory in Macedonia strengthened the positions of both sides and continued the stalemate on the southwestern European front.

On 30 August 1916 a pro-entente faction of the Greek army assumed authority in Salonika. Venizelos became the leader of this movement and formed a government that declared war on the Central Powers on 23 November. For the next eight months, during the "national schism," Greece had two governments—a pro-entente government in Salonika headed by Venizelos, and a neutral government in Athens under the leadership of King Constantine. An entente force landed at Pireaus, the port of Athens, on 29 November in an attempt to depose King Constantine, but loyalist Greek resistance forced the British and French troops to withdraw on 1 December. This loyalist victory was ephemeral. It only increased the determination of the Entente Powers and the Venizelos forces to take control of the entire country.

During the war, no effective government existed in Albania. The German princeling William of Wied (1876–1945), established as ruler of the newly independent country by the 1913 ambassadors' conference in London, had decamped from his new domain upon the outbreak of war in September 1914. Soon thereafter, Greek troops moved into the southern part of the country, which they called Northern Epirus; Italians occupied the port of Valona (Vlorë) in the center on 28 December 1914; and Montenegrins returned to the region of Scutari. By 1916 the Central Powers occupied Albania north of the Voyusa River, and the Entente Powers occupied it to the south. By 1916 the southeastern European front extended all the way from the Aegean Sea in eastern Macedonia to the Adriatic Sea in Albania. Soldiers from all four Central Powers faced a varied force of British, British colonial, French, French colonial, Russian, Serbian, and eventually Greek units. Albanian units served on both sides.

This southeastern European front was the most cosmopolitan effort in the entire war.

Like Italy, Romania had been allied to Austria-Hungary and connected to the Triple Alliance since 1883. At the outbreak of war in 1914, however, little political pressure emerged to uphold alliance obligations, other than the personal inclinations of the Hohenzollern King Carol, who died soon after the war began. Carol's nephew Ferdinand (1865–1927), who succeeded him, was less inclined to follow family traditions. While Romania's major irredentist interests lay in Hungarian-ruled Transylvania, other aspirations led many Romanians to look east to Russian-ruled Bessarabia. Given Romania's geographic vulnerability to an attack by either Austria-Hungary or Russia and Bulgaria's hostility resulting from the Second Balkan War, a policy of waiting was prudent for the Bucharest government. In the summer of 1916 the Romanian government, encouraged by the initial success of the Brusilov offensive, decided to intervene in the war on the side of the Entente Powers.[9] The timing of the Romanian intervention was poor. On 27 August, as the Russian offensive waned, the Romanians declared war on Austria-Hungary and invaded Transylvania with most of their army. They succeeded in occupying some areas of Transylvania against very light Hungarian resistance. At the same time, the Russians extended their front south as far as the Dobrudzha, thereby weakening it.

Russian intervention could not deter the Central Powers' determination to punish Romania. On 1 September a mainly Bulgarian army, along with some Austro-Hungarian, German, and Ottoman units, under the command of von Mackensen invaded Dobrudzha. The Bulgarians smashed a weak Romanian counterthrust farther up the Danube near Russe at the beginning of October. Von Hindenburg and Ludendorff sent General von Falkenhayn to direct the campaign against Romania. The Austrians rushed reinforcements from the Italian front to Transylvania. In late September and early October 1916 Austrian and German forces defeated the Romanians at Hermanstadt (Cluj) and Kronstadt (Brasov). Von Falkenhayn's forces crossed the Transylvanian Alps while another force under the command of von Mackensen crossed the Danube near the Bulgarian town of Svistov. Between them they overran Wallachia. Bucharest fell on 6 December. The Romanian government and the remnants of the

Romanian army retreated to Iaşi, where they regrouped under the protection of the Russian army. By the beginning of 1917 the Romanians had lost 350,000 men, and the Central Powers occupied half their country. No other country had intervened in the war with greater consequence or cost. The Central Powers' victory added Romanian food and material resources to their war effort. The division of this bounty, however, caused great acrimony. Disagreements over the allotment of Romanian foodstuffs and the disposition of the fertile Dobrudzha regions caused antipathy among the Central Powers that continued until the final days of the war.

The eastern fronts did not offer an opportunity for decisive victory for either side. The battlefields were too scattered and too remote. They did, however, offer the opportunity for exhaustion and defeat.

Even though the Germans had a significant ally on the Russian front in Austria-Hungary, the military weakness of this ally increasingly forced the Germans to assume a dominant role in the east. After the Brusilov offensive, the Germans effectually controlled the Austro-Hungarian army. This situation would be duplicated in the Second World War when the Germans assumed pro forma control over the Italian armed forces after their failures in Greece and North Africa in the fall of 1940.

A German defeat in either the west or the east would mean the end of the German war effort. Russian weakness became apparent early in the war, however. After the initial invasion of East Prussia in August 1914, Russia posed little offensive threat to Germany.

The smaller countries in the east lacked the military power to gain decisive victories. The Italians, Montenegrins, Romanians, and Serbs all sapped the resources of the Entente Powers. The Bulgarians and Ottomans drew on the strength of the Central Powers. These eastern European battlefields exhausted both sides. In doing so, they hindered the accumulation of military capacities on the western front for a decisive battle. In the east, during the first phase of the First World War, there was no victory, only defeat.

Chapter 4

AMERICAN INTERVENTION, 1917–1918

The origins of American intervention in the First World War lay in the naval struggle that had been an important factor in precipitating the war and began in earnest at the outbreak of war. The British-imposed blockade on Germany to strangle its industrial economy and German attempts to break the blockade were important issues that led to U.S. entry into the war. In particular, American outrage over the German naval strategy provided a basis for action against the Germans.

At the beginning of the twentieth century, all the Great Powers had indulged in a frenzy of warship construction. Rivalry between the traditional European naval power Great Britain and the upstart Germany had been a major reason for the British to seek the shelter of the Triple Entente alliance. Yet at the start of hostilities in 1914, the fighting was largely confined to land. These costly fleets, the prides of their respective nations, played little part in the fighting.

Nevertheless, some naval engagements occurred in all the bodies of water surrounding Europe. Entente navies controlled the Mediterranean Sea, but German and Austrian submarines, or U-boats (*unterseebooten*), challenged their dominance. The addition of the German warships *Goeben* and *Breslau* to the Ottoman navy enabled the Ottomans to dominate the Black Sea through much of the war. Even so, the Russian Black Sea fleet made a successful landing on the Ottoman coast near Trebizond. This was in marked contrast to the British and French failure on the other side of the Ottoman Empire at the Dardanelles. The Adriatic became an area of intense naval fighting between small ships of the Austro-Hungarian and Italian fleets. In the major engagement in the Adriatic, the Habsburg navy under the command of Admiral Miklós Horthy (1868–1957), the future Hungarian regent, sailed on 15 May 1917 to attack the barrage of ships and floating batteries blocking the Strait of Otranto. This resulted in a rare Austro-Hungarian success.

The most critical of the naval arenas, however, was the North Sea. At the beginning of the war the British imposed a naval blockade on the Germans, with the intention of preventing the importation of the raw materials and foodstuffs required by the sophisticated German economy. Initially, neither the British nor the Germans deployed their battleships against each other. When German U-boats sank three outdated armored cruisers—the *Aboukir, Cressy,* and *Hougue*—on 28 August 1914, that led the British to move their blockade from the European coast to the English Channel and the expanse of the North Sea between Scotland and Norway. The loss of these ships also reinforced the danger of committing valuable symbols of national strength to immediate battle. Minefields and warship patrols maintained the British blockade of industrial Germany.

The British also enjoyed some local successes in the North Sea with their surface fleet. For instance, at Heligoland Bight on 28 August 1914, a large British force sank three German light cruisers and one destroyer. At Dogger Bank on 24 January 1915, the Royal Navy achieved another victory, sinking the German armored cruiser *Blücher*.[1] These engagements caused the Germans to adopt a cautious policy for their surface fleet.

The Germans' success with their U-boats and the losses suffered by their surface fleet encouraged them to increase the use of submarines to challenge the blockade. Originally, these craft were intended for coastal patrols, but they ventured farther out into the ocean to sink vessels bringing supplies to Britain. The Germans also sought to impose a similar blockade on the British. On 4 February 1915 they declared a war zone around the British Isles and indicated that they would attack without warning any merchant ships entering that zone. By May the U-boats had sunk more than a hundred ships.

On 7 May 1915 the German submarine *U-20* sank the British passenger ship *Lusitania,* causing the loss of more than a thousand lives, including 128 U.S. citizens. Images of drowned women and children exercised a powerful influence on the American public. The sinking of the British liner *Arabic* on 19 August further provoked American opinion. American protests led the Germans to reduce the U-boat blockade around the British Isles on 18 September. They had no desire to add the United States to their enemies.

By 1916 the British blockade was proving effective against Germany. The German General Staff understood that it needed to take action to undermine the blockade and erode the British fleet's numerical advantage. Also, the German navy did not wish to remain in port while the German army was engaged in a ferocious struggle at Verdun. In May 1916 the commander of the German High Seas Fleet, Admiral Reinhard Scheer (1863–1928), undertook the war's only major naval offensive in European waters involving the main British and German battle fleets. The German fleet sailed out into the North Sea, intending to challenge and destroy a portion of the British fleet.[2] Admiral John Jellicoe (1869–1935) bore the dubious distinction of being the "only man who could lose the war in an afternoon,"[3] since a British defeat would presumably destroy the blockade and might even open Britain up to a German invasion. Contact between the two fleets occurred on the afternoon of 31 May 1916 about a hundred miles west of the Danish Jutland Peninsula. Initially, the Germans had the advantage, inflicting serious damage on the British fleet and sinking the battle cruisers *Indefatigable, Invincible,* and *Queen Mary.* Jellicoe's subordinate, Admiral David Beatty (1871–1936), calmly observed, "There seems to be something wrong with our bloody ships today."[4] The Germans had not encountered only a portion of the British Grand Fleet, as expected, but the entire fleet. When they recognized their peril, the outnumbered Germans turned around and, as evening descended, ran back to port. Admiral Jellicoe performed the classic naval maneuver of "crossing the T" of the German fleet twice and managed to sink the battle cruiser *Lützow.* Nevertheless, Admiral Scheer was able to lead the High Seas Fleet back to safety. Jellicoe received some criticism for not pursuing the German fleet with sufficient aggression. The British certainly lost an opportunity to inflict great damage on the High Seas Fleet and perhaps even eliminate it as a factor in the war.

The results of the Battle of Jutland were mixed. The Germans gained a tactical advantage. They inflicted heavy casualties on the British, sinking fourteen British ships, including three battle cruisers, and killing 6,094 British sailors. In contrast, the Germans lost eleven ships, including one battleship, and 2,551 sailors. Admiral Scheer did not succeed in significantly reducing the British numerical advantage, however. Even more critically, the Germans did not break the blockade; the chokehold on their economy remained in place. Although the situation demanded aggressive action, the German High Seas Fleet did not make another major attack for the remainder of the war. Despite the lack of a great British success at Jutland, the German High Seas Fleet was not a significant factor in the war.

The British blockade continued to constrict the German economy. Neither the imposition of strict rationing, the use of substitute goods, nor the conquest of most of agriculturally rich Romania in the autumn of 1916 alleviated the widespread food shortages in Germany. So severe was the lack of foodstuffs that the winter of 1916–1917 was known as the "turnip winter" because that root vegetable became the staple of the German diet.

Under these circumstances, the German command decided that it had no choice but to resume unrestricted submarine warfare. As early as 10 June 1916 Admiral Scheer proposed a return to this strategy. Not until 9 January 1917, however, did Kaiser Wilhelm order unrestricted submarine warfare to begin on 1 February. The German high command hoped to impose the same economic strictures on Britain that Germany was enduring. The Germans recognized that the resumption of submarine warfare was likely to involve the United States in the war. Nevertheless, they hoped that Britain could be defeated before the Americans could intervene or, failing that, that the U-boats could interdict American troop ships crossing the North Atlantic.

Two days after the Germans' announcement, the United States severed diplomatic relations with Germany. The Germans' failure to accept his offer of mediation in December 1916 had disappointed President Woodrow Wilson. Also, their return to submarine warfare directly contravened his explicit policies from 1915. Finally, a German success threatened the considerable economic investments that American agricultural, banking, and industrial interests had made in the entente cause. The balance of trade with the entente nations had completely swung around to the American advantage. All three major Entente Powers had incurred large debts to American concerns by the end of 1916.

Then, on 23 February, the American government learned through British intelligence that German foreign minister Arthur Zimmerman (1864–1940) had offered the southwestern United States to Mexico as an incentive to enter the war. The United States had already intervened in Mexico with more than 12,000 troops in 1916. This ludicrous suggestion, contained in the so-called Zimmerman telegram, further inflamed American public opinion against Germany.

As a result, on 6 April 1917 the United States declared war against Germany. The Americans also broke off relations with Austria-Hungary and the Ottoman Empire at this time. Only on 7 December 1917, however, did Washington declare war on the Habsburg Empire. The United States never declared war on the Ottoman Empire, nor did it ever sever diplomatic relations with Bulgaria. American intervention in the European war was based on moral, economic, and Mexican concerns. The European issues that had begun and fueled the war had little relevance for the Americans.

Initially, the American declaration of war had little impact on the European conflict. Up until 1917 the American army was small and relied on volunteers to fill its ranks. As war with Germany became increasingly likely, much of the American army was mired in northern Mexico, fruitlessly pursuing Mexican revolutionary Pancho Villa (1878–1923). Thus, the Americans had to draft, train, and equip an army. Then they had to transport that army across the Atlantic to the battlefields of Europe. U-boat activity in the North Atlantic made this no certain thing. Meanwhile, events in Europe began to turn in favor of the Central Powers.

Even before U.S. entry into the war, the rule of the Romanov dynasty in Russia collapsed. Tsarist absolutism had undergone significant change since the 1905 revolution. The October Manifesto that year had permitted a two-tiered representative body and had imposed legal limitations on the tsar's power. The outbreak of war in 1914, however, impeded further progress toward the development of a modern democratic society in Russia. The lower house of the Russian parliament, the Duma, had little role in the management of the war. Tsar Nicholas II, who had assumed personal command of the army in 1915, thus bore major responsibility for the failed war effort; while in the capital, his German-born wife and her adviser Rasputin undermined public confidence in the government. In February 1917, after massive antiwar and antigovernment demonstrations in the Russian capital Petrograd, tsarist authority collapsed. Military authorities at Russian headquarters informed Nicholas that he no longer enjoyed the confidence of the army.[5] The tsar had been devoted to the entente cause, and his abdication after several days of disorder was at least in part intended to ensure Russia's continued participation in the war.

In these circumstances, the Duma assumed power as the provisional government. It pledged to uphold Russia's obligation to its allies and remain in the war. The Duma had little experience with authority, however. Russia's military position at the front continued to deteriorate. Also, as the tsarist government collapsed, the Petrograd soldiers' and workers' council, called the Soviet, formed. The Petrograd Soviet acted as a check on the actions of the provisional government and loomed as a threat to its existence. The Germans recognized the potential danger posed by a revived Russia, and to counter this problem, they facilitated the return of a number of exiled radical politicians to Russia. Among these was the leader of the Bolshevik (majority) faction of the Social Democratic Party, Vladimir Ulyanov, known as Lenin (1870–1924). From the moment he returned to Russia in April 1917, Lenin worked through the Petrograd Soviet to seize power from the provisional government and institute a policy of accelerated Marxist revolution. Lenin was convinced that conditions in Russia were ripe for his attempt to hasten the historical process and thus also hasten the material development of Russia. Day by day, as the war continued and conditions deteriorated, his slogan "peace, land, bread" gained the attention of the peoples of Russia.

The consequences of the fall of the House of Romanov reverberated throughout the other dynastic states—the Habsburg, the Hohenzollern, the Ottoman, and even the House of Savoy. The immediate advantage, however, was for the Central Powers. The struggle to establish a post-tsarist order clearly detracted from the Russian war effort. The next place to undergo significant military disaffection because of the war, however, was republican France.

At the beginning of 1917 the Germans altered their strategy. The fighting at Verdun had exhausted their reserves in manpower and material. To address this situation, Hindenburg and Ludendorff ordered a return to a defensive strategy. With Operation Alberich, named for the malicious dwarf of Wagnerian mythology, the Germans shortened their lines in the west.[6] They withdrew from exposed and unfavorable defensive positions to meticulously prepared lines about twenty miles to the rear. These positions, in northern France between Arras and Soissons, became known as the Hindenburg Line to entente soldiers or the Siegfried Line to Germans. The Germans cut down trees, leveled buildings, poisoned wells, placed booby traps, and generally scorched the earth. They also employed their considerable technical skills to construct new lines, build concrete bunkers, and reinforce machine gun nests with clear fields of fire. In February they began to withdraw to these positions. They shortened their lines by about twenty-five miles and replenished their reserves with the troops no longer needed for frontline duty. By April the German withdrawal was complete.

That same month, a new French offensive began. General Robert Nivelle, the new French commander in chief, decided to employ the rolling barrage tactics developed at Verdun. Nivelle, who had replaced Joffre in December 1916, was convinced that the rolling barrage, together with the entente's numerical superiority, could rapidly achieve a breakthrough on the western front. On 16 April the Nivelle offensive began, with the main thrust aimed at German positions between Soissons and Reims, just east of the Hindenburg Line. Supporting British attacks to the west began at Arras on 9 April. After three days, the offensive failed. The rolling barrage was too far ahead of the advancing infantry, and the shortened Hindenburg Line enabled the Germans to further concentrate their manpower. The French sustained more than 120,000 casualties and achieved no significant gains.

Even worse for the French, the Nivelle offensive was the catalyst for the discontent and war weariness that became manifest in the French army. Years of slaughter and deprivation had eroded morale. Beginning on 17 April strikes and mutinies erupted in the French ranks. Troops sent to the front baaed at their officers like sheep going to the slaughter, and withdrawing troops accused those taking their place of prolonging the war. Some soldiers deserted, and many others refused orders, especially ones to attack. Briefly, the French army was paralyzed.

On 15 May General Pétain replaced Nivelle as commander of the French army. He dealt with this emergency with a relatively humane program that improved the quality of food and wine supplied to the troops and permitted some home leave. Nevertheless, at least fifty French soldiers were executed. By the end of June 1917 the mutinies were over, and it appeared that they cured the French command of its offensive proclivities. If attacked, the French army would respond. Otherwise, it would remain largely on the defensive until the arrival of American soldiers and supplies permitted a renewal of offensive action.

Interestingly, the Germans evidently failed to detect any indication of unrest across no-man's-land. Whether they might have been able to take advantage of the disarray in the French ranks remains an open question. A German offensive at this point might have renewed the patriotic spirit in the French army. In any event, the relative quiescence of the French army gave the Germans on the western front a much-needed respite.

With the Russian army disintegrating and the French army in stasis, General Haig decided that the British army would have to assume the responsibility of pressing the Germans until the arrival of the Americans. He developed a grand plan to break through the German lines in Flanders. In doing so, he hoped to outflank the Germans in the west and clear the Belgian coast of the German U-boats and surface raiders stationed there.

The offensive began with a preliminary bombardment. Then on 7 June the British detonated a huge amount of explosives placed by British miners tunneling under German positions at Messines Ridge. The resulting explosion, which could be heard across the English Channel, destroyed the forward German positions. British and Dominion troops surged forward and took the ridge. Haig failed, however, to follow up on this success. Not until the end of July did he renew the offensive in Flanders. The British bombardment initiating this action, called Passchendaele or Third Ypres, destroyed many of the water-containing dikes in this low country. Rains added to the gooey mess through which the British soldiers attempted to advance.[7] Some soldiers drowned in the mud. The fighting continued until November, but despite heavy casualties, the British were unable to make much headway. Even after this failure, Haig attempted another attack at Cambrai in November. There, for the first time in the war, the British deployed a significant number of tanks, fielding 374 of them. Although these armored weapons demonstrated great potential, they were not reliable enough to sustain the attack. On 3 December Haig called it off.

The fighting at Passchendaele and Cambrai inflicted heavy casualties on both the British and the Germans. The British army never developed discipline problems like those in the French and Russian armies. Nevertheless, after the 1917 offensives the British were exhausted. They too had to await the Americans before engaging in another major effort on the western front.

While the British were bearing most of the burden against the Germans, the Russian provisional government attempted to pursue the war. Under the leadership of Alexander Kerensky (1881–1970), the provisional government initiated an offensive in Galicia on 1 July 1917, hoping to replicate the success of the Brusilov offensive the previous year. It also wanted to demonstrate its own commitment to the Entente Powers. With the Americans and their virtually unlimited resources committed to the entente effort, the provisional government hoped that Russia would emerge on the side of victory. Although the Kerensky offensive enjoyed some initial success, it quickly ran out of energy. On 19 July German and Austro-Hungarian forces counterattacked and soon regained all lost territories. The provisional government suffered an additional setback on 1 September when the Germans, employing new infiltration methods developed by General Oskar Hutier (1857–1934) and Colonel Georg Bruchmüller (1863–1948), swept around Russian positions and into the fortress of Riga. These infiltration tactics, which relied on surprise, involved a short, intensive artillery barrage, followed by small groups of assault troops moving forward rapidly, avoiding strong points, and seeking communication and command targets. The shock troops in the forefront of these assaults were specially trained and highly motivated. Often they received priority in the distribution of Germany's dwindling food and material resources. Riga fell on 3 September, signifying the complete military collapse of the provisional government. In a little more than two months, the government itself would collapse.

The Central Powers gained another important success in October 1917. After their earlier victories on both the western and eastern fronts, the Germans decided to attempt to knock Italy out of the war. This would eliminate any danger to their faltering Austro-Hungarian allies from the southwest. On 24 October an Austro-German force initiated an attack along the Isonzo front against the Italians. Using the same infiltration tactics that had proved so successful at Riga, the Austro-German attackers quickly broke through the Italian defenses. Overwhelmed by the initial attacks, the Italians retreated in disarray eighty miles to the Piave River, where they succeeded in establishing defensive positions by 12 November.[8] The Austro-German force, having advanced to within thirty miles of Venice, had outrun its logistical support and expended its energies, but it had also achieved a great victory. The Italians lost more than 300,000 men, and for the time being, at least, Italy was out of the war.

The Central Powers achieved one more success at the beginning of 1918. This was their greatest victory in the entire war. In a swift action on 7 November (25 October, according to the old Russian calendar), the Petrograd Soviet, under the leadership of Lenin, ousted the provisional government from power. Several days later it took control of Moscow. To implement Lenin's concept of accelerated historical development, the new Soviet government immediately indicated its intention to implement Lenin's "peace, land, bread" slogan. The other members of the Entente Powers, anticipating the arrival of significant American forces in the next year, had no interest in Lenin's proposal for a general peace. The Central Powers, however, accepted a Soviet armistice proposal on 28 November. Subsequently, on 22 December, delegations met in the Polish city of Brest-Litovsk. The Germans proved impervious to the Soviet attempt at propaganda, whereas the Soviet delegation was shocked by the extent of German demands. A Soviet attempt to finesse the problem by refusing further negotiations, characterized as "no war, no peace," utterly failed in the face of a German–Austro-Hungarian advance that occupied most of Byelorussia and Ukraine. The Central Powers signed a peace treaty with independent Ukraine on 9 February, putting additional pressure on the new Soviet government. Lacking a viable military force, it had few options but to reach an accommodation with the Central Powers. On 3 March the Soviet government signed a peace treaty with the four Central Powers. Under the terms of the Treaty of Brest-Litovsk, Russia withdrew from Estonia, Courland and Livonia (Latvia), Byelorussia, Ukraine, Finland, and Georgia. The Soviets also ceded Batum to the Ottoman Empire. These losses amounted to one-third of the population of the Russian Empire and most of its industrial resources.

The Germans did not intend to annex these areas directly. They envisioned them as satellite states between Germany and Russia, connected to Germany by economic, military, and even dynastic ties. Political entities emerged in Lithuania, Latvia, Estonia, Finland, Byelorussia, and Ukraine. In addition, the Soviet government made economic concessions to the Central Powers, granting access to foodstuffs and natural resources. The Treaty of Brest-Litovsk made Soviet Russia a more purely Russian state and undoubtedly enabled the Soviet government to stabilize and extend its control over the country. The Treaty of Brest-Litovsk was the Central Powers' greatest success in the war.[9] After more than three years of hard fighting and heavy losses on the eastern front, the Central Powers had prevailed and won the war in the east. This gave them an opportunity to win the war in the west before the appearance of American men and material made victory by the exhausted Central Powers unlikely.

Nevertheless, the Germans and Austrians had to retain significant numbers of troops in the east to enforce the peace and gather foodstuffs. German troops continued eastward into Ukraine even after Brest-Litovsk because of the chaotic conditions there. By 5 April they occupied Kharkov, the second largest city in Ukraine. On 1 May they seized the naval base at Sevastopol.

On 7 May 1918 the Central Powers signed a peace treaty with Romania, the Treaty of Bucharest. Only a rump portion of Moldavia remained under the control of the Romanian government in Iași after the Central Powers' victory in 1916. With Russia out of the war, the Romanians were isolated. The Austro-Hungarians obtained some territorial advantages in the Carpathians, and all the Central Powers enjoyed considerable economic gains, including access to Romanian grain. The disposition of the fertile Dobrudzha region, however, remained problematic for the rest of the war. The Bulgarians claimed most of it, in opposition to the interests of the other three Central Powers. With the Treaty of Bucharest, the Central Powers had defeated or at least silenced all their eastern European opponents.

Even before the peace settlement in the east, the Germans were preparing to make one final attempt to win the war in the west before the arrival of the Americans. The victories in the east had given them a slight numerical advantage in the west for the first time in the war. Nevertheless, they recognized that they were at the extreme limit of their ability to continue the war. The opportunities created by the victories in the west and the east were unlikely to offset the masses of American manpower and material already on their way to Europe. In November 1917 the Germans started to prepare for a major offensive in the west in the spring of 1918. They undertook five major efforts, at first directed mainly against British forces. Ludendorff was convinced that the key to victory in the west was the defeat of the British. With the British out of the war, the Germans could then turn on the French.

General Ludendorff opened his first offensive, called Operation Michael, or the Emperor's Battle (*Kaiserschlacht*), on 21 March 1918.[10] He chose the region between Arras and the Oise River, at the juncture between the British and French armies. This area included most of the

Somme battlefields of two years before. Ludendorff hoped to drive a wedge between the British and French armies and pin the British army up against the English Channel. In these circumstances, the British might well decide to take their army home. A British evacuation would leave him free to deal with the French and give the Americans no place to land their forces on the European continent. As the German offensive unfolded, one British army collapsed; another withdrew. The Germans managed to advance forty miles. By 23 March their long-range artillery, consisting of 15-inch naval guns firing 280mm projectiles and mounted on railway carriages, fired seventy-five miles into Paris. Although they had found a way across the trenches, the German success was tactical, not strategic. Their drive fell short of Amiens and did not turn the British. Forward forces outpaced supplies. Also, the Germans suffered heavy casualties, especially among the elite shock troops. Entente defenses recovered and slowed the German advance. By 3 April Operation Michael ground to a halt. That same day, pressured by the German success, the entente forces on the western front finally adopted a unified command structure. French General Ferdinand Foch (1851–1929) became the overall commander.

The results of Operation Michael were encouraging for the Germans. On 9 April Ludendorff launched the second of his three spring offensives, Operation Georgette. Here again, he hoped to push the British against the Channel. This offensive took place to the west in Flanders, around the town of Ypres. Its initial blow fell on the Second Portuguese Division serving in the line alongside the British. The Portuguese had entered the war in March 1916 because of ambitions to expand their African holdings at the expense of the German colonies. Their troops, long in the line and poorly led, soon collapsed in the face of the German onslaught. Once again the Germans made tactical gains, especially in the southern area of the battle around the town of Armentieres. Most of the territory the British had seized the previous autumn at Passchendaele was lost. Firm Belgian resistance, however, withstood a German attempt to sweep around the British in the north. By the end of the month Operation Georgette had exhausted its strength, for the same reasons Operation Michael had run out of steam. Again, Ludendorff had failed to gain a decisive result and had further depleted the strength of his forces. Meanwhile, American troops continued to arrive in France.

Ludendorff was determined to try again. On 27 May the third German offensive of the spring, Operation Blücher, began against the French army north of the Aisne River. This was intended to be a diversionary attack before a major effort against the British in Flanders. By 30 May the Germans had crossed the Aisne and reached the Marne. This encouraged Ludendorff to sustain the effort there. The Germans' proximity to Paris distracted him from his original intent. Too much elasticity of planning led the Germans into a forty-mile salient that was difficult to supply and defend. Ominously for the Germans, at Cantigny in Picardy at the end of May, an American infantry division repulsed their efforts to advance. Although limited in scope, this was the first American victory of the war.

In the summer Ludendorff continued his offensive efforts. Operation Gneisenau began on 9 June with the intent of filling out earlier advances between Noyon and Montdidier. It gained only about six miles before ending on 14 June in a French counterattack. Gneisenau was Ludendorff's final success. Tactical success continued to dazzle him, while strategic victory still eluded him.

Ludendorff made one more attempt to win the war in the summer of 1918. On 15 July he undertook the Champagne-Marne offensive, resulting in the Second Battle of the Marne. German troops advanced for three days until a counteroffensive ordered by General Foch ended their progress and slowly forced them back. This was the beginning of the German defeat on the western front. They had exhausted their manpower and material resources in their 1918 offensives but had failed to achieve victory. They could not contain the counteroffensive by an enemy invigorated by fresh American troops and tons of American supplies. This French counteroffensive ended the German threat to Paris and forced Ludendorff to call off his plans for a renewed effort in Flanders.

Throughout the summer the entente slowly pushed the Germans back. Heavy fighting developed around Amiens beginning on 8 August and around the German-held Saint-Mihiel salient on 12 September. This was the first effort in the war planned and implemented by an American force. It was also the largest American military undertaking since the American Civil War. By 16 September the Americans had cleared the salient. A major Franco-American effort occurred in the Meuse-Argonne beginning on 26 September. As at Saint-Mihiel, the American forces sustained heavy casualties. This fighting lasted until the end of the war in November. By this time, the Americans and French had reached the Meuse River. The Hindenburg Line in particular proved to be a formidable obstacle. In all this fighting the Germans did not break, conducting a fighting retreat in good order. Nevertheless, their ebbing strength was increasingly apparent. Ludendorff himself later called 8 August the "Black Day" of the German army, not because of significant German combat losses but because of the large numbers of demoralized German soldiers who gave themselves up to attacking British and Canadian troops east of Amiens. Five days later von Hindenburg and Ludendorff informed the German government that the offensives had failed, but this information did not reach the Reichstag until 2 October.

Well before this "Black Day," the failure of the U-boat campaign was evident. The Entente Powers had adopted a number of measures to combat the U-boats, including the development of audio sensors, better depth charges, and increased mine barrages in the North Sea and English Channel along U-boat routes. Probably the most effective anti–U-boat action was the convoy system, whereby destroyers and other anti–U-boat craft escorted cargo and troop ships from North Atlantic ports in Canada and the United States to Britain. Access to some German codes enabled the convoys to avoid U-boat locations. On 22 April 1918 the British implemented another anti–U-boat action when they attempted to block the pens in the Belgian ports of Zeebrugge and Ostend by sinking ships in front of them. This effort was not successful. German U-boats continued to operate until the end of the war, but with decreasing effectiveness.

The Germans developed the tactical ability to break the trench stalemate on the western front, but Ludendorff was unable to harness these tactics to an overall strategy to win the war in the west. The near German success in the 1918 offensives lent credence to the "stab in the back" lies (that is, that betrayal on Germany's home front had undermined its military efforts) that circulated in Germany after the defeat.

Meanwhile, the other Central Powers found themselves in growing difficulties elsewhere. The Balkan front had been relatively quiet since the fighting in 1916. In 1917 the Greek governmental dichotomy was resolved when the entente forced King Constantine to abdicate. The Salonika government then merged with the Athens government and joined the entente. Bulgarian defenses had held against entente assaults throughout

1917. At the beginning of 1918, despite strong Bulgarian objections, the Germans withdrew most of their troops from the Balkans to participate in the western front offensives. By the summer of 1918, the Bulgarian soldiers in Macedonia were hungry, exhausted, and demoralized. Entente forces mounted an offensive against them, beginning with a strong artillery attack on 14 September. Many of the Bulgarian defenders held, but on 16 September the entente forces, mainly French and Serbian soldiers, broke through the Bulgarian positions at Dobro Pole. The breach in their defenses forced a general Bulgarian retreat toward the prewar frontiers. Austria-Hungary and Germany had exhausted their ability to send meaningful assistance to the Macedonian front. By this time the Bulgarians were contemplating war against their Ottoman ally. Furthermore, revolutionary disorders had exploded among the Bulgarian troops, some of whom marched on Sofia to demand a republic. Bulgarian soldiers had been at arms, with two years' interruption, since 1912. These soldiers were angry at the military defeat and exhausted from six years of war. Because of all these problems, the Bulgarian government signed an armistice in Salonika on 30 September.[11] The last country to join the Central Powers was the first to leave. The fighting had started in the Balkans, and it ended there first. On 4 October Tsar Ferdinand abdicated in favor of his son, Boris III (1891–1943).

With Bulgaria out of the war, the Ottoman position became untenable. The Ottomans had enjoyed some recent successes in the Caucasus and had obtained Batum and Kars at Brest-Litovsk. Their soldiers had advanced into the region and, in the face of weak resistance from the post-tsarist Armenian government, had briefly occupied Baku on the Caspian, the capital of Azerbaijan. At the same time, the Ottomans suffered a serious defeat in Palestine and Syria. Entente forces were still a long way from Constantinople, but with Bulgaria out of the war, entente forces from the Salonika front moved through Thrace toward the Ottoman capital. On 30 October the Ottomans signed an armistice with the Entente Powers at Mudros on the island of Lemnos in the Aegean Sea.

Like the other Central Powers, Austria-Hungary was bereft of food and material resources, especially in the more industrialized Austrian part of the empire. After the Germans' spring successes, the Austro-Hungarian army attempted an offensive along the Piave front on 15 June, designed to crush the Italians between an attack from Tyrol and an attack across the

Piave River. After successfully crossing the river, the Austrians were unable to maintain logistical connections when it flooded and washed away temporary bridges. This was the Austro-Hungarian army's final offensive. An Italian counterattack threw the Austrians back across the Piave, but the Italians failed to follow up on their success, not moving until October. By that time the Austro-Hungarian army was in disarray. Many soldiers had deserted in anticipation of the collapse of the empire and the formation of national states. The Italians finally attacked across the Piave on 23 October.[12] Austrian resistance broke after several days of fighting, and most of the Austrian casualties were prisoners, indicative of the extent of their demoralization. On 30 October the Italians reached Vittorio Veneto. That same day the Austrians asked for an armistice, which was signed on 3 November.

The Bulgarian collapse made the inevitability of defeat clear to the German command. A strategy of defense in the west could not succeed with entente forces moving up from Macedonia into Serbia and Hungary. On 29 September Ludendorff suffered a mental breakdown. Negotiations for an armistice began on 5 October and continued until November. As the extent of the German collapse became clear to the entente, it pressed its advantage. In the meantime, the German fleet mutinied at Kiel on 30 October rather than accept orders to embark on a suicide mission against the British fleet in the North Sea. Revolutionary agitation broke out throughout Germany. On 9 November the German kaiser, upon learning that he no longer had the confidence of the army, abdicated and fled to the Netherlands. Two days later, at 11 A.M. on 11 November, the armistice with the Entente Powers went into effect. The war was over.

American intervention had proved critical for the entente victory. Desperation resulting from the success of British naval strategy caused the Germans to return to the U-boat strategy in 1917, even though it had so antagonized the Americans two years earlier. Nevertheless, at the time of their entry in the war, the Americans were not prepared to intervene in Europe militarily. Before American forces appeared in Europe, the stalemate ended in a series of Central Powers successes and Entente Powers defeats. By the end of 1917 the Central Powers had achieved victories on all their European fronts, creating an opportunity for the Germans to win the war. Ludendorff's spring and summer offensives in 1918 were a race to defeat the British and French on the western front before the Americans' considerable manpower and material resources could be brought to bear. The U-boats singularly failed to stop the Americans from crossing the North Atlantic. Without the influx of American resources, the Entente Powers might have succumbed to the Germans' spring offensives in 1918. Even if they had managed to hold out, they might have been forced to reach a negotiated end to the war because of exhaustion. For the first time in modern history, an external power had provided the decisive edge in a European conflict. The first phase of the century of conflict was coming to a conclusion.

Chapter 5

PEACE SETTLEMENT

The failed settlement of the First World War had its origins in the aims of the belligerents. Both sides quickly framed their objectives in mainly geographic terms. At first no one envisioned a political or ideological alteration of Europe. Once the fighting began, the military dictated the course of events, not the diplomats, who had singularly failed in the summer of 1914. Fighting, not talking, determined the war aims.

At the onset of the war, the Entente Powers sought to expand their territories in Europe and thus limit Germany and Austria-Hungary. The Belgians wanted to annex Luxembourg. Even though young Grand Duchess Marie Adelaide (1894–1924) of Luxembourg had compromised herself with the German occupiers of her country, Belgian expansion aroused little enthusiasm among the other Entente Powers, especially France. The British had few territorial aspirations on the continent. They wanted to curtail the power of the German fleet and especially the U-boats. The French wanted the return of Alsace-Lorraine; they also wanted to annex Germany's coal-rich Saar region and hoped to undermine the unity that had held Germany together since 1871 and thus reestablish the balance of power in Europe that had existed before that time. Belgium, Britain, France, and Portugal all aspired to parts of the German colonial empire.

In 1914 the Russians were more ambitious than their allies. They sought the annexation of East Prussia, along with additional Polish and Ukrainian lands in Austrian Galicia and Bukovina. Their advocacy of a Poland under the Romanov dynasty aroused little enthusiasm among German and Austrian Poles, let alone Russian Poles. The Russians enjoyed more success in Galicia among the Ukrainian population. Russian troops occupied eastern Galicia from the fall of 1914 until the summer of 1915, and briefly again in the summer of 1916. They also held Bukovina from October 1914 to June 1915 and again from June 1916 to July 1917. In the Constantinople Agreements of 18 March 1915, the British and French assented to Russia's ancient *desirata* of Constantinople and the straits. This became Russia's primary war aim.

With the 26 April 1915 Treaty of London, Britain, France, and Russia recognized Italian claims to Austro-Hungarian territories in the eastern Adriatic, including Trieste and much of Dalmatia and the Adriatic islands, the port of Valona in Albania, southern Tyrol, and Trentino. The Italians also had territorial ambitions in Anatolia.

The Romanians entered the war after signing a treaty with the Entente Powers on 17 August 1916 that promised them the Austro-Hungarian territories of the Banat of Temesvár, Bukovina, and Transylvania and a border with Hungary on the Tisza River. The Serbs claimed Bosnia-Hercegovina, Dalmatia, parts of southern Hungary, and access to the Adriatic through northern Albania. Greek ambitions were far reaching. They sought to acquire Bulgarian-held western Thrace, but even more ambitiously, they hoped to realize the *Megale Idea* (Great Idea) of obtaining Constantinople and parts of Anatolia to restore the Byzantine state extinguished by the Ottomans in 1453.

Significantly, most of these claims did not overlap. Only the Italian and Serb claims to Dalmatia conflicted. The Corfu Declaration of 20 July 1917, in which Serbian, Croat, and Slovene representatives called for the establishment of a united Yugoslav state after the war, represented a rejection of Italian claims to the eastern Adriatic. Otherwise, the geographic separation of the Entente Powers ensured that they did not compete among themselves for the Central Powers' European territories.

During the course of the war the Entente Powers had little opportunity to implement their territorial programs. In most cases entente troops did not physically intrude on the European territories of the Central Powers until the end of the war. The western front was almost entirely in Belgium and France. The French army managed to occupy only a few villages in southern Alsace. The Italians struggled to reach a few isolated alpine areas of Austria-Hungary. In the east the Russians were a little more successful, occupying eastern Galicia and Bukovina. They combined these two areas into a single *guberniia* and Ukrainianized the administration to some degree. The Serbs enjoyed only ephemeral successes at the beginning of the war in Bosnia and Hercegovina, and the Romanians had no success in occupying their objectives in Transylvania.

The Central Powers no less than the Entente Powers developed specific, mainly territorial war aims. Austro-Hungarian war aims were relatively modest. The Habsburg government had little interest in acquiring neighboring territories and adding to the already complicated ethnic mix of the empire. The Austrians wanted to punish Serbia and ensure that it could not threaten the empire, but this did not necessarily mean the direct annexation of Serbia. The Austrians did, however, seek to annex the Lovčen, a Montenegrin mountain looming over the Austro-Hungarian Adriatic naval base at Cattaro. They also obtained small border changes in Transylvania under the 1918 Treaty of Bucharest with Romania. Otherwise, the Austrians wanted to control Albania and sought a Polish state tied to the dual monarchy through the Habsburg dynasty. As the war persisted, food became a primary war aim for Austria-Hungary. The Austro-Hungarians urged the signing of the treaties of Brest-Litovsk and Bucharest as a means of securing sustenance for their hungry cities.

The Bulgarians wanted to obtain Macedonia from Serbia and Greece and regain Dobrudzha from Romania. The Austrians and Germans promised these territories to Bulgaria as inducements to join the war. The Ottomans also ceded the lower Maritsa valley to Bulgaria. The failure of the other Central Powers to grant all of Dobrudzha to Bulgaria under the Treaty of Bucharest was a source of great disappointment and irritation to the Bulgarians. Even as the Bulgarian army retreated from Macedonia in September 1918, the Bulgarian government hectored the Germans about this issue.

German aspirations were wide ranging. As early as 9 September 1914 German chancellor Theobald von Bethmann-Hollweg (1856–1921) specified that Germany wanted to control a Polish state and the Baltic provinces of Russia.[1] In the west, Germany wanted Belgium and specific parts of France, including Belfort, Briey, and the Channel coast from Dunkirk to Boulogne. The Germans also envisioned their establishment of economic and political hegemony over most of the continent under a concept called *Mitteleuropa*. This central European idea included the Netherlands and Switzerland as well as most of eastern Europe. German geographer Friedrich Naumann (1860–1919) elucidated this concept in a book appropriately titled *Mitteleuropa* published in 1915. Like many Germans, Hindenburg and Ludendorff found the *Mitteleuropa* concept appealing, although they attempted to implement the plan in much more direct terms than those envisioned by Naumann. The *Mitteleuropa* idea eventually came to pass in a much less coercive form at the beginning of the twenty-first century with the creation of a European Union based on a strong and reunited Germany.

The Treaty of Brest-Litovsk provided a clear indication of German plans. They wanted to establish the buffer states of Finland, Poland, Ukraine, Lithuania, and Courland between Germany and Russia. These states would all to be tied to Germany both politically and economically, as would Romania under the Treaty of Bucharest. This German vision of a new Europe was at once both medieval and modern. It employed ties of blood as well as economic incentives to link the eastern fringe to the center.

Ottoman aspirations in Europe were mainly at the expense of Central Powers ally Bulgaria. The Ottomans wanted the Maritsa valley returned and sought to regain western Thrace, lost to Bulgaria in the Balkan Wars. The return of these areas to Ottoman control would have enhanced the security of Constantinople on the European side. The Ottomans' demands made them problematic allies with Bulgaria throughout the war.

The Central Powers, more compact and more proximate than the peripheral Entente Powers, developed several intra-alliance conflicts over their territorial war aims. For instance, Austrian and German plans for Poland were inconsistent. Neither the Austrians nor the Germans wished to cede their own Polish territories to the "self-governing" Polish state they envisioned. Both Austria and Germany intended the new state to have dynastic links with themselves, and they quarreled over the eastern border of the new state while making peace with and seeking foodstuffs from the newly independent Ukraine at Brest-Litovsk.

Bulgarian insistence on the annexation of most of Dobrudzha created another conflict among the Central Powers. Bulgarian claims to Dobrudzha extended back to the ephemeral San Stefano Treaty of 1878. The Austrians and Germans favored a condominium in Dobrudzha so they could more easily exploit the food resources there. The Ottomans sought to finagle their interest in Dobrudzha for the retrocession of the Maritsa valley and western Thrace, causing great outrage in Bulgaria.

Because of their initial success in the west and general successes in the east, the Central Powers were able to implement some of their aims. The Austrians never determined the extent of their annexationist claims, and they failed to establish any institutions more permanent than military governments in Serbia, Montenegro, and Albania.

The Bulgarians directly annexed Macedonia. On the northwestern Macedonian frontier, they came into conflict with the Austrians in occupied Albania and Kosovo over the precise delineation of the frontiers. Here the Bulgarians adhered to the same Slavic cause that had produced conflict between the Austrians (as Albanian advocates) and the Serbs in the fall of 1913. The Bulgarians established rigorous occupation governments in southern Serbia up to the Morava River and in the part of Greek Macedonia they occupied.

In the west the Germans annexed Luxembourg, which had been a member of the German Confederation until 1866. They installed military governments to administer occupied Belgium and France. German officials made some effort to favor the Flemish areas of Belgium because of linguistic and cultural connections and because of plans to establish a German presence on the English Channel. The prospect of annexation to Germany found little support among the Flemish population.

In Poland the Austrians and Germans announced on 6 November 1916 that a "self-governing" Polish state would be established after the war. They permitted the formation of a regency council and a Polish army, but neither of these aroused much enthusiasm. In the Baltic the Germans pursued a dynastic policy to tie the region closely to the Reich. In Lithuania, under German occupation since March 1915, a national council, the *Truba*, met on 18 September 1917 in Vilnius with German sanction. The Germans planned to place a German prince, Wilhelm Urach of Württemberg (1897–1957), on the throne of a restored Lithuania; he even took the Lithuanian title Mindaugas II. After the occupation of southern Latvia in 1917, the Germans planned for a duchy of Courland tied to Germany through the Hohenzollern dynasty. Kaiser Wilhelm wanted the title duke of Courland for himself. The Germans also recognized Finnish independence with the Treaty of Brest-Litovsk and provided 12,000 troops to assist Finnish nationalists fighting a civil war against Soviet-backed Finnish communists. The Germans and Finnish nationalists quickly won this conflict in the spring of 1918, and the Finns offered their throne to

Wilhelm II's brother-in-law, Friedrich Karl of Hesse-Kassel (1868–1940). Although the Finns succeeded in preserving their independence, the German collapse in the fall of 1918 made the offer moot. The Germans also established a Byelorussian National Council at the beginning of 1918 to form a political basis for the separation of this region from Russia. Only a few of the educated elite of this poor and ethnically mixed region claimed a Byelorussian identity.

The Ottoman advance into the Transcaucasian region in 1918 brought about the annexation of Batum and Kars, territories lost to the Russians with the 1878 Treaty of Berlin. The Ottomans entered Baku on 15 September 1918, but at this late date they were unable to establish any kind of permanent presence. After the October 1918 armistice, Ottoman forces withdrew from this region.

The failure to achieve immediate victory in 1914 aroused great concern in the German government. Nevertheless, it made no diplomatic efforts to achieve a favorable resolution of the conflict until 1916. During the Battle of Verdun and the Brusilov offensive in the summer of 1916, the hard-pressed Germans met with Russian representatives in Stockholm, Sweden, to discuss a negotiated peace between Germany and Russia.[2] The future of Poland was an obstacle, but contacts continued through the end of the year. At the same time, von Bethmann-Hollweg contacted the Americans, seeking their mediation to end the war. This had no result. Hindenburg and Ludendorff, who assumed power in 1916, would consider nothing less than a military victory for Germany.

The failure of either side to realize clear victory at the beginning of the war led even the Americans to attempt to find a peaceful solution as early as 1915. That year American industrialist Henry Ford (1863–1947) embarked on a futile mission to Europe to persuade both sides to end the war. In 1916 Colonel Edward M. House (1858–1938), a confidant of President Wilson, proposed a peace conference based on the return of Alsace-Lorraine to France, the restoration of Belgium, and access to the warm sea for Russia. This had little appeal for the Central Powers. On 18 December 1916 President Wilson formally requested both sides to state the conditions they would accept. The Entente Powers replied on 10 January 1917, calling for the Germans and Austrians to evacuate virtually all the territories they had occupied during the war, including Belgium, Serbia, and parts of France, Romania, and Russia. The Central Powers failed to present a clear program to Wilson, despite an earlier indication of interest in a negotiated peace. On 22 January Wilson called for "peace without victory." On 19 July 1917 the German Reichstag passed a resolution calling for peace without annexations or indemnities. The Reichstag, however, could not prevail against the annexationist program of the Hindenburg-Ludendorff dictatorship or against the successes of German arms in 1917. The Reichstag was not alone in its war weariness.

In February 1917 the Austro-Hungarians, who were barely maintaining a war effort, approached the French government through Sixtus of Bourbon-Parma (1886–1934), an officer in the Belgian army and the brother of Empress Zita of Austria-Hungary (1892–1989), inquiring about terms for a separate peace. This yielded no result. The next year, however, the French published the correspondence of Prince Sixtus. This had the consequence of binding the Austrians, who initially denied the approach, even more tightly to their German allies.

At the same time, some French politicians were calling for negotiations. In 1917 Joseph Caillaux (1863–1944), a former minister of finance, urged a negotiated peace, although he insisted on the return of Alsace-Lorraine. The French government refused to consider Caillaux's proposals. His appeals for peace resulted in his arrest in January 1918.

The Bolshevik seizure of power in Russia, with its call for immediate peace and self-determination for the peoples of Russia, posed a huge challenge for the increasingly war-weary populations of both sides. President Wilson responded on 8 January 1918 with his Fourteen Points.[3] Wilson intended his points not only to be the basis for ending the current war but also to ensure that there could be no future war; he also hoped to counter the appeal of Lenin's call for a peace with no annexations. The Entente Powers, eager to hasten the appearance of American troops on the western front, quickly accepted the Fourteen Points as the basis for a peace settlement. After the failure of the German offensives became clear in the summer of 1918, the German government also accepted them as the basis for a negotiated peace.

The first five points addressed issues that Wilson perceived to be general causes of war: (1) no secret diplomacy, (2) freedom of the seas, (3) removal of economic barriers among nations, (4) arms reduction, and (5) impartial adjustment of colonial claims. The next eight points addressed specific European issues that Wilson understood to be the basis for conflict: (6) German evacuation of Russia; (7) restoration of Belgian independence; (8) return of Alsace-Lorraine to France; (9) adjustment of Italian frontiers according to nationality; (10) autonomous development for the peoples of Austria-Hungary; (11) restoration of Serbia, Montenegro, and Romania and access to the sea for Serbia; (12) autonomy for the peoples of the Ottoman Empire and free passage for all through the straits; and (13) an independent Poland with access to the sea. The fourteenth point returned to a general issue: establishment of a League of Nations for the resolution of any future conflicts and disputes. From their inception, the Fourteen Points were an ambitious and idealistic means of addressing a complex subject. After the Germans signed the armistice on 11 November, however, the Fourteen Points lost much of their attraction for the entente governments. The British and especially the French considered them to be naïve. Georges Clemenceau (1841–1929), the French prime minister, remarked that God himself needed only ten commandments, but Wilson required fourteen.

Wilson announced his intention of personally participating in the peace process, forcing the other entente leaders to do so. He sailed for Paris, the agreed-on location of the meeting, in December 1918. In doing so, he became the first American president to visit Europe while in office. He arrived to great acclaim, but when the peace talks began, much of his popularity waned.[4]

The first major action of the assembled entente representatives was to exclude the German delegation, claiming that the defeated foe had no part in the peace talks. This gave the Germans little reason to support the results of the Paris process, which they called the *Diktat*, or dictated peace.

Other problems soon arose. The Italians fully expected to realize the territorial gains in the eastern Adriatic promised by the 1915 Treaty of London.[5] Wilson firmly rejected this assumption, since the population of these areas was overwhelmingly Croat and Slovene. The angry Italian delegation walked out of the conference. They returned, however, to obtain only South Tyrol (Trentino), Istria, and a few small areas in the Adriatic, including the island of Lagosta, the Adriatic port of Zara, and the Albanian island of Saseno and port of Valona. The combined population of these areas amounted to about 500,000, the same number of Italian military losses in the war. (By comparison, the Americans sustained about

60,000 military deaths in the war.) Italy's huge sacrifices but relative lack of military success in the war created great frustration, and the results in Paris left the Italians greatly disappointed.

Much more serious were two disputes that developed between the French and the Americans. The first of these involved the French demand for reparations. The northern part of France had been the main location of the western front and had consequently suffered tremendous physical damage because of the fighting and the deliberate destruction by the Germans. The Americans opposed the imposition of heavy financial burdens on defeated Germany, considering this to be an obstacle to the creation of a permanent peace. The other problem lay in the French attempts to divide Germany. In particular, the French hoped to separate the area west of the Rhine River from the remainder of Germany. To this end, they sponsored a Rhineland separatist movement that aroused little enthusiasm. After some wrangling, the Americans and French reached a compromise. The Americans agreed to the imposition of an indemnity on Germany, although they refused to accept any direct payments. In return, the French abandoned the prospect of an independent Rhineland but secured the right to occupy the Rhineland. Although this settlement represented a retreat from Wilson's idealism, he accepted it to secure the success of the League of Nations.

The conditions of peace imposed on Germany were stringent.[6] They included the loss of territories in the east to a new Polish state, including parts of West Prussia, Posen, and lower Silesia; the loss of Alsace-Lorraine to France; and the loss of Eupen and Malmedy to Belgium and North Schleswig to Denmark. In addition, all German overseas colonies were lost. Strict limitations were imposed on the German armed forces; they were permitted only a small army of 100,000 men, a coastal navy, and no air force. Tanks and heavy artillery were forbidden. Germany also had to agree to pay an indemnity of an as yet uncalculated amount. Finally, Article 231 of the treaty required that Germany acknowledge responsibility for causing the war. These terms shocked even some entente delegates and appalled the Germans. Nevertheless, they had no choice but to agree (although they did so under protest): the British blockade remained in force, the German military was bereft of supplies and reserves, and social revolution threatened. The victorious Entente Powers and vanquished

Germany signed the Treaty of Versailles on 28 June 1919, five years to the day after the assassination in Sarajevo.

Similar harsh treaties requiring territorial loss, military limitations, and indemnity payments were imposed on the other Central Powers. The Treaty of St. Germain, signed on 10 September 1919, forbade the over-whelmingly German rump of Austria, now merely an alpine tail stuck on the head of the region around Vienna, from unifying with Germany. Bulgaria, its dream of Macedonia dashed once again, lost its Aegean coast to Greece and small western areas to the new Yugoslav state under the Treaty of Neuilly, signed on 27 November 1919. Hungary suffered the loss of two-thirds of its prewar population and three-quarters of its territory with the Treaty of Trianon, signed on 4 June 1920. Although most of these losses did not involve ethnic Hungarians, several million Hungarians found themselves in the new state of Czechoslovakia, the greatly augmented Romania, the new state of Yugoslavia, and even rump Austria. Bulgarian and Hungarian refugees poured into the defeated states from territories assigned to others. In the 10 August 1920 Treaty of Sèvres, the Ottoman Empire suffered a fate similar to that of the Habsburg Empire in 1918. Eastern Anatolia was divided into Armenian and Kurdish national states. The British took Mesopotamia, the French took Syria, and the Greeks occupied eastern Thrace and Smyrna (Izmir) and its hinterland. The vital passage between the Mediterranean and the Black Sea was to be supervised by an International Straits Commission.

The conditions forced on the defeated Central Powers in Paris were less harsh than those they imposed on their own defeated foes at Brest-Litovsk and Bucharest. Still, a less onerous peace might not have been so firmly rejected by the Central Powers and might have enabled them to more easily integrate into postwar Europe. There is no doubt that this would have lessened the chance of renewed conflict in an exhausted Europe. In any event, European conflict began again as soon as another generation of Austrian, Bulgarian, German, Hungarian, and other males became old enough to serve as soldiers to overturn the Paris peace settlement.

In fact, fighting continued in several locations even as diplomats attempted to create a new Europe out of the remains of the old one. A radical Hungarian government headed by communist Béla Kun (1888–1939) made a desperate attempt to retain much of historic Hungary. This resulted in fighting in Slovakia against the forces of the new Czechoslovak state, and it provoked the invasion of the Romanian army in the fall of 1919. The Romanians defeated the forces of the Hungarian radicals and occupied Budapest in November 1919. Fighting also developed around areas in Silesia claimed by both the Germans and the new Polish state. There, the German *Freikorps* (volunteers supposedly unaffiliated with the regular German army) were generally successful in maintaining German authority.

The most severe and destructive fighting occurred in a horribly complex war in Russia. The multifaceted fighting there defies easy analysis, but it can best be understood as three distinct conflicts—a Russian civil war, foreign intervention in Russia, and national independence movements—that were interactive and contemporaneous.

Opposition to Lenin's Soviet government began immediately after the Bolshevik seizure of power. By the spring of 1918 it had erupted into civil war in several locations. The concessions made by the Soviets at Brest-Litovsk helped fuel the conflagration. Supporters of the Soviet regime became known as the Reds, and its opponents became known as the Whites, whether they were monarchists or militarists or belonged to any of the various noncommunist political movements, from liberals to socialists.

The first important center of opposition to the Soviet regime developed in the lower Don and Kuban regions of southern Russia. There Cossack forces, seeking to maintain the entitlements they had enjoyed under the tsarist and provisional regimes, proclaimed a Don republic on 13 November, soon after the Soviet seizure of power. A number of officers who traveled to the Don region to escape from the Soviet government formed the Volunteer Army, which made common cause with the Don Cossacks and became the first significant White force. After a series of travails, including the death in action of the original commander, General Lavr Kornilov (1870–1918), in May 1918, the White forces came under the command of General Anton I. Denikin (1872–1947).[7] The White Army surrounded Tsaritsyn (later Stalingrad; now Volgograd) in the fall of 1918 but failed to take it. Had Tsaritsyn fallen then, Denikin's forces might have made contact with White forces in the upper Volga region, allowing them to present a united front against the Reds. In October 1919 Denikin mounted a major offensive that took him as far as Orel. Political naïveté hampered Denikin's efforts, however. He failed to address the very social and political issues that had engendered the Russian revolutions. His slogan "Russia one and indivisible" found little support among peasants intent on keeping the land they had seized or among Ukrainian and other nationalists. Opposition from Ukrainian nationalists and Nestor Makhno's (1889–1934) anarchist (Black) forces behind Denikin's lines weakened his command and logistical abilities as the front expanded, and he suffered defeat south of Tula in October 1919. By March 1920 Denikin's army had retreated all the way down to the Crimea.

Later, one of Denikin's subordinates, General Baron Peter von Wrangel (1878–1928), offered a viable social program, including land reform. He was the only White leader to do so. During the Polish invasion of Ukraine in the summer of 1920, Wrangel briefly occupied much of southern Ukraine, but his forces were too few to sustain their initial success. Wrangel had to retreat to the Crimea in the fall of 1920. In November 1920 the remaining White forces evacuated the Crimea by sea and scattered throughout Europe.

Another major source of opposition arose in the upper Volga region. The Constitutional Convention (*Komuch*), closed down by Lenin after a one-day session in January, reconstituted itself in Samara in May 1918. In ousting the local Red forces, it received assistance from the Czechoslovak Legion, which had been organized chiefly from Czech and some Slovak prisoners of war from the Austro-Hungarian army. The Czech Legion had expected to fight against the Central Powers on the eastern front, but the Treaty of Brest-Litovsk, had made this impossible. The legion began to move east on the Trans-Siberian Railroad to Vladivostok, where it could embark on ships headed to France and service on the western front. As it did so, it came into conflict with the Reds. Extending along the railroad all the way from the Volga to Vladivostok, the Czech Legion became the best-organized force in Siberia. In May 1918 it came into conflict with Red forces and became enmeshed in the Russian civil war, at first supporting the White forces. *Komuch* troops briefly held Kazan and Simbirsk. After a brief retreat, the Whites resumed their westward offensive. As they approached Ekaterinburg on 16 July 1918, the local Red authorities, acting on Lenin's orders, killed the tsar and his family, who were confined there. Conflicting centers of authority weakened the western Siberian anti-Red governments. On 18 November Admiral Alexander Kolchak

(1874–1920) overthrew the government and established a White military dictatorship at Omsk. He professed to be the leader of all White forces and the "supreme ruler of Russia," but he was never able to exercise this claim. Kolchak's forces advanced westward in the winter of 1919, taking Perm and moving toward Vyatka.[8] But his army became overextended, and the resurgent Red Army stopped Kolchak's army before it reached the Volga. After the Whites suffered a major defeat at Ufa on 9 June 1919, they fell back on the Trans-Siberian Railroad. Siberia had few human or material resources to sustain Kolchak's movement, and his brutal policies alienated the thin population of this vast region. The Reds captured Kolchak at Irkutsk and executed him on 7 February 1920.

In northwestern Russia, White forces organized in Estonia under the leadership of General Nikolai Yudenich (1862–1933) briefly threatened Petrograd during the fall of 1919. These Whites reached the outskirts of the former capital but were too few to actually take the city or even mount a siege. They quickly retreated to Estonia and were interned there. A White force in Latvia, the Western Volunteer Army commanded by General Pavel Bermondt-Avalov (1884–1973), cooperated with German Freikorps against Latvian and Lithuanian nationalists. It had little local support other than from Baltic Germans. In the far north, a White government formed in Archangel and Murmansk. As in Siberia, a military officer, General Evgeni Miller (1867–1937), seized control and remained in power until 1920. After the evacuation of American, British, and Canadian troops from the region, this government could not defend itself against Red attacks. Archangel fell to a Red Army offensive on 21 February 1920, while the more remote Murmansk held out until 13 March.

The Whites were never able to coordinate their forces from their four main areas of control. Nor did their presence on the periphery of Russia give them access to the main human and material resources located in the center of the country. Finally, the Whites were never able to articulate a viable political program. They were against the Reds, but it was often difficult for the peasants they encountered to ascertain exactly what the Whites stood for.

In addition to the Red versus White conflict, Black anarchist forces led by Makhno operated successfully in much of the southern Ukraine against both Reds and Whites.[9] Although Makhno, a convicted criminal, committed many outrages against civilian populations, his forces were not markedly anti-Semitic, unlike those of the Reds and Whites. After the White defeat, Makhno eventually eluded pursuing Red forces to reach safety in Romania. He died an alcoholic in Paris.

In the Tambov region of central Russia, so-called Green bands fought the Reds. These were armed peasants who opposed communist collectivization and confiscation. They essentially sought a social revolutionary program of government based on peasant power. The Reds were unable to suppress the Green movement until 1921.

Amidst the civil war, German and Austrian troops occupied large areas of in the west as a result of the Treaty of Brest-Litovsk, and entente troops intruded into Russia in the north at Murmansk and Archangel and in the Far East at Vladivostok. This foreign intervention added another element to the chaos in Russia. British and Canadian forces landed in the north beginning in June 1918, ostensibly to prevent the war supplies landed at Archangel and Murmansk from falling into German hands. Americans arrived in September. A mixed force appeared in the Far East beginning in August 1918. The largest component of this force was Japanese, with Japan sending more than 70,000 troops to Siberia. The French maintained a brief presence, from December 1918 to April 1919, in Odessa. A British mission lent considerable advisory and material support to Denikin's efforts in south Russia.

The interventionists' lack of clear purpose and their soldiers' eagerness to return home, especially after the 11 November 1918 armistice, led to their withdrawal in 1920. The last Czechoslovak troops left Vladivostok on 2 September 1920. The interventionists departed from Archangel in September 1919 and from Murmansk the next month. The Japanese remained the longest, staying in the Far East until 1922 and in northern Sakhalin until 1925. Most of the entente forces soon forgot the cold and confusing Russian episode. Many Russians remembered it, however, and the underlying resentment resurfaced during the Cold War.

While the civil war raged and the foreign forces occupied the fringes of Russia, a third issue added to the disarray in Russia. Many of the non-Russian peoples seized the opportunity presented by the Russian revolutions to assert their national independence. Those in the west, such as Poles, Byelorussians, Lithuanians, Finns, and Ukrainians, were able to do so initially with some German assistance. The Byelorussian National Republic was unable to survive the withdrawal of the Germans at the end of 1918, however. The next year the Baltic nations found themselves fighting both Germans and Reds. In Ukraine a particularly complicated situation arose. From 1918 to 1921 a *Rada* (council) government, pro-German General Pavlo Skoropadsky (1873–1945), the Reds, Denikin, nationalist Symon Petlura (1879–1926), and the Poles held sway in Ukraine at various times. Control in Kiev changed hands eighteen times during this period.

The interventionists remained largely indifferent to the national independence movements. In the Baltic the British navy provided some assistance to the Estonians and Latvians. Both Reds and Whites opposed the national independence movements, although the Reds initially claimed to support national self-determination. By 1921 the Reds, after their victory in the civil war, were able to suppress the national movements in Ukraine and the Caucasus. Mainly Turkic Muslims in central Asia, known as *Basmachis,* continued fighting until the late 1920s.

The most important of the national liberation conflicts was the Russo-Polish War of 1919–1921. The new Polish state under General Jósef Piłsudski (1867–1935) attempted to reestablish the frontiers of the prepartition 1772 Polish Commonwealth consisting of Byelorussia, Lithuania, and Ukraine. In June 1920 a major offensive effort carried the Poles and their Ukrainian allies as far as Kiev and Minsk. A Red Army counteroffensive under the command of the so-called Red Napoleon, General Mikhail Tukhachevsky (1893–1937), swept the Poles back to the gates of Warsaw by August. Tukhachevsky was a young officer of noble origin who had distinguished himself in the Imperial Russian Army and then joined the Reds in the Russian civil war. At Warsaw, Piłsudski advanced through a gap in the Red lines and broke the invaders' attack.[10] The failure of Red troops in the south to close with those in the north helped secure the Polish success. The Poles forced part of the Red Army into German East Prussia. This presaged the German-Russian cooperation that would doom Poland less than twenty years later. The Polish victory, called the "Miracle on the Vistula," guaranteed the independence of the new Polish state. The Treaty of Riga, signed the next year, extended Polish frontiers into Byelorussia and Ukraine, although Minsk and Kiev remained with the Soviets. The Riga treaty also ensured the Polish-Soviet hostility that would reignite in September 1939.

The civil war, foreign intervention, and national independence movements all occurring in the territories of the Russian Empire extended conflict over a vast area and caused tremendous loss of life and infrastructure. In the end, control of the central core of Russia between Petrograd and Moscow proved critical for the victorious Reds. The complexity and brutality of these conflicts would be matched in twentieth-century Europe only by the fighting in Yugoslavia during the Second World War. Millions of inhabitants of the former Russian Empire died prematurely during this period from war, disease, and starvation, and hundreds of thousands fled. Precise figures are elusive. The Soviet state that emerged after the chaotic and cataclysmic fighting was hampered by the loss of population and a damaged economic infrastructure.

Other conflicts continued on the periphery of Europe. In the west, in Ireland, a rebellion against British rule broke out in April 1916 in Dublin. The Germans made an abortive attempt to assist the so-called Easter Rebellion at the outset, but after a week of fighting, the British managed to suppress it. In the aftermath of the rebellion, the British moved to loosen the ties between Britain and Ireland, but events outran British intentions. Nationalist agitation increased, and guerrilla warfare spread throughout the country. British attempts to end the fighting using hastily recruited troops known as Black and Tans (because of the colors of their improvised uniforms) only made matters worse. Fighting between Irish nationalists and British troops continued until 1921, when a Free State of Ireland (Eire) was proclaimed that included only the mainly Catholic southern areas. Northern Ireland remained under British control. Fighting between Irish supporters of the Free State and more radical Irish republicans, who rejected accommodation with the British and the separation of largely Protestant Northern Ireland from the Catholic south, continued for another year.

Meanwhile, at the eastern edge of Europe, fighting erupted between Greek and Turkish forces. The Greeks sought to expand their position in Anatolia at the expense of the defeated Ottoman government. This represented the implementation of the *Megale Idea* of Greek nationalism that sought to reestablish the Byzantine Empire. In May 1919 a Greek army occupied Smyrna (Izmir) on the west coast of Anatolia in anticipation of its assignment to Greece in the peace settlement (the Treaty of Sèvres gave most of this region to Greece). The Greeks subsequently extended their control over the hinterland. A resurgent Turkish army under the leadership of Mustafa Kemal, the former Young Turk and hero of the defense of Gallipoli and the future Atatürk, contested these Greek attempts to extend their control of Anatolia. At the Battle of the Sakarya (Sangarios) in central Anatolia in August and September 1921, Kemal's Turkish forces defeated the overextended Greeks, who then slowly withdrew to the Aegean. Greek troops evacuated Smyrna in September 1922, accompanied by hundreds of thousands of Greek civilians. With this disorganized exodus, more than 3,000 years of Greek presence in western Anatolia ended. The dream of the *Megale Idea* was over. The Greeks also had to evacuate Adrianople, which they had occupied in 1920. And in 1924 they left southern Albania, where they had supported a Greek state called Northern Epirus, although they did not abandon their claims to this region. After the Greek defeat, the Turks negotiated a new treaty at Lausanne, Switzerland, in 1923 that relaxed the conditions of the Treaty of Sèvres. This Treaty of Lausanne provided some hope to the Germans, Bulgarians, and Hungarians that their treaties could be revised.

The first cycle of the twentieth-century European conflict defied a facile and complete resolution. The Paris peace settlement was remarkably fragile, lasting only two decades. Many of the forces unleashed by the conflict remained active even after the formal attempts to settle it, especially and confusingly in Russia. Only in the early 1920s did conflict temporarily reach an exhausted stopping point.

Chapter 6

PRESERVING THE PEACE, UNDERMINING THE PEACE

The peace settlement achieved at Paris was fragile from its inception. Britain would not be a major supporter. The elimination of the German High Seas Fleet and the U-boats assuaged British security concerns, while the responsibilities of a global empire placed increasing demands on Britain's flagging energies. Immediately after the war, the Irish quest for independence provided a major distraction from continental affairs. Italy, largely because of its contention that its rewards did not match its losses in the war, was a problematic advocate for preservation of the peace. Germany, though exhausted and defeated, remained demographically and economically the main power in Europe. The Paris *Diktat* found few supporters there. Russia had to recover from seven years of war, revolution, and civil strife, together with the entwined problems of famine, plague, and destruction. Defeated by Germany in the war and shunned by the Entente Powers at Paris, Soviet Russia had little reason to support the peace settlement.

Between these two temporarily enfeebled powers, a weak and quarrelsome belt of thirteen eastern European states stretched from the Arctic Circle to the Mediterranean. The major beneficiaries of the settlement in eastern Europe, chief among them a restored Poland, a greatly enhanced Romania, and the new states of Czechoslovakia and Yugoslavia, supported the peace settlement. Former German allies Hungary and Bulgaria unabashedly sought revision of the settlement. All sought to survive.

The United States, a major factor in the military victory of the Entente Powers, rejected the terms of the settlement and the League of Nations. Afterward, the Washington government retreated into isolationism. Under these circumstances, preservation of the Paris peace settlement was problematic from its inception.

Preserving the Peace

The onus of responsibility for maintaining the provisions of the settlement fell on France. Though determined to preserve the peace, the French lacked the demographic and economic resources to manage a bitter and recalcitrant Germany. Nevertheless, a number of important mechanisms and resolutions for the preservation of the Paris peace settlement existed.

One important factor in maintaining peace and stability in Europe was the League of Nations.[1] Headquartered in Geneva, the League provided a framework for the distribution of international aid and the resolution of international disputes. The absence of the United States, Germany, and Soviet Russia greatly hampered the League's function, and perhaps fatally, it lacked a viable enforcement mechanism to carry out its decisions. Nevertheless, the League of Nations managed some real successes and worked hard to resettle the large numbers of refugees and displaced persons resulting from the war. It also made available small loans for reconstruction projects to repair war-related damage. Although it lacked any viable enforcement mechanism and the participation of some of the Great Powers, the League functioned as Wilson had envisioned it—as a world forum for the resolution of international conflicts. For instance, in 1920 it persuaded the Swedish-speaking inhabitants of the Åland Islands, situated in the Baltic between Sweden and Finland, to remain under Finnish rule (the islanders had sought affiliation with Sweden), but with wide autonomy. The League also arranged for the withdrawal of Greek troops from southern Bulgaria and restitution for damaged property after a punitive incursion in 1925.

In the aftermath of the war the League of Nations oversaw the establishment of new frontiers for Germany. It managed to hold reasonably fair plebiscites in the disputed regions of northern Schleswig on the Danish-German border and in southern Carniola on the Austrian-Yugoslav frontier. The League-supervised plebiscites divided the ethnically complex region of Upper Silesia between Germany and Poland and adhered to the decision of the voters in Allenstein and Marienwasser to remain a part of East Prussia. It also oversaw governments in Memel (Klaipeda) until 1923, when Lithuanian troops turned it out; in Saar, until this region was returned to Germany in 1935 after a plebiscite; and in Danzig, where the League-sponsored government provided a stable regime until the German invasion of Poland in September 1939. All these areas had German-speaking majorities, having been part of the Second Reich. Memel, at the northeastern extreme of imperial Germany, was the main port for the Lithuanian hinterland. In Saar, France had assumed control of the iron ore mines as a part of reparations. Danzig served as the main port for the new Polish state. The present-day obscurity of most of these issues is testament to the League's success. Despite its obvious weaknesses, the League of Nations proved to be a viable support for the recovery and stability of Europe after the war.

Several disarmament conferences also buttressed the peace settlement. Chief among these was the Washington Naval Conference of 1921–1922. The resulting Washington Naval Treaty imposed limits on the British, French, Italian, Japanese, and U.S. surface fleets and a ten-year "battleship building holiday." An agreement signed in London in 1930 supplemented the Washington treaty for the United States, Britain, and Japan. In addition to the signatories to the Washington agreement, Germany joined the London accord. With these agreements, the British accepted limits on their naval forces for the first time. The French and Italians, however, never agreed to all the terms of the London conference.

The Kellogg-Briand pact represented the ultimate effort to ensure the 1919 peace settlement and maintain the stability of Europe. U.S. Secretary of State Frank Kellogg (1856–1937) and French Foreign Minister Aristide Briand (1862–1932) were the chief sponsors of this agreement, which was signed in Paris in August 1928. The forty-five signatory nations bound themselves to forsake aggressive war once and for all. This pact was part of an effort by the French to engage the Americans and draw them away from isolationism. The concept of a world without war was admirable then and remains so today. Nevertheless, the Kellogg-Briand agreement did little to stem the bellicose intentions of those nations determined to overturn the settlement of 1919.

As noted earlier, the French assumed primary responsibility for maintaining the Paris peace settlement. The Americans, disappointed by the failure of their idealistic efforts to rearrange Europe and ensure an eternal peace, had withdrawn from the continent and returned across the Atlantic. The British, relieved by the self-destruction of the German High Seas Fleet at Scapa Flow in May 1919, assumed that their security was assured. The French found some support for their task when they concluded an alliance with Belgium in 1920. After the invasion of 1914, France and Belgium had shared an antipathy to the Germans and agreed to cooperate against them. The settlement of 1919 dispersed German territories in Africa and Europe to both Belgium and France and reinforced their need for cooperation. The Franco-Belgian alliance hardly made up for the disinterest of the British, but it was of some utility in coordinating defensive measures during the 1920s. Belgian troops supported the French incursion into the Ruhr in 1923. After 1935, however, Belgium abrogated the alliance with France and adopted a policy of independent self-defense.

The French also sought to establish a presence in eastern Europe. They wanted to replace their vanished tsarist Russian ally as a source of pressure on Germany's eastern frontier and to establish a barrier, or *cordon sanitaire,* against the communist forces that had seized power in Russia. The French first established an alliance with Poland. French assistance had been important in the Polish victory over the Soviets in 1921, and that same year, France and Poland signed a formal alliance. Poland remained France's most important continental ally until 1939. Wedged between Germany and Soviet Russia, and hostile to both after incorporating parts of the kaiser's and the tsar's empires, Poland needed allies.[2] The Wilno (Vilnius) dispute precluded friendly relations with Lithuania, as did the Teschen (Cieszyn) quarrel with Czechoslovakia. Polish gains in the west and north at the expense of German territory guaranteed bad relations with Germany. Only Poland's relatively short Latvian and Romanian frontiers were friendly. Even so, because of its much smaller population and less developed economic base, Poland could not fully replace tsarist Russia as a serious threat on Germany's eastern border.

French diplomacy also facilitated the construction of a frail alliance system among the new states of Czechoslovakia and Yugoslavia and a greatly expanded Romania. A Czechoslovak-Romanian-Yugoslav agreement—actually, three bilateral agreements—came about in 1921. Thereafter, a series of individual agreements linked these countries to France—Czechoslovakia in 1924, Romania in 1926, and Yugoslavia in 1927. This overall arrangement became known as the Little Entente, evoking the memory of its much larger and stronger prewar predecessor. The Little Entente was of little use against Germany, however. Only Czechoslovakia, because of its long border with Germany, its strong industrial infrastructure, and its well-trained and -equipped army, offered the French any real security value. The Romanians and Yugoslavs had no borders and no security problems with Germany, although they did share borders with the revisionist powers Bulgaria and Hungary. The Little Entente gave the Romanians little support against Soviet Russia, its major Great Power threat. The Yugoslavs obtained some aid from the Little Entente against Italy, their main antagonist. The chief function of the Little Entente was to serve as a check against Hungarian revisionism. All three members had significant Hungarian minorities within their frontiers, and together, the three countries had much larger populations and armed forces than Hungary. In 1921 threats from the Little Entente prevented the restoration of the Habsburg dynasty in Hungary. Although the Little Entente did restrain Hungarian ambitions, it could do little against the German, Soviet, or Italian aggressions that threatened its members. And although each member of the Little Entente had a connection to France, the alliance could not work out any viable relationship with France's Polish ally, largely due to Polish resentment over the Czech seizure of the city of Teschen and its environs in lower Silesia in 1920, while the Poles were preoccupied by the war with Soviet Russia.

France was prepared to support the peace settlement with more than just security systems. When the Germans defaulted on their reparation payments, one Belgian and five French army divisions crossed the Rhine River in January 1923 and assumed control of the important Ruhr industrial district. They were determined to control Germany's industrial production to facilitate their own reconstruction and to prevent the Germans from rebuilding and restoring their economic and military strength.

The Germans could not resist this invasion with military means. Nevertheless, the majority of the Ruhr population refused to cooperate with the occupiers. Attempts by the French and Belgians to foster Rhineland separatism found little support among the German population and ended with the assassinations of its major adherents. The Berlin government supported resistance financially, but at the cost of ruining the German currency and the German economy. By the autumn of 1923 the German mark was utterly worthless.

At this point, American economic intervention ended the crisis and rescued the German economy. The Dawes Plan, formulated by American banker Charles Dawes (1865–1951), utilized American loans to stabilize the German mark, enabling the Germans to resume reparation payments. In return, the French agreed to evacuate the Ruhr and left by August 1925. The American economic intervention restored European equilibrium for the time being. For the second time in seven years, the Americans had come to Europe to establish a new order. The Americans did not withdraw immediately this time. A committee headed by American businessman Owen D. Young (1874–1962) announced the Young Plan in 1929. It sought to soften the payment schedules of the Dawes Plan, spreading out German reparations so that payments would not be completed until 1988. The pending Great Depression eradicated any advantages the Young Plan might have bestowed on the European and American economies.

Several other regional arrangements attempted to provide some local stability. One was the Balkan Pact, signed in 1935 by Romania, Yugoslavia, Greece, and Turkey.[3] This agreement was directed mainly against the possibility of Bulgarian revisionism, but provisions were made for potential Bulgarian adherence to the pact. The Bulgarians demurred, however, refusing to agree to the status quo for Balkan borders. Because of the strong Italian influence in Albania, King Zog's (1895–1961) government was not invited to join. The Balkan Pact, especially with the participation of Bulgaria, had the potential to be a force for stability in southeastern Europe. By the time it was signed, however, all its members were vulnerable to German economic encroachment. All were eager to align their frail economies with that of the Third Reich.

In northeastern Europe, Finland, Estonia, Latvia, and Poland signed a nonaggression and mutual consultation pact in Warsaw in 1922.[4] The Wilno dispute precluded the addition of Lithuania; a state of war continued to exist between Lithuania and Poland, and Lithuania's seizure of Memel from the League of Nations had alienated the international community. All the signatories, which were part of the former tsarist empire in whole or in part, feared Soviet ambitions that might include the reincorporation of their states. This Warsaw Pact, anchored by Poland and Finland but weakened by the absence of Lithuania, could not act as a bulwark against Soviet expansionism without support from Germany or Scandinavia. That support was not forthcoming, and by 1925 the pact had lapsed. Only an Estonian-Latvian alliance remained, but this provided little security to either partner.

In 1934 the three small Baltic states—Estonia, Latvia, and Lithuania—signed an agreement for mutual consultation in foreign affairs. This Baltic Entente provided little basis for regional stability. The Wilno problem prevented cooperation between the Baltic Entente and Poland, and the agreement never realized its potential. In any event, the Baltic states, located precariously between Germany and Soviet Russia, were unlikely to determine their international situation alone or together.

The Ruhr invasion and it aftermath persuaded the French that a strict enforcement of treaty provisions was beyond their capacities. France's weakness necessitated some accommodation of its eastern neighbor, so French Foreign Minister Briand initiated an effort to reach some agreement with Germany by ameliorating the Paris peace settlement. The result was a series of negotiations including Belgium, Britain, France, Germany, and Italy in Locarno, Switzerland.[5] Representatives from France's two main eastern allies, Czechoslovakia and Poland, also participated in the talks. The agreements reached at Locarno, which supplemented and ameliorated the Treaty of Versailles, were signed in London on 1 December 1925. The Germans guaranteed the French and Belgian frontiers, and in return, France and Belgium agreed to pull their troops out of the Rhineland, which was to become demilitarized. The last French soldiers left the Rhineland in June 1930. A British guarantee of the Franco-German border—in effect, ensuring French possession of Alsace-Lorraine—further assuaged the Paris government. The next year, 1926, Germany joined the League of Nations and obtained a seat on the permanent council. A subsequent agreement resulted in the French evacuation of the Saar region. The Locarno treaty thus helped stabilize the international situation in western Europe; however, it increased tensions in eastern Europe. To Czechoslovakia and Poland, it seemed that their French ally had increased its own security at their expense. Although Germany had accepted its western frontiers as permanent, the question of its eastern frontiers remained open.

German Foreign Minister Gustav Stresemann (1878–1929) sought to deal with these eastern issues. He calculated that with Alsace-Lorraine secure, the French would be less likely to support their eastern allies in any territorial dispute with Germany. This would force Czechoslovakia and Poland to make concessions to Germany in return for guarantees of security. Despite some hope for an "Eastern Locarno," no such agreement ever came about during the period of the Weimar Republic. The main point of the agreement in the west was to provide Berlin with greater freedom of action in the east. The problems of the eastern borders, however, remained intractable. After Hitler came to power, any arrangement guaranteeing the permanence of Germany's frontiers with Poland and Czechoslovakia became impossible.

Probably the most important factor that preserved the peace and the settlement was the overwhelming sense of exhaustion and horror that pervaded Europe in the aftermath of the war. The millions of dead and the millions of physical and psychological casualties throughout Europe reinforced the desire to avoid another war. This sensibility remained stronger in those countries that had emerged on the winning side. In the aftermath of victory, the British and French never wanted to make such sacrifices again. Time eroded this antiwar feeling, however, and the sense of war horror faded more quickly among those on the losing side. The Germans' sense of injustice over the terms of the peace settlement undermined their desire not to experience war again.

These stabilizing factors, chief among them the League of Nations and general revulsion for war, provided Europe with about fifteen years to recover from the devastation of the First World War. Ultimately, they could not prevail against all the efforts to undermine the settlement.

Undermining the Peace

The major factor undermining the Paris peace settlement of 1919 was the intractable attitude of Germany. Most Germans absolutely rejected the Treaty of Versailles. Even before the formal signing of the treaty, the German army began to prepare for a future conflict. The German army command rejected responsibility for defeat and encouraged the idea that domestic traitors had caused Germany's catastrophe. This became known as the *dochstoss,* or stab in the back, legend.

The *Reichswehr* (German army), limited by the terms of the treaty to 100,000 men, resorted to various expedients to maintain its forces in the face of this restriction. The German army continued to support military units throughout Germany as well as in eastern Europe and the Baltic

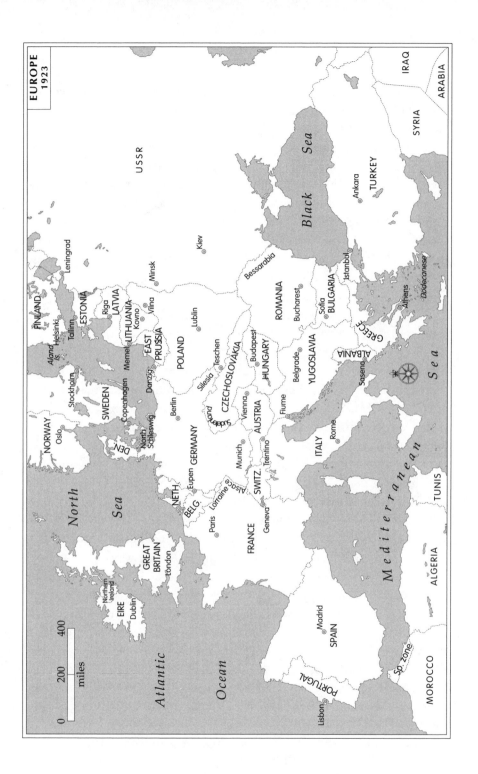

EUROPE
1923

region—the so-called Freikorps units composed of German servicemen and volunteers. They fought to preserve German military interests and the German imperialistic goals in the east. The Reichswehr provided equipment and training for these units, which were particularly important in Silesia, where fighting continued until after the plebiscite in 1921. The Freikorps fought against the Poles to preserve German rule in upper Silesia and also played a convoluted role in Estonia and Latvia. There, they supported the nationalists against the communists and then fought against the nationalists in the expectation of receiving land. They also supported the brief White Russian effort of General Bermont-Azorov. These Freikorps units varied greatly in terms of size, leadership, and composition. They represented, above all, a nationalistic German armed force.

Most of the Freikorps units accepted formal dissolution in 1921.[6] The concept lingered in the Black Reichswehr, officially called the *Arbeits-Kommandos*. These "work units" represented an early attempt to evade the military limitations of the Versailles treaty. The Reichswehr also supported a number of other paramilitary organizations, such as the veterans' organization *Stahlhelm* (Steel Helmets) and the Nazi *Sturmabteilung* (Assault Detachments), as well as shooting clubs and parachute and glider organizations. These were intended to provide specific training that could be useful in the future, when a revived Germany would cast aside the limitations of the treaty and rapidly expand its army.

The German army found other means to evade the terms of the treaty. Although forbidden to maintain a General Staff, the Reichswehr hid its existence in the *Truppenamt,* the military personnel bureau. From there, officers continued the tradition of planning for future war contingencies. The *Ruesamt,* the Economic General Staff, amassed large quantities of raw materials (enough to equip twenty-one divisions) so that another blockade of the German coasts would not have such a devastating effect on German industry. The German navy also prepared for war. In 1931 the first "pocket battleship," the *Deutschland,* was launched. Two others, the *Admiral Graf Spee* and the *Admiral Scheer,* soon followed. These small but powerful warships were intended to evade restrictions on the German navy. The German military leadership, having failed to prepare adequately for the previous war, was determined to be ready for the next one.

The common interests of Weimar Germany and Soviet Russia were obvious. Both needed to recover from the effects of military defeat, and neither had any interest in preserving the Paris peace settlement. This community of interest resulted in a diplomatic and economic agreement in 1922 known as the Rapallo treaty.[7] German and Russian delegates attending the Genoa conference met separately at Rapallo, where they signed an agreement that dispensed with mutual claims resulting from the settlement and granted both parties favorable economic relations. The Germans agreed to provide technical assistance to Soviet Russia, enabling the Russians to rebuild after the devastation of the civil war. In return, the Russians agreed to provide raw materials, which the Germans used to restore their economy and to stockpile reserves in anticipation of another conflict. A lack of raw materials had been a serious problem for the Germans during the war.

The German army, pursuing policy aims not always congruent with those of the Berlin government, made a number of arrangements with its Russian counterpart. It agreed to provide technical training and other assistance to the Red Army, which had only come into existence during the Russian civil war and had much to learn from the German officers, who were already adroit practitioners of the art of war. In return, the Germans obtained the right to train soldiers in Russia, out of sight of those powers intent on upholding the terms of the Paris peace settlement. In a facility near Kazan, German soldiers maneuvered with tanks and fired heavy artillery. German airmen also flew in the vast skies over Soviet Russia. The Rapallo agreements were the logical consequence of the exclusion of Weimar Germany and Soviet Russia from the Paris peace settlement.

The Rapallo treaty aside, Soviet Russia was mainly concerned with material reconstruction after the losses of the First World War and the Russian civil war. An interest in China also distracted the Soviets. Only in 1929 did the Soviets sign the Litvinov Protocol with the neighboring states of Poland, Estonia, Latvia, and Romania. Named for Soviet Foreign Minister Maxim Litvinov (1876–1951), this protocol renounced the use of force. The Litvinov Protocol provided little real security for the neighbors of Soviet Russia, however, as its intention was more important than its application.

The Italian government, despite having fought on the side of the Entente Powers and having participated in the Paris peace settlement, had little interest in preserving the settlement. The territories Italy had gained in Trentino, South Tyrol, and Istria contained a significant population of non-Italians, mainly Germans and Slovenes. Many Italians thought the peace settlement had deprived them of territories on the eastern shore of the Adriatic that had been promised by the 1915 Treaty of London as the price of Italy's entering the war on the side of the entente. But all Italy obtained in this area was the small Dalmatian port of Zara, several Adriatic islands, and some areas in Albania. In their first demonstration of power since obtaining independence in 1912, Albanian forces compelled the Italians to evacuate Valona in 1920. The Italians retained only the island of Saseno, which they regarded somewhat grandiosely as the "Gibraltar of the Adriatic."

Indicative of the Italian sense of thwarted gains was the Fiume (Rijeka) episode. At Paris in 1919 the Italian government had insisted on obtaining the Adriatic port of Fiume on the basis of national self-determination, since a plurality of its population was Italian. Before the war Fiume had been the major maritime outlet for Hungary, and the Paris settlement intended it for the new Yugoslav state. In September 1919 a ragtag force led by futurist poet Gabrielle d'Annunzio (1863–1938) seized the city and proclaimed it a free state. When the Italian navy shelled d'Annunzio's headquarters, he fled. Italian forces occupied the city in 1921. When Benito Mussolini came to power the next year, he was firmly supportive of annexationist aims. In 1924 the Pact of Rome signed by Italy and Yugoslavia recognized Fiume as Italian.

Benito Mussolini (1883–1945) had been born in impoverished circumstances in Romagna. His blacksmith father named him for Mexican president Benito Juarez (1806–1872). Mussolini's education was sporadic, and his initial political inclinations were socialist. He opposed the Italian war in North Africa, but with the outbreak of the First World War, he underwent a change of heart, became an advocate of war, and enlisted. Mustered out of the army in 1917 after a training accident, he adopted an increasingly strong nationalist position. After the war he organized groups of disaffected veterans into groups called *I fasci*. These bands combated communism, which found many adherents in Italy after the Bolshevik Revolution, and maintained the camaraderie of the front. After three years of nationalist agitation, Mussolini's followers marched on

Rome in 1922. Neither the Italian army nor the police force opposed this demonstration of former comrades in arms. This audacious act led King Victor Emmanuel III (1869–1947) to appoint Mussolini prime minister. Upon obtaining control of the Italian government, Mussolini adopted an equivocal foreign policy that tended to uphold the peace settlement in western Europe but was increasingly aggressive in eastern Europe.

Under Mussolini, Italy directed its policy against Albania, Greece, and Yugoslavia on the eastern shore of the Adriatic. In August 1923 Italian General Enrico Tellini and several members of his staff were murdered in northwestern Greece while working on the delimitation of the Greco-Albanian frontier. Although the perpetrators were unknown, Mussolini used the incident to bombard and then occupy Corfu, where Italian forces remained for one month. This show of force demonstrated Italian dominance in the Adriatic.

It also indicated Italy's interest in Albania.[8] The Italians had strong economic interests in the underdeveloped land across the Adriatic. Until 1918 Austria-Hungary had held Italian ambitions in check, but after the collapse of their rival, the Italians could proceed unimpeded. Mussolini supported the aspirations of Ahmed Zogu (1895–1961) to rule the poor, backward country as president of the republic. Although Zogu had come to power in 1924 with the help of the Yugoslav army, he found Yugoslav proximity stifling. In 1927 the Pact of Tirana confirmed Italian predominance in Albania. The Italians had already founded the Albanian National Bank in 1926 and provided much of the capital. Zogu's assumption of the title Zog I, king of the Albanians, on 1 September 1928 also received Italian support. This title indicated Zog's interest in Albanian populations in Kosovo, Macedonia, and northwestern Greece and, to a certain degree, Italy's support for these claims. Mussolini sent large amounts of economic, military, and technical aid to his Albanian protégé.

Albania did not represent Mussolini's only eastern European interest. He also extended Italian influence into the two eastern European revisionist states Bulgaria and Hungary. In 1930 Tsar Boris III of Bulgaria married Giovanna (1907–2000), daughter of Italian King Victor Emmanuel III. Under Admiral Horthy, Hungary pursued a revisionist policy and gravitated politically toward Mussolini's Italy. The slogan *nem nem soha* (no no never) emphasized the Hungarian rejection of the Trianon settlement and the intention to support Hungarian populations in Czechoslovakia, Yugoslavia, and especially Romania. In 1927 Hungary and Italy signed a friendship treaty in Rome.

Under peasant leader Aleksandŭr Stamboliski (1879–1923), Bulgaria made an effort to turn away from the nationalist policies that had led to defeat in the Second Balkan War and the First World War. He sought reconciliation with the old Serbian enemy in the new state of Yugoslavia. In April 1923 Stamboliski signed the Treaty of Niš, establishing a rapprochement between Bulgaria and Yugoslavia. Shortly thereafter extremist elements in the Bulgarian army and Macedonian organizations overthrew Stamboliski's peasant government and murdered him and many of his supporters. They cut off the hand that had signed the agreement with the hated Serbs. Bulgaria then resumed a revisionist foreign policy focused on the acquisition of Macedonia.

The revisionist powers supported terrorist groups. Chief among these were the Ustaša and the Internal Macedonian Revolutionary Organization (IMRO). The Ustaša, founded in 1929–1930 and led by Ante Pavelić (1889–1959), was an organization of Croatian extremists who advocated the establishment of an independent Croatia. Soon after founding the Ustaša in Yugoslavia, Pavelić fled to Italy to avoid arrest. The Italians offered the Ustaša training facilities and other support. During the 1930s the Ustaša committed terrorist acts in Yugoslavia and formulated a small uprising. After the assassination of King Alexander of Yugoslavia (1888–1934) the Italians kept the Ustaša under strict control.

IMRO began in Salonika, in Ottoman Macedonia, in 1893. Its objective was autonomy for Macedonia, although the meaning of autonomy was vague. IMRO had played an important role in the Ilienden uprising of 1903 and had generally supported Bulgarian aims during the Balkan Wars. After the Bulgarian defeat in 1918 IMRO directed its efforts primarily against the new Yugoslav state, seeking the unification of Macedonia and Bulgaria. The organization regularly launched raids into Yugoslav Macedonia and played an important role in the overthrow and murder of Stamboliski in 1923. It ruled southwestern Bulgaria (Pirin Macedonia) with no interference from Sofia until the Bulgarian military organization *Zveno* (Link), tired of the constant infighting in IMRO, seized power in 1934 and outlawed the organization. Bulgaria's revisionist foreign policy remained unchanged.

In 1934 the revisionist powers Bulgaria, Hungary, and Italy and the Ustaša and IMRO terrorist organizations cooperated in the 9 October assassination of Yugoslav King Alexander and French Foreign Minister Louis Barthou (1862–1934) in Marseilles during the king's visit to France.[9] The actual assassin, Vlada Georgiev Chernozemski, also known as Veličko Georgiev Kerin (1897–1934), was a member of IMRO and had received aid from Hungary and Italy. His three accomplices were all Ustaša men.

Despite the terrorist disruptions in eastern Europe, the Germans remained the chief advocates of change in Europe. In 1931 Chancellor Heinrich Brüning (1885–1970), in an effort to gain a foreign policy success and to mollify the increasingly strident nationalist voices in his country, proposed the establishment of a customs union between Austria and Germany. The actual initiative had originated with the Austrians. After the collapse of the Habsburg Empire, the German inhabitants of the alpine and capital regions had not sought independence; instead, they preferred inclusion in Germany. The Paris peace settlement prohibited this, because Germany could not expand in the aftermath of defeat. Brüning's proposal was an allusion to the customs unions that had preceded German unification in the nineteenth century, and it was a clear indication of a movement toward the unification (*Anschluss*) of Austria and Germany. This proposal was also a clear violation of the Treaty of St. Germain, and its implementation would have represented a significant erosion of the Paris peace settlement. Strong opposition from France, Italy, and the Little Entente forced Berlin and Vienna to abandon the scheme.

The greatest assault on the Paris peace settlement came not from the revisionist powers Germany, Italy, Hungary, and Bulgaria or from the various terrorist organizations but from the collapse of the European economic system. A web of war debts, reparation payments, and the Dawes Plan had bound the European economies to the American economy. When the American economy fell into the abyss in 1929, it pulled the Europeans along with it. A wave of economic depression and unemployment swept over Europe. The failure of the Viennese bank *Kreditanstalt* in 1931 effectively spread the economic problem throughout Europe. Only the command economy of Soviet Russia, itself in deep crisis, escaped the depression. By 1932 the rate of unemployment in Germany approached 50 percent. This economic disaster undermined political stability and abetted extreme political ideas. Totalitarian solutions to political and economic problems became appealing to many Europeans. The Paris peace settlement could not withstand the pressures of totalitarianism.

In little over ten years after its inception, the Paris peace settlement was in serious danger of dissolution. Although imposed by the military victory of the Entente Powers and maintained by France and by international institutions, it could not withstand the combined rejection by the revisionist powers and the economic collapse of Europe. With Britain and the United States remote from Europe, France was unable to maintain the settlement assisted only by Belgium and by eastern European allies. Neither strict enforcement nor amelioration of the settlement terms mollified the Germans. Germany—still the main economic power and potentially the strongest military power in Europe, in spite of its 1918 defeat—never accepted the settlement. Although a member of the entente, Italy became disaffected by the settlement terms and increasingly pursued a revisionist policy, especially toward southeastern Europe. Soviet Russia, excluded from the settlement, found an advantage in cooperating with Germany. Finally, the economic collapse of Europe at the beginning of the 1930s undermined democratic support for the settlement. Under these circumstances, the European truce prevailed for only a little more than ten years. Nevertheless, this was one of the longer periods of relative peace in twentieth-century Europe.

Chapter 7

GERMANY RESURGENT

By the early 1930s Europe had again polarized into two hostile camps—those countries that supported the 1919 settlement, and those that sought its revision. Unlike the situation before 1914, no formal arrangement united the adherents of these positions. Only their mutual desires to maintain or overturn the status quo guided their policies. Several factors complicated the situation. Britain, as it had been before 1914, was equivocal about any commitment to the continent. The states in eastern Europe, divided into the two camps and then divided among themselves within the camps, were weak economically, militarily, and politically. Because of these weaknesses, they were unable to undertake initiatives such as the Balkan states had done to instigate events in 1912 and 1914. Soviet Russia, though cooperating with Germany in many areas, was enigmatic in terms of the direction of its policy. Italy had interests in both camps: although Mussolini sought a greater territorial and political role in Europe for Italy, a revival of German power did not necessarily offer any great advantage.

The general truce held until 1933. It ended with the appointment of Adolf Hitler as German chancellor on 30 January 1933. Hitler had been born in 1899 in Braunau am Inn, in the Austrian region of the Habsburg Empire, to Alois Hitler (1837–1903), a minor customs official, and Clara Pölzl Hitler (1860–1907). He grew up in the nearby city of Linz and received a standard education, but he failed to attain his goal of acceptance into art school. After years of aimlessness in Vienna and a move to Munich to evade military service in the Austro-Hungarian army, he found purpose as a volunteer in the German army during the First World War. There he served on the western front, attaining the rank of corporal and several decorations. After his discharge he found direction as a political agitator in the National Socialist German Workers' (Nazi) Party. Hitler advocated not merely the revision of the peace settlement but its utter destruction. He urged that Germany dominate Europe even beyond the position of power attained before 1914. This idea undoubtedly found support among most of the German people, because regardless of whether they sought European domination, most Germans supported the revision of the peace settlement.

Hitler advocated another foreign policy goal: the attainment of *Lebensraum* (living space) in the area east of Germany.[1] This idea was not merely an amplification of Naumann's *Mitteleuropa* concept. It combined elements of social Darwinism and the experience of Germany's victory against Russia in the First World War with the Pan-German concept of expansion into eastern Europe. Hitler, drawing on an amalgamation of these ideas, insisted that Germans lacked sufficient geography to contain their energies. Only by means of Social Darwinist expansion, whereby the Germans attained control over the food and material resources of eastern Europe and Soviet Russia, and the Slavic inhabitants were displaced, could Germany continue to develop as a nation politically, socially, and economically. Hitler's concept was exploitative and coercive in relation to the local, non-German populations. It lacked precise parameters but was directed mainly against eastern Europe and Soviet Russia. The appeal of lebensraum for the German population is difficult to gauge, but it did offer a means of avoiding the great food and material shortages imposed by the blockade of 1914–1918. Undoubtedly, this idea contained a large element of extreme nationalist fantasy. Nevertheless, it remained a pillar of Hitler's foreign policy.

Hitler's foreign policy required Germany to go to war. To realize his goals, Germany would have to reiterate an operational scheme similar to the Schlieffen Plan. First, Germany would have to overcome France, which was the chief buttress for the peace settlement as well as Germany's major rival for power in Europe. After that, with most of Europe under German control, German soldiers would move east into Soviet Russia to establish the basis for a Greater German Reich that would last a thousand years.

Hitler began to implement his foreign policy objectives immediately upon his assumption of power in 1933. One of his first steps was to take Germany out of the League of Nations. On 14 October 1933 Hitler announced that Germany would withdraw from the League and from ongoing disarmament talks. This demonstrated Hitler's hostility to the Paris peace settlement and his disinclination to suborn the interests of Germany to any country or institution.

At the beginning of 1934 Hitler concluded his first important diplomatic agreement—a nonaggression pact with Poland. Hitler's rise to power in 1933 had so alarmed the Poles that Polish dictator Jósef Piłsudski had made an oblique proposal to the French for a preventive war against Hitler's Germany in 1933, suggesting that Polish troops would occupy the free city of Danzig, East Prussia, and upper Silesia, while the French would occupy the Rhineland. The French declined to undertake such a risky policy, given that their previous action against Germany in the Ruhr had brought them little benefit.

The German-Polish agreement brought Germany a measure of security on the eastern frontier. This security gave Germany the time to prepare to attain its foreign policy goals. The pact with Poland also undermined the French security system. Poland was France's main continental ally, so the agreement with Germany indicated an abatement of French influence in Warsaw. Finally, the German-Polish nonaggression pact indicated the end of the old German-Russian entente established at Rapallo. Hitler had already ordered most German military personnel withdrawn from Soviet Russia. Germany's anti-French and anti-Russian orientation became overt. At this time, Hitler rejected overtures from Soviet dictator Josef V. Stalin (1879–1953) to renew the military and economic agreements originating at Rapallo.

In July 1934 the Nazis' premature attempt to seize power in Austria resulted in the murder of Engelbert Dollfuss (1892–1934), the Austrian prime minister. Dollfuss had established a clerical-fascist regime in Vienna the previous year, but only recently had he secured his position by pounding socialist opposition areas in Vienna with army artillery. The Nazis objected not to Dollfuss's ideology but to his Austrian separatism. The coup attempt aroused great opposition among some of Austria's neighbors, particularly Italy. Mussolini had little desire to share an alpine frontier with Germany, and the German minorities in Trentino and South Tyrol remained a source of discomfort. Italy had also managed to extend its influence to the north with the signing of the Rome Protocols of February 1934, establishing an Austrian-Hungarian-Italian alliance.

This countered the Little Entente and briefly extended Italian influence into the Danubian region.

Upon receiving news of the events in Vienna, *Il Duce* mobilized his army and ordered troops to the Brenner Pass. This effort maintained Italian influence north of the Alps for the time being, and it bought Austria four more years of independence. Italian military strength, however, would prove no match for German nationalism.

At the beginning of 1935 Hitler gained an important foreign policy success. In a 13 January plebiscite, the inhabitants of Saarland voted overwhelmingly for reunification with Germany. The French had insisted on the separation of the coal-rich region from Germany in 1919, and the League of Nations had governed Saar since then. The plebiscite offered three choices: reunification with Germany, linkage to France, or a continuation of the League of Nations mandate. The French had failed to endear themselves to the population; nor did the option of a continued League of Nations presence in the region receive many votes. The reincorporation of Saar into Germany was Hitler's first expansion of German territory and his first step toward the creation of a Greater German Reich.

Hitler also expanded the German military. In March 1935 he ordered the reinstatement of conscription and the repudiation of all other military aspects of the Treaty of Versailles. Germany began the process of restoring its military power, based on the preparations begun by the German army in 1919.

German rearmament produced some alarm in Europe. One result was the diplomatic emergence of Soviet Russia. Moscow had already joined the League of Nations in 1934, a year after the Germans abandoned the world forum. After the Germans began to revive their military, Stalin adopted a policy of collective security, concluding mutual assistance agreements with both France and Czechoslovakia. For the French, the agreement with Russia helped offset the German-Polish pact of the previous year. The appearance of Soviet Russia in the European diplomatic arena did not have as great an impact as it might have. This was largely due to the strong distaste for the Soviet regime and its leader throughout Europe. If not for this ideological revulsion, Russia might have resumed its Triple Entente role of an eastern counterweight to German power in Europe.

Demonstrating some concern about the military revival of Germany, Britain, France, and Italy concluded an agreement at Stresa, Italy, in 1935 to oppose further German action. This Stresa front proved ephemeral. British interest faded after the conclusion of a shortsighted naval agreement with Nazi Germany in June 1936 that limited the German navy to 35 percent of the British fleet. The British continued to think of security only in terms of their navy. The Germans had little interest in a renewed naval competition with the British, since the German surface fleet had not proved particularly effective in the previous war. The Italian attack on Ethiopia a year before had distracted the Italians from the problem of German rearmament. Hitler's pro-Italian attitude in the Ethiopian war earned him Mussolini's gratitude.

In 1936 the process toward renewed war in Europe accelerated. On 7 March Hitler sent the new German army across the Rhine to establish a presence in the Rhineland. He justified this action because of the Franco-Soviet pact. Both the Treaty of Versailles (implicitly) and the Locarno treaty (explicitly) forbade the presence of the German military in the Rhineland. Most senior German military leaders advised against this action, since the German army was not yet ready to confront France. German troops received instructions to retreat across the Rhine if the French army responded to their advance. It did not. They French were not prepared for war.[2] As a result, Hitler gained an important victory at no cost. This may have been the best opportunity to stop Hitler without resorting to war.

That same year, civil war erupted in Spain.[3] For Spain, the glories and responsibilities of Great Power status were centuries past. Most of its remaining colonial possessions had been lost in the war with the Americans in 1898. Only a troublesome part of Morocco, a corner of the Sahara in northwestern Africa, a mainland enclave in equatorial Africa, and a few fetid islands remained. An economic revival beginning in 1914 with the outbreak of war had exacerbated tensions between the traditional and propertied classes and the workers and peasants. Complicating the Spanish political situation were the demands of the Basque and Catalan minorities for autonomy. The monarchy passed in 1931 without much resistance, and a democratic republic replaced it. The February 1936 elections brought a leftist government to power, and that July, the military, supported by traditionalist forces, revolted against the republic. Those who supported the republic—termed Republicans—included unions, peasant organizations, and Basque and Catalan autonomists. Those who opposed it—called the

Nationalists—included the Roman Catholic Church, the military establishment, and the fascist Falange organization. Army general Francisco
Franco (1892–1975) soon emerged as the Nationalist leader.

When the fighting began in 1936, the insurgents controlled Spanish
Morocco, a piece of territory around Cadiz, and a northern piece extending from the Atlantic Ocean to the French frontier. To the north, primarily Basque forces held the southern shore of the Bay of Biscay; in the south
and along the Mediterranean coast, loyalist soldiers maintained Republican rule. The Nationalist forces conducted primarily an offensive war,
while the Republicans generally remained on the defensive. Neither side
refrained from atrocities. The war proceeded on the northern front against
the Republican Basques and in the south mainly against the Republican
stronghold at Madrid. By March 1937 the Nationalists had joined their
two pieces of territory. Six months later the Basque north had fallen to the
Nationalists. The Nationalists then concentrated against the Republicans
in the south. In July 1938 the Nationalists broke through Republican-held
territory on the Mediterranean north of Valencia. This success divided
the remaining Republican territory into two parts and made continued
Republican resistance unlikely over the long term.

From the beginning of the war, foreign influence intruded into Spain.
The Germans appeared at the beginning of the fighting, sending supplies
and advisers. German pilots transported many Nationalist troops from
Spanish Morocco to Spain. The Germans also contributed the Condor
Legion, an air corps that provided the Nationalists with heavy air support and bombing capacity. Notoriously, the Condor Legion bombed the
Basque-held town of Guernica on 26 March 1937. The Spanish civil war
provided the Germans with the opportunity to test weapons, tactics, and
men. They also had a strong interest in obtaining the Spanish iron ore and
wolfram necessary for armor.

Mussolini had even greater objectives in his support of the Nationalists. He hoped to extend Italian influence to the western Mediterranean
and possibly gain control of one or all of the Balearic Islands. He sent four
divisions of Italian troops, as well as submarines to interfere in Spanish
waters. Ostensibly, these Italians were all volunteers. The Italian effort
represented the greatest foreign presence in the Spanish civil war, yet it
brought Italy few benefits. Perhaps the only real advantage Mussolini
realized from his intervention was the clear indication that the Italian

military was not prepared for war. For instance, an Italian force of three divisions suffered a reverse north of Guadalajara in March 1937 as it bore down on Madrid. The relative ineffectiveness of the Italian troops stood in marked contrast to their German counterparts.

The Spanish Republic did not lack foreign support. Volunteers from all over Europe and North America fought for it in the so-called International Brigades. These were intended to demonstrate leftist solidarity with the Republican cause and opposition to fascism. The Republicans gained the most aid, however, from Soviet Russia. Stalin saw this struggle as an opportunity to oppose his ideological enemy and extend his influence over the leftist movement. His agents made strong efforts to take over most aspects of the Republican effort, but the resulting infighting only undermined the Republican cause. Whatever military experience these Soviet agents gained during the war was soon lost when many of these same officers fell victim to Stalin's paranoid purges upon their return to Russia.

At the Battle of Guadalajara in March 1937 the complexity of the forces fighting in Spain was apparent. Italian volunteers fighting in the Garibaldi Battalion of the International Brigades fought against their Italian army countrymen. An Italian civil war ensued when these two groups encountered each other. The Battle of Guadalajara was a Republican defensive victory. Unfortunately, the Republicans could not sustain their success.

By 1939 the Republican forces were exhausted. Much of the foreign support had eroded. Barcelona fell to the Nationalists on 28 February 1939, and one month later the Nationalist forces took Madrid without resistance. The remnants of the Republican forces retreated across the French frontier. Spain was devastated; its economic infrastructure was destroyed. Perhaps half a million people had died. The Nationalist victory added a significant member to the revisionist coalition in Europe, but because of the widespread destruction of the civil war, Spain's participation in further events was limited. Real recovery from the destruction and trauma of the civil war did not begin until Franco's death in 1975.

The Spanish civil war also completed the rapprochement between Nazi Germany and fascist Italy. Although ideologically aligned in general, their nationalisms conflicted mainly over the issues of Austria, South Tyrol, and Trentino. Cooperation in Spain eased Italian concerns about

Germany. In November 1936 the two revisionist powers formed an informal Rome-Berlin axis. The term indicated a Europe orbiting around an axis extending between the German and Italian capitals and an alignment of their foreign policies.

Except for the fighting between the Reds and the Whites in Russia in 1918–1921, the Spanish civil war was the most ideologically based conflict in Europe during the twentieth century. The Nationalists were authoritarians, while the Republicans were democrats with strong socialist and communist support. Even here, however, nationalism was important. Much of the Nationalist support came from the Falange movement, consisting of Spanish fascists. On the other side, Basques and Catalans fought the Nationalists to maintain and expand the rights they had gained under the Republic.

While the war raged in Spain, Hitler accelerated preparations for the realization of his foreign policy goals through war. By 1937 Germany was recovering economically, and plans were under way to build the material foundations for war. These preparations depended to a considerable degree on the extension and strengthening of German economic influence in eastern Europe. The Germans offered manufactured goods and military equipment to the eastern Europeans in return for foodstuffs and raw materials. These products were intended to provide the material basis for war until the Germans realized the rewards of lebensraum in Soviet Russia.

The depression had devastated the economies of eastern Europe, and the German economic revival offered some hope to them. Bulgaria and Hungary were already inclined toward German revisionism because of their defeats in the First World War. The Franco-Soviet agreement of 1935 had startled some French allies in the region, especially Romania. All the governments in the region, except for Czechoslovakia, had become authoritarian by this time. All the eastern European regimes (with the possible exception of Czechoslovakia) abhorred communism and feared Soviet Russia. For these countries, an economic and political relationship with Nazi Germany was preferable to one with communist Russia. The Germans signed economic agreements with Hungary and Yugoslavia in 1934, and by 1937 they had signed agreements with all the Danubian states. Only Czechoslovakia and Poland remained aloof. In this way, the Germans implemented the *Mitteleuropa* concept to realize the lebensraum scheme.

On 5 November 1937 Hitler met with Foreign Minister Konstantin von Neurath (1873–1956), Minister of War Werner von Blomberg (1878–1946), air force commander Marshal Hermann Göring (1893–1946), army commander General Werner von Fritsch (1880–1939), navy commander Grand Admiral Erich Raeder (1876–1960), and an adjutant, Colonel Friedrich Hossbach (1894–1980), who took notes. At this meeting, which became known as the Hossbach conference, Hitler indicated that he wanted to realize lebensraum in the east no later than 1943. He stated that after that date, their enemies would be too strong; he also hinted that his own health precluded plans beyond that time. The first steps toward realizing that goal, Hitler insisted, would be the annexation of Austria and Czechoslovakia. The leaders of the German military raised objections to Hitler's projections, but he remained determined to implement his strategy.

At the beginning of 1938 Hitler renewed his attempts to annex Austria.[4] This was actually the third time in the past seven years that the German Reich had attempted to resolve the issue of the German state to the south. Chancellor Brüning had proposed a German-Austrian customs union in 1931, and the Nazis' 1934 coup attempt in Vienna had resulted in the murder of Dollfuss and caused great alarm south of the Alps in Italy. Now, with the establishment of good relations between Germany and Italy, German plans for the annexation of Austria could proceed.

Hitler signaled his intentions by inviting the Austrian chancellor, Kurt Schuschnigg (1897–1977), to Berlin on 12 February 1938. He then demanded that Austria accept political and military domination by Germany. The next month Schuschnigg desperately attempted to preserve Austrian independence by announcing a plebiscite on the issue. Hitler responded by ordering mass demonstrations by Austrian Nazis and creating an atmosphere of unrest throughout Austria. German troops then moved into the country to restore order. On 12 March the German army undertook its first official foreign venture since 1918 when it rolled into Austria. For the most part, the Austrian population greeted the arrival of German troops with bouquets of flowers and enthusiasm. The bloodless Austrian campaign became known by Wehrmacht personnel as the *Blumenkrieg*, or Flower War. Hitler himself arrived in Vienna the evening of the twelfth. Evocative of its medieval origins, Austria became known as the Ostmark province of the Reich. The Austrian republic had failed to bring its citizens political or economic stability, and nostalgia for the pre-1918 imperial days faded quickly. For many Austrians, as well as many Germans, the subsequent annexation (*Anschluss*) of Austria was the realization of a German nationalist dream dating back to 1848: the establishment of a German Reich including all Germans. Hitler, naturally, was the major beneficiary of this establishment of a Greater Germany. Austrian independence found few foreign defenders. By 1938 no Europeans envisioned a war to prevent German unity.

The Wehrmacht's movement into Austria demonstrated that it had many logistical and maintenance problems to work out. However, the annexation of Austria brought the Reich an additional army that could be directly incorporated into the German armed forces, linked by a common language and the experience of an alliance during the First World War. It gave Germany an additional six million Germans who were, for the most part, enthusiastic about their incorporation into a Greater German nationalist state led by one of their own. It placed Germany on the frontiers of southeastern Europe, where the foodstuffs and raw materials necessary for the realization of Germany's foreign policy objectives could be obtained. Finally, the annexation of Austria placed Germany on three sides of Hitler's next victim—Czechoslovakia.

Czechoslovakia was the most successful of the postwar eastern European states to emerge wholly or partially from the old Austro-Hungarian state. Under the leadership of its founder, Tomáš Masaryk (1850–1937), Czechoslovakia maintained a viable democracy throughout the interwar period. Among European states east of the Rhine River, only Finland managed a similar feat during the interwar period. Czechoslovakia enjoyed a strong industrial economy anchored by the huge Škoda works in Plzeň (Pilsen). This industrial economy enabled Czechoslovakia to field a well-trained, well-armed, and well-equipped army that was prepared to defend the country from behind extensive fortifications built into the Sudeten, Ore, and Bohemian hills that formed the country's borders with Greater Germany. The Little Entente and a formal alliance with France buttressed Czechoslovak foreign policy.

Czechoslovakia had some serious weaknesses, however. One was the binational nature of the state. The western Czechs dominated the state economically, militarily, and politically. Naturally, this caused considerable resentment among the less industrialized Slovaks in the east. Czechoslovakia's German and Hungarian enemies sought to take advantage of this Slovak resentment. The other major weakness was the existence of a large German minority population concentrated along the German and Austrian frontiers. These Sudeten Germans, as they came to be called, numbered three million people, or about one-fifth of the population of Czechoslovakia. Although the Prague government granted and upheld extensive minority rights for these Germans, they increasingly responded to the siren calls wafting from Nazi Germany. After the *Anschluss* these Nazi appeals to a Greater German nationalism became irresistible to the Sudeten Germans. Their position was critical to Germany, because the border regions where they resided contained the Czechoslovak defensive fortifications.

Less than a month after the *Anschluss,* in an attempt to provoke the Prague authorities, Hitler instructed his Sudeten German minions to increase agitation for autonomy within Czechoslovakia. The Czechs refused to be intimidated and ordered partial mobilization of their army in May. At the same time, the British and French governments warned that general war could ensue from this crisis, and Soviet Russia offered support for its Czech ally. At this point, Hitler ordered the German armed forces to prepare for an autumn attack on Czechoslovakia, called Operation Green. Some senior officers, most notably the chief of the General Staff, General Ludwig Beck (1880–1944), had strong misgivings about engaging in a war that Germany could not win. Beck resigned in protest, but other German generals dutifully prepared for Operation Green. In September, with plans for war in place, Hitler renewed his pressure on the Czechs. The British had no formal agreement to defend Czechoslovakia. Although the French did have a treaty obligation, they were not inclined to fight for Czechoslovakia without British assistance. Soviet promises of aid were contingent on French action, and the Little Entente was of little value against the Germans. The Romanians and Yugoslavs were already in economic thrall to Germany.

A series of three conferences sealed the fate of Czechoslovakia.[5] At the first, held in Berchtesgaden on 15 September, British Prime Minister Neville Chamberlain (1869–1940) accepted Sudetenland autonomy. At the second, in Godesberg on 22 September, Hitler demanded that the Germans occupy the region; a later plebiscite would determine its final status. Finally, representatives from four of the principal powers—Prime

Minister Edouard Daladier (1884–1979) of France, Chamberlain, Hitler, and Mussolini—met at Munich on 29 September. There, they agreed that Germany could assume immediate possession of the Sudetenland; no plebiscite would occur. In return, Hitler forswore any additional territorial demands in Europe.

Notably absent from the deliberations at Munich were representatives from Soviet Russia and from the other primary country involved, Czechoslovakia. President Eduard Beneš (1884–1948) hovered outside the conference room, awaiting word of his country's fate. When he learned that Czechoslovakia would lose the Sudetenland and, with it, the country's defenses, he returned to Prague to inform his government. Many Czech generals insisted on a fight, but Beneš maintained that a fight would be hopeless. He insisted that whatever happened, the nation had to survive. Ironically, when German generals inspected the Czech fortifications, they acknowledged that these would have enabled the Czechs to sustain a strong defense.

The British and French were not yet prepared to embark on a European war.[6] Not even the secret entreaties of dissidents with links to upper-level German military and diplomatic circles could persuade the British and French to act. A conspiracy had materialized in the German army to arrest Hitler if he ordered the invasion of Czechoslovakia, but British and French acquiescence to Hitler's demands completely undercut that plot. Hitler's stance as a unifier of European Germans was never higher. In the aftermath of Munich, any covert action against him by military conspirators became impossible. Soviet aid was not forthcoming without French involvement, and in any event, Poland and Romania were unlikely to permit Soviet troops passage through their territories.

Later in the autumn of 1938 the Czechs suffered further territorial diminution. On 2 October the Poles seized the region around Teschen (Cieszyn) in Czech Silesia. This was the territory the Czechs had occupied in 1920 while Poland was at war with Soviet Russia. One month later the Germans and Italians arbitrated Hungarian claims to Czechoslovak territory with the "First Vienna Award," which granted the southern fringe of Slovakia and Ruthenia, the so-called *Felvidék,* to Hungary. This area had a Magyar population of over 800,000.

The remaining part of Czechoslovakia, now virtually defenseless, became a German satellite. In this rump state, the Slovaks and Ruthenians demanded and obtained greater autonomy. Hitler had no intention of permitting even quasi–Czech independence. In spite of his promises at Munich, he issued orders in October 1938 for the occupation of the remainder of the state. On 14 March Slovak nationalists, acting in collusion with Hitler, declared independence. Slovakia, under the leadership of a Catholic priest, Father Jozef Tiso (1887–1947), thus became Germany's first satellite state. The next day German forces occupied the western part of the Czechoslovak Republic, declaring it to be the Protectorate of Bohemia and Moravia under German rule. This was Hitler's first acquisition of non-German territory. In the east, Ruthenia enjoyed two or three days of self-proclaimed independence before occupation by Hungarian troops.

When the Germans occupied rump Czechoslovakia, they obtained the equipment of the Czech army. Czech tanks, trucks, and armaments were of good quality, and this equipment enabled the Germans to maintain the growth of their army. It also was critical in supporting the upcoming German offensives in Poland, western Europe, and Soviet Russia. In addition, the Germans took over the important Czech arms- and vehicle-producing capacities of the Škoda works in Plzeň. This arms complex provided equipment for the Austro-Hungarian army in the first phase of the Long War and for the Czechoslovak Republic in the interim. It then manufactured military equipment for the German army in the second phase of the Long War. Although the Czechoslovak army did not participate in the second phase of the Long War, Czech equipment and Czech productive capacities were of great importance to the Wehrmacht.

One week later, on 22 March, Hitler demanded the return of Memel to German rule, and the Lithuanians had no choice but to agree. The annexation of Memel was Hitler's last bloodless conquest. Had he stopped there, he could have been hailed as a twentieth-century Bismarck who unified the German people and restored the power of the German Reich. The logic of lebensraum, however, precluded stopping at the shores of the Baltic.

After the takeover of Bohemia, Moravia, and Memel, Hitler wasted little time in claiming the territories of his next victim—Poland. The Germans demanded the annexation of Danzig and the right to construct an extraterritorial railroad and road linking East Prussia with the main part of Germany. These demands were just pretexts for the invasion of Poland. The Poles refused the German demands, and on 22 April the Germans denounced their nonaggression pact with the Poles.

After the destruction of rump Czechoslovakia, Hitler's aggressive intentions became clear to even the most obtuse. Obviously, he was intent on more than German unification; he sought European domination. The Italians, though not eager to go to war, sought to take advantage of this situation. On 7 April Italian troops occupied Albania, meeting only scattered resistance from the Albanian army they had helped train and equip. King Zog, together with his wife and days-old son and heir, fled the country. Italian King Victor Emmanuel III accepted the Albanian crown. The Italian occupation of Albania was really only a formality, as Italians had dominated the economic and security infrastructure of the nation for some time. The presence of the Italians across the Adriatic did represent a potential threat for Albania's Greek and Yugoslav neighbors, however.

Mussolini's other response to the reality of a European war was to tighten his relations with Nazi Germany. On 22 May 1939 Hitler and Mussolini signed the "Pact of Steel," which was a mutual assistance agreement.[7] Although it placed Italy solidly on the German side, Mussolini warned Hitler that Italy was not prepared to go to war before 1943. Italy stood to gain economic and perhaps territorial concessions in the wake of a German victory. The advantages of the Pact of Steel to Germany were not readily apparent. Italy had little to offer in terms of material or military aid for realization of the lebensraum objectives. Hitler consistently overrated Mussolini and Italy.

The British and French hastened to rectify their previous mistake of relying on Hitler's promises. They offered security guarantees to Poland, Romania, Greece, and Turkey in the spring of 1939. These guarantees were of limited value, however, because of geography. From their locations in northwestern Europe, Britain and France could have only a limited impact on eastern Europe and could not offer direct military assistance. In this circumstance, the position of Soviet Russia became critical. The British and French made some efforts to negotiate with the Soviets, but these were hampered by the anti-Soviet attitude of the Polish government. The Poles, having fought the Soviets less than twenty years before, refused to consider the presence of Soviet troops in their territory. Polish Marshal

Edward Rydz-Śmigły (1886–1941) remarked, "With the Germans we risk losing our freedom, with the Soviets we would lose our souls."[8] The British and French were unable to offer credible inducements to the Soviets to conclude an agreement. They were loath to offer territorial incentives that would infringe on eastern European sovereignty. All they had to go on was their shared concern about Nazi aggression and the recognition that Soviet Russia would be the chief victim of the lebensraum policy.

Stalin understood that the Soviet position was advantageous and that the western states were not reliable. They had, after all, spurned his aid during the Munich conference the previous year. Under these circumstances, he made overtures to Germany, most obviously by replacing Foreign Minister Maxim Litvinov, an advocate of collective security, with Vyacheslav Molotov (1890–1986) on 3 May. The Soviets were eager to reach some kind of arrangement quickly because of events in the Far East. For the past two years, probing Japanese attacks along the Mongolian and Far Eastern borders had become a source of growing concern. Stalin did not want to face simultaneous enemies in Europe and Asia.

On 21 August Soviet authorities invited German Foreign Minister Joachim von Ribbentrop (1893–1946) to Moscow. There, he and Minister Molotov signed a pact on 23 August 1939.[9] It contained pledges of nonaggression and assurances of neutrality in case one of the states went to war. It also contained secret clauses that recognized Soviet spheres of influence in Finland, Estonia, Latvia, eastern Poland, and Bessarabia. The Germans obtained rights to western Poland and Lithuania. In a subsequent agreement in September, the Germans traded Lithuania for the Białystok region of Poland. Eastern Europe was completely under German and Russian domination. The fourth partition of Poland ended Polish independence.

The Nazi-Soviet Pact surprised the rest of Europe. Even so, it offered both parties real advantages.[10] For the Germans, the pact ensured that they would not get bogged down again in a two-front war. The agreement with Soviet Russia doomed Poland and made the rapid implementation of a campaign in the west possible. It also provided a basis for the renewal of German-Russian trade agreements. The Germans would utilize the Russian raw materials gained under these agreements to undertake their wars elsewhere—and eventually against the Russians themselves. Hitler stayed focused on his goals. He insisted, "Everything I do is directed against Russia."[11]

The pact offered solid advantages to Soviet Russia as well. It extended Soviet frontiers by creating a buffer zone in the west and approximately reestablishing the old tsarist borders. This gave the Soviets considerable security against a German attack. It also bought the Soviets the time they needed to rebuild their military leadership, which Stalin had destroyed by his purges. They also needed time to deal with the Japanese threat in the Far East. Stalin was cognizant of the danger from Nazi Germany, but apparently he hoped for a stalemate in western Europe when the Germans attacked, just as had happened in 1914. The Russians could then assume the role taken by the United States and intervene decisively on whichever side offered the greatest advantage. In such a case, the Germans' ability to realize their lebensraum goals, whether they won due to Russian aid or lost due to Russian intervention, would be severely limited.

When Adolf Hitler came to power in Germany in 1933, the European truce in place since 1918 began to fall apart. Only combined, determined action by European powers to uphold the peace settlement of 1919 could have prevented war. Britain and France, in particular, had the opportunity to prevent a wider war if they had opposed Hitler militarily soon after he assumed power. But they were not willing to do so until Germany's dismemberment of rump Czechoslovakia in March 1939, when Hitler's intentions became obvious. He outmaneuvered the western powers with the Nazi-Soviet Pact. This gave him Russian support to defeat Poland and acquiescence in the defeat of France. Neither individual states nor collective action by several states nor the League of Nations could contain Hitler's ambitions. Only a renewal of the conflict would do that.

Chapter 8

RENEWED WAR

Twenty years after the conclusion of peace, war again erupted in Europe. In the early morning of 1 September 1939, German forces invaded Poland on the pretext of a contrived Polish provocation at the Silesian border town of Gleiwitz. All advantage lay with the attackers. The Germans fielded well-trained forces motivated by the promises of Nazi ideology.

The Germans enjoyed another major advantage over their opponents. They were developing a new strategy for waging war called *Blitzkrieg,* or lightning war. Based on the assault tactics of the First World War developed by General Oskar von Hutier and Colonel Georg Bruchmüller, blitzkrieg depended on surprise, exploitation of breakthrough, command at the front, and other shock tactics. To a considerable degree, blitzkrieg was assault tactics on wheels and tracks. During the First World War, German shock troops had depended on their own physical strength. Beginning on 1 September these soldiers stormed into battle in armored personnel carriers and tanks. The German air force, the *Luftwaffe,* functioned as flying artillery, seeking command and control, concentration, and supply targets to ensure maximum disruption in front of the advancing German forces.[1] Most German forces, however, moved forward on foot to exploit the confusion and disorder caused by the blitzkrieg attacks. Throughout the war, horsepower moved the better part of German artillery and supplies. A determination not to repeat the perceived mistakes of 1914–1918, years of planning and training, and experiences in Spain helped formulate this idea.

The blitzkrieg strategy was predicated on the German General Staff's realization that Germany lacked the economic resources to win a prolonged war.[2] The foodstuffs and natural resources of *Mitteleuropa* could not sustain Germany for long. German war planners believed that civilian material and food deprivations had been major factors in the 1918 collapse, and they were determined to avoid that situation again. This meant limited amounts of military armament and equipment and maximized resources for German civilian consumption. War would have to be waged on a limited basis, which meant that Germany would have to forgo some means of waging war. For instance, although Hitler had vague plans for a global policy that required an extensive navy, Germany would not invest in an expensive surface fleet. The High Seas Fleet had provided Germany with little advantage during the initial round of fighting in 1914–1918. If Germany could not obtain a quick triumph, another defeat like that of 1918 loomed.

No European armies developed effective countermeasures against this strategy. The French, remembering the heavy losses sustained in their World War I offensives and drawing on their experiences at Verdun, determined to take a defensive posture. Beginning in 1931 they constructed a line of fortifications extending along the border between France and Germany from the Alps to the Ardennes. These fortifications were known as the Maginot Line, named after French Minister of Defense and Verdun veteran André Maginot (1877–1932). Largely completed by 1935, these emplacements consisted of concrete machine gun positions, artillery, and reinforced troop bunkers. Essentially, the Maginot Line was an updated trench system. It provided intense fire and strong shelter against a frontal attack; however, it lacked flexibility and inhibited French policy. This "Maginot mentality" provided little incentive for the French to leave the safety of their fortifications and pursue the Germans in the Rhineland in 1936 or to aid the Czechs in 1938.

The destruction of the German High Seas Fleet in 1919 had infused the British with a false sense of security. Although they had considered the idea of mechanized forces in the aftermath of the war, they never developed a consistent plan for the use of armor. The British had been interested in Italian General Gulio Douhet's (1869–1930) concept of air offensives since the First World War. Appalled by the heavy casualties on the Italian front, Douhet had proposed the use of large bombers to attack Austrian civilian targets to destroy Austrian morale. The British only awoke to their own vulnerability from the air after Munich, and more so after the German dismemberment of rump Czechoslovakia in March

1939. Only then did the British begin to prepare a program of air defense, including the development of the Spitfire fighter and the construction of radar emplacements along the southern and eastern coasts.

The Red Army of Soviet Russia had developed in the 1920s and early 1930s in part with German assistance. General Mikhail Tukhachevsky, a junior guards officer in the tsarist Russian army during the war, had led much of that development. During the civil car he joined the Red Army and rose to the rank of general. Known as the "Red Napoleon" because of his youthful command, he led his forces to the gates of Warsaw in 1920. In 1937 Tukhachevsky and most other senior Red Army officers became victims of Stalin's purges. As much as half the officer corps was killed, imprisoned, or exiled to the Soviet penal system. Among these victims were most of the high-ranking officers, including fourteen of sixteen four-star generals, sixty of sixty-seven three-star generals, and all eight admirals. Many veterans of the Soviet effort in the Spanish civil war suffered the same fate upon their return to Russia, depriving Red forces of their experience. The Red Army was thus decapitated on the eve of the outbreak of fighting.

The Italian armed forces had made some technical advances during the 1920s, but Italy lacked the natural resources, especially oil, to sustain them. By 1939 much of Italy's equipment was of limited utility. The Italian military, with its major investment in older technology, was unable to modernize. Italian senior commanders were often distinguished not by professional prowess but by sycophantism toward Mussolini. Although many Italian soldiers gained experience fighting in Ethiopia in 1935–1936 and in the Spanish civil war, material constraints limited the utility of the lessons learned there. The Italian forces were not prepared technically or logistically for war in 1939.

The Germans faced a new entente, known as the Allies, during the second round of the Long War. The British and French reprised the roles they had taken in the first round of fighting. In place of tsarist Russia, however, was the much smaller but determined Poland. When the Germans attacked, the Poles were well prepared psychologically to defend their homeland, but they lacked the numbers and the equipment to do so. Initiating Operation White (*Fall Weiss*), German forces attacked Poland on three sides from their own territory and from their Slovak satellite state. Slovak units also participated in the invasion. The Poles were determined to defend their borders and especially the industrialized areas of upper Silesia. This allowed the Germans to cut off and surround the forward Polish forces early in the campaign. Nevertheless, the Poles resisted fiercely. Reputedly, their cavalry attacked German tanks, but such incidents were more likely attempts by the cavalry to break out of encirclement. By 9 September German advance units had reached Warsaw. That same day at the Bzura River, the Poles mounted a strong counterattack that thwarted the German offensive for several days.[3] The Poles were counting on the usual turn in the weather from dry summer to wet autumn to muddy the roads and cloud the skies and slow the German attack. In September 1939, however, the weather remained sunny and dry.

The Germans' behavior toward the Polish civilian population exhibited the same fury they had unleashed on Belgian and French civilians in 1914. Unlike the German victims at the beginning of the First World War, some Polish civilians may have actually fired on German units. In response, German army and *Schutzstaffel* (SS) units executed thousands of Polish Catholics and Jews. These actions were preliminary to the massive atrocities the Germans committed in their invasion of Soviet Russia two years later.

On 17 September Soviet Russian forces invaded Poland from the east. Stalin was eager to take his share of the spoils before the Germans occupied all of Poland. The decisive Soviet victory over the Japanese at Khalkin Gol, along the border between Russian-controlled Mongolia and Japanese-controlled Manchukuo (Manchuria), at the end of August had eliminated a source of concern for Stalin. The Polish staff had failed to anticipate an attack from the east, so most Polish troops were deployed in the west. With attacks across their western, southern, and eastern frontiers, the Poles could not hold out for long. After the Soviet invasion, the Polish army continued its stubborn resistance. This enabled some Polish units to escape to Romania and fight later elsewhere. The Polish government crossed over into Romania on 18 September, one day after the Russian invasion threatened to trap it. After heavy casualties, Warsaw surrendered on 27 September. The Polish garrisons on the Hel Peninsula near Danzig held out until 2 October.

Poland's allies proved to be little help. France and Great Britain dutifully declared war on Germany on 3 September, but the defensive mentality pervasive in these two countries afforded the Poles small comfort.

With the bulk of German forces deployed in the east, the French had the opportunity to launch an offensive into western Germany; instead, they remained for the most part in their Maginot positions. The French army managed to occupy only a small part of the Saar. Nor did any large-scale air effort ensue, owing to French concerns about German retaliation on civilian targets. The Poles lost 70,000 dead and 133,300 wounded; the Germans 11,000 killed and 30,000 wounded, with 3,400 missing; and the Russians 966 killed and 2,002 wounded.

Hitler directly annexed the Polish Corridor, Polish Silesia, and the region south of East Prussia into Greater Germany. The remainder of German-occupied Poland became a German colony under a general government. Slovakia annexed the small districts of Spiš and Orava.

Some Polish forces managed to escape through Romania and Hungary. Polish soldiers fought throughout the war on most European battlefields, as did Polish airmen in European skies and Polish sailors in European waters. The Poles' continued resistance of German and Russian aggression was epitomized by a plaque in a Polish cemetery near the Monte Cassino battlefield in Italy that read, "We Polish soldiers, for your freedom and ours devote our souls to God, our bodies to the soil of Italy, and our hearts to Poland." But the Poles made another important contribution to the defeat of Nazi Germany: the Enigma machine. Polish espionage agents secured a copy of this German coding machine in the late 1920s and learned how to use it. The Poles made this information available to their British and French allies, and Enigma provided valuable intelligence throughout the war. Like all intelligence, however, Enigma's worth was limited. The Poles knew the Germans' intentions but could not stop them. Nevertheless, it was better to know the enemy's aims than not to know.

With the defeat of Poland imminent, Stalin implemented other aspects of the Soviet pact. On 29 September the Estonian foreign minister signed an agreement in Moscow to permit the presence of Soviet Russian armed forces on Estonian territory. On 5 October the Latvians agreed to the same conditions, and on 11 October the Lithuanians accepted the inevitable. In compensation, the Russians returned Vilnius, recently taken from the Poles, to Lithuania. The small Baltic states, with a combined population of only about five million, could not hope to mount any resistance to the Russian demands. Nor could they expect help from abroad.

They were isolated geographically from France and Great Britain, and the other important power, Germany, had secretly acquiesced (at least temporarily) in the extension of Russian influence in the region. The Russian military quickly occupied the Baltic states, restoring Russian control of the eastern Baltic Sea and providing an additional buffer against any aggression from their German allies.

Having obtained satisfaction from Estonia, Latvia, and Lithuania, the Russians turned to the northernmost Baltic state, Finland. Like the other three, Finland had been part of the tsarist empire before the Russian revolutions. The Soviet government had long recognized that an independent Finland controlling several rocky islands in the Gulf of Finland and extending to within twenty miles of Leningrad represented a potential threat. During the interwar period, Finland had enjoyed good relations with Great Britain and Sweden. More ominously, German intervention in 1918 had secured Finnish independence.

Talks between Moscow and Helsinki had begun in 1938, but they intensified in the autumn of 1939. The Soviets sought land protection for Leningrad and their Arctic port Murmansk, both of which were proximate to the Finnish frontier. The Finns, however, rejected a not unreasonable Russian offer of a territorial concession of 5,500 square kilometers of territory north of Lake Ladoga in return for the cession of all islands in the Gulf of Finland, territorial adjustments in Karelia and in the far north, and the lease of the Hanko Peninsula at the mouth of the Gulf of Finland. The memory of more than a century of hated Russian rule remained strong in Helsinki. Without a declaration of war, Russian attacks on Finland began on 30 November.

The ensuing "Winter War" was really two conflicts.[4] In the Karelian Peninsula between Leningrad and the Finnish city of Viipuri (Vyborg), the fighting resembled that on the western front in 1914–1918. Russian forces sustained heavy casualties as they unsuccessfully assaulted strongly fortified Finnish positions. North of Lake Ladoga, the forest fighting was conducted largely along woodland roads and across frozen lakes. The Russians mounted eight major, widely dispersed thrusts into Finnish territory. Only the attack in the far north on the weakly held Arctic port of Petsamo succeeded. Everywhere else, determined Finnish resistance stopped the Russian thrusts. The Finns adopted hit-and-run tactics, aided by the use of skis and white clothing, as well as their Finnish-manufactured submachine guns. The Finns began to eliminate the invaders by surrounding the Russian units that were advancing slowly on forest roads and chopping them up into smaller and smaller pieces. By the turn of the year, the Finns, led by former tsarist officer and war of independence hero Field Marshal Baron Carl Gustav von Mannerheim (1887–1951), had inflicted serious losses on the invading Russians.

The Russians then regrouped and renewed their offensive in the Karelian Peninsula in February. Concentrating huge numbers of troops and relying on massive artillery barrages, the Russians used frontal attacks to push the outnumbered and exhausted Finns back to Viipuri. Russian forces then attacked over a frozen arm of the Gulf of Finland to avoid Finnish fortifications near Viipuri. This broke the Finnish resistance. The Finns agreed to a cease-fire on 13 March 1940. A treaty signed in Moscow deprived Finland of the Karelian Peninsula, including Viipuri; Finland's entire Lake Ladoga shoreline; the islands in the Gulf of Finland; and territory east of the town of Salla in the far north. This last territory was taken to move the Finnish frontier farther west of the Murmansk railroad. These territorial concessions undoubtedly improved the security of Leningrad. However, the Winter War also demonstrated the fundamental weakness of the Russian army. The problems resulting from Stalin's decapitation of the Russian armed forces were manifest in the confusion and lack of initiative prevalent in the Russian army. Russian forces lost as many as 200,000 dead, while the Finns lost 25,000. In June 1941 the Finns would try to regain their territories by joining the Germans in their attack on Soviet Russia.

The Germans observed with some glee the weaknesses the Russian army demonstrated in the Winter War. They also began to focus on the strategic opportunities north of the Baltic. The occupation of Norway could secure timber and fish for the war effort, and it could enable the Germans to avoid the total blockade the British had imposed during 1914–1918. The German navy argued that control of the Norwegian port of Narvik would also assure the winter transport of Swedish iron ore to Germany. (During the summer months, iron ore from the northern Swedish mines of Kiruna was shipped to Germany via the port of Luleå, down the Gulf of Bothnia. But during the winter, when the gulf was frozen, the ore went by rail across the border to Narvik.) Also, the deep fjords of the Norwegian coast could serve as excellent havens for German submarines.

The Winter War also drew the attention of the British and French to northern Europe. The David and Goliath struggle of the Winter War naturally attracted public sympathies throughout much of the world. Seeking a means to continue the war, but reluctant to confront the Germans directly, the British and French militaries contemplated aid to the Finns as a way to undercut Germany's Russian ally. The British and French staffs prepared a force to intervene in the Winter War on the side of the Finns. The expected arrival of this force was undoubtedly a factor in prolonging Finnish resistance to the Russian invasion. The British and French force needed Norwegian and Swedish cooperation to reach Finland, however, and although the Swedes sympathized with the Finns, they refused to compromise their neutrality. The Swedish position made the deployment of this force impossible.

As the Stockholm government's insistence on strict Swedish neutrality became clear, the British and French began to consider alternative locations to utilize the force they had assembled. They turned their attention to Norway as a potential new arena in the war against Germany. Control of Norway could supplement the British blockade and increase the isolation of Germany, and control of Narvik would impede the transportation of Swedish iron ore to Germany. The Allies thus began to contemplate the occupation of Narvik.

By March 1940 the interests of both belligerent sides converged on Norway. Since regaining independence in 1905 after five centuries of foreign rule, Norway had pursued a policy of neutrality. The Norwegian government indicated that it would defend its territory against any incursion, however. Whether the Norwegians would have responded as strongly to British-French attacks as to German attacks remains an interesting conjecture. In any event, the Germans arrived first. On the night of 8–9 April, in an operation dubbed *Weserübung* (Weser River exercise), German naval task forces moved into Norwegian waters. Soon afterward German parachute troops descended on Norwegian airfields. In short order the Germans controlled the important ports of Bergen, Narvik, Stavanger, and Trondhiem, as well as the airfields in Oslo and Straventer.[5] Only at Oslo did the surprised Norwegians administer a rebuff. In the Oslo fjord an ancient Norwegian fortification sank the new German cruiser *Blücher*, with considerable loss of life. A paratroop assault supported by infantry took Oslo later on the ninth.

At the same time, the German army and naval units quickly overran Denmark. This was necessary to ensure communications and logistical support for the campaign in Norway. The Danes had fought stubbornly in defense of Schleswig-Holstein in 1864, but by 1940 their armed forces were small and armed with antiquated weapons. Also, the topography offered no obstacles to the German attack. The Danes surrendered within three hours of the German attack. Resistance was futile.

The British navy reacted quickly to the German offensive. Although it sank several German ships, it could not prevent the German landings. Nevertheless, the show of force encouraged the Norwegians to oppose the German advance in central Norway. British and French troops, part of the force originally intended for Finland, landed at Namsos and Andalsnes, and the British initiated a counterattack at Narvik. German control of the skies, however, proved an effective counter to British control of the seas. By 3 May the British had withdrawn most of their forces, except around Narvik. There, in the far north and at the extreme range of German aircraft, the British finally took the town on 28 May, supported by French and Polish units. On 3 June, however, because of critical events in western Europe, the Allied force reembarked on British ships. The Norwegian campaign was over. It was a costly campaign for both sides. The British lost 4,500 sailors and soldiers, the Norwegians 1,500, and the French and Poles around 500. The Germans lost 5,500 men and much of their navy. Nevertheless, this was probably the German navy's greatest success in the war.

One important consequence of the Norwegian campaign was a change of leadership in Great Britain. Winston S. Churchill (1874–1965) became prime minister upon the resignation of Neville Chamberlain (1869–1941). Throughout the 1930s Churchill had strongly opposed the German resurgence, and he immediately promised vigorous prosecution of the war.

Before the conclusion of the Norwegian campaign, the Germans initiated their long-anticipated offensive against France. Since the beginning of the war in September 1939, the Franco-German frontier had seen little fighting. This period of inactivity became known as the "Phony War" or *Sitzkrieg*. Hitler had wanted to begin an offensive in November, but the need to recover men and equipment after the rigorous Polish campaign and unfavorable climatic conditions caused a postponement of the action.

This provided the Germans with the opportunity to prepare thoroughly for the offensive. By chance, plans for the German offensive fell into Allied hands in January 1940 due to the inadvertent landing of a German courier plane in Belgium, forcing the Germans to reevaluate their plans.[6] The result was Operation Case Yellow (*Fall Gelb*), also known as the Sickle's Cut (*Sickelschnitt*). This plan was based on the ideas of General Erich von Manstein (1887–1973), but it also corresponded with some of Hitler's own ideas. Whereas the compromised plan had actually reprised the Schlieffen Plan, with a greater arc through the Netherlands, the Sickle's Cut sent a strong force into the Netherlands and Belgium, merely intending to give the appearance of the Schlieffen Plan. This attack was largely diversionary, devised to draw mobile British and French forces up into the Low Countries. A strong armored column would then thrust through the lightly defended Ardennes, a hilly, forested region in southern Belgium and Luxembourg. The armored column would then race to the English Channel, cutting off those Allied units that had rushed to the aid of the Low Countries. The German objective was the rapid and total defeat of these mobile forces and thus of France.

The German attack began on the morning of 10 May, with the Germans invading the Netherlands, Belgium, and Luxembourg with air, airborne, and ground forces. British and French units moved into Belgium as far as the Dyle River. The invaders quickly overwhelmed the Dutch, whose forces were unable to cope with the speed of the German advance. Even the opening of dikes to flood the land and slow the attackers' advance failed to stop the Germans. The bombing of Rotterdam on 13 May broke Dutch resistance, and the Dutch government surrendered two days later. By this time, the British and French had begun to withdraw from the Dyle.

The Belgians fared little better. As in 1914, they depended on forts to forestall a German invasion. Their key fort, Eban Emael, north of Liège, fell to an airborne attack on the first day of the German offensive. This German success echoed the rapid victory at Liège twenty-six years earlier. The Belgian army fell back toward the North Sea.

To the south, the main German thrust advanced rapidly to the Meuse River. It crossed this obstacle on 15 May and raced for the English Channel. It reached Abbeville on 19 May, effectively cutting off the Allied

WESTERN EUROPE
WORLD WAR II

0   100   200
miles

Shetland
Islands

Orkney
Islands

NORWAY

Oslo

SWEDEN

Stockholm

North
Sea

Skaggerak

DEN.

Copenhagen

Baltic
Sea

GREAT
BRITAIN

London

Amsterdam

NETH.

Hamburg

Berlin

Dunkirk

English Channel

Antwerp

BEL.

Liege

GERMANY

Dresden

Brussels

Bastogne

NORMANDY

Paris

LUX.

Maginot
Line

SUDETENLAND

PROTECTORATE
OF
BOHEMIA AND MORAVIA

Lake
Constance

Vienna

Bay
of
Biscay

FRANCE

Bern

SWITZ.

AUSTRIA

to
Ger.

Trieste

to
It.

Milan

CROATIA

SPAIN

ITALY

Corsica

Adriatic
Sea

Rome

Anzio

Balearic Islands

Sardinia

Tyrrhenian
Sea

Taranto

M E D I T E R R A N E A N

S E A

Sicily

forces in Belgium from France. These forces, now trapped, saw no option but evacuation by sea. They converged on the French port of Dunkirk (Dunkerque), where, beginning on 26 May, an improvised British flotilla consisting of Royal Navy and civilian craft began to take Allied soldiers across the water to Britain.[7] The Belgian surrender on 28 May increased the urgency of the evacuation.

Nevertheless, for several days the Germans remained passive. The reason for their failure to attack the British evacuations remains unclear. Bad weather prevented the use of the Luftwaffe for several days. The exhaustion of the German troops, the expectation of continued fighting against the French to the south, and hope for a negotiated settlement with Britain are other possible explanations. German attacks eventually began on 1 June, but by then, the opportunity to destroy the Allied forces had passed.

The evacuations, which ended on 2 June, succeeded in taking home almost the entire British Expeditionary Force and some French troops. Left behind, however, were all the British equipment and a sizable French force. Two additional British divisions not caught in the German trap in Belgium were evacuated through Le Havre, Saint-Nazaire, and several other French ports. This was a major German victory. Only the panache with which the British had carried out the evacuations gave the enterprise a thin veneer of success.

After their victory at Dunkirk, the German forces turned south and moved into France. The French government declared Paris an open city. The Germans entered it on 14 June and moved to the rear of the Maginot Line. Ironically, the strength of the Maginot Line had initially compelled the Germans to attack successfully elsewhere. On 22 June a French government led by the hero of Verdun, Marshal Henri-Philippe Pétain, signed an armistice in the same railway car used for the 1918 armistice ceremony. In the western campaign the British and French plus the Belgians and Dutch lost 90,000 men, while the Germans lost around 30,000. This represented a stunning success for the Germans. In six weeks they had achieved the victory that had eluded them during four years of war from 1914 to 1918. After the victories in the west, Hitler annexed Alsace and Lorraine from France and Eupen and Malmedy from Belgium. Alsace, Lorraine, and part of French Flanders were administered by the German authority in Brussels.

The German losses at Versailles in 1919 had been restored. German forces occupied western and northern France, while southeastern France remained unoccupied for the time being. The Italians annexed several border areas, and France east of the Rhone came under Italian influence. On 30 June German troops occupied the Channel Islands—the only British territory the Germans would control during the entire war. Europe was under German rule, to an extent comparable to Napoleon's Europe after the Treaty of Tilsit in 1807.

The German occupation of France and the eviction of Great Britain from the continent reverberated throughout eastern Europe. The speed of the German success made the improvement of Soviet Russian security imperative. Stalin seized the opportunity to complete the destruction of Baltic independence by rigging plebiscites and accepting the resulting "requests" of Estonia, Latvia, and Lithuania to be incorporated into the Soviet Union. Latvia and Lithuania became Soviet Socialist Republics on 5 August, and Estonia joined them the next day.

The main eastern European result of Germany's western European victories, however, was the rape of Romania. The defeat of Britain and France eliminated any chance of western assistance for Romania, and Stalin moved quickly to implement the relevant provisions of the Nazi-Soviet Pact. On 26 June the Romanian government acceded to the Soviets' demand for Bessarabia and the northern part of Bukovina (although Bessarabia was mentioned in the pact, Bukovina, a former Habsburg province, was not). These acquisitions put Soviet Russia on the Danube and placed almost the entire Ukrainian population under Stalin's control. Other demands on Romania followed that summer. On 30 August the Second Vienna Award, arbitrated by Hitler, granted northern Transylvania to Hungary. This placed most of the Transylvanian Magyar population under the rule of Budapest but left a substantial Romanian minority under Hungarian rule. On 7 September the Treaty of Craiova restored southern Dobrudzha to Bulgaria, which it had lost to Romania in the 1913 Treaty of Bucharest. Romania, which had emerged from the 1919 settlement as the most aggrandized eastern European state, was greatly weakened by these losses. After the disastrous summer of 1940, German protection was Romania's only alternative. This seemed evident to the Bucharest government, despite Germany's role in Romania's dismemberment. German troops entered Romania in October.

The Germans were the big beneficiaries of the rape of Romania. They had placated Bulgaria and Hungary at Romania's expense. At the same time, they had secured control of the oil fields of Ploeşti, vital to the German war effort. Above all, they had secured economic and political control of the largest country in southeastern Europe. And all this had been accomplished at virtually no cost to themselves. Because of the national catastrophe, feckless King Carol II (1893–1953), whom many Romanians held responsible for their country's amputations, fled in a hail of gunfire. His son Michael (1921–) succeeded him on the throne, but General Ion Antonescu (1882–1946) assumed real power, replacing King Carol's royal dictatorship with a military dictatorship.

As the Germans were establishing their brutal control over Romania, the conflict with Britain was intensifying. After Dunkirk, Hitler had expected the British to negotiate, and he had been willing to do so, since his immediate plans did not include direct conflict with Britain. Then Prime Minister Churchill signaled his determination to remain in the war by ordering an attack on the French fleet anchored near the Algerian port of Oran at Mers el Kébir. On 3 July a British fleet appeared off the French naval base at Mers el Kébir and ordered the French to join the British, sail to the French West Indies, or scuttle itself. Upon the French refusal, the British opened fire on their erstwhile allies, sinking or damaging several warships and killing more than 1,200 French sailors. Churchill recognized that if the relatively modern French fleet had fallen under German control, the consequences could have been fatal for Britain. This attack at Mers el Kébir demonstrated that the British would remain in the war to fight for their national existence.

By waiting for the British to negotiate, the Germans lost an opportunity to launch a rapid invasion. In the aftermath of Dunkirk the British army, though intact, was bereft of its equipment and scattered throughout southeastern Britain. A swift and determined assault immediately after Dunkirk might have taken the island. German attention was on France, however. When it became clear that the British were determined to stay in the war, the time had passed for an airborne assault. Since the Germans did not control the sea, they would have to control the air before attempting to implement Operation Sea Lion, the code name for the invasion of Britain. The Germans began intensive air attacks on 12 August, although they had been making sporadic attacks for about a month. From the beginning of the fight, the advantage lay with the British. They were flying over their home skies and could retrieve any pilot who survived being shot down. The Germans could not. The British also had radar sites throughout the southern and eastern parts of their country that could warn them of an approaching German attack.

The British advantage increased after 7 September when the Germans intensified their attacks on London and correspondingly eased attacks on purely military targets such as airfields and radar emplacements. Increasingly heavy losses of pilots and airplanes caused the Germans to reduce their bombing attacks by the end of October. Operation Sea Lion had never been very realistic, and in December it was deactivated. By then, the German General Staff was planning its attack on Soviet Russia and could not afford further losses of pilots and aircraft.

The German victory over France had another important consequence. Italy entered the war by attacking the French while they were in extremis. In September 1939 Mussolini had declined to fulfill his obligations to Germany because of a lack of material preparation. The defeat of France offered opportunities that proved impossible for Mussolini to resist. On 10 June Italian forces "stabbed France in the back" with an attack in the Alps, but the Italians made little headway against determined French resistance. For this effort, the armistice assigned Italy a few small areas in the Alps.

The Germans formalized their relationship with Italy and Japan with the signing of the Tripartite Pact in Berlin on 27 September 1940. This alliance provided a formal framework for German hegemony in Europe. Hungary, Romania, and Slovakia joined in the agreement in November. The adherence of other European states would follow.

Having tasted blood, Mussolini was eager to engage in further military endeavors. He wanted to demonstrate Italian military prowess to the world in general and to Hitler in particular. Mussolini's target was Greece, as its conquest would give Italy control of the eastern Mediterranean. Mussolini tried to provoke Greece on 1 August 1940 with the sinking of the Greek light cruiser *Elli* off the island of Tinos by an Italian submarine. The Greek government, wanting to stay out of the war, refused to be drawn in by this Italian action. Adopting a more direct approach, and without informing his German allies, Mussolini ordered Italian forces in Albania to attack Greece on 28 October. The Greek army responded with a spirited defense of its homeland.[8] Albanian roads to the Greek border were almost nonexistent, and Albanian ports were inadequate to maintain logistical support for the Italian army. As a result, the Italian invaders soon bogged down in difficult mountainous terrain. A strong Greek counterattack on 14 November threw the Italians back and brought most of southern Albania under Greek control. Exhaustion and its own difficult logistical situation halted the Greek army's advance outside of Valona in early December.

The Italian invasion of Greece provided the British with an opportunity to pursue the war against Germany's weaker ally. Royal Air Force (RAF) units landed in Greece on 3 November. Greek dictator General Ioannis Metaxas (1871–1941) was reluctant to provoke the Germans by allowing the British army to take up positions in his country. Even after the Italian attack, he hoped for German mediation. Soon after the RAF's arrival in Greece, carrier-launched Royal Navy airplanes inflicted a serious defeat on the Italian navy, striking the Italian fleet at Taranto on 12 November.[9] The British used airplane-launched torpedoes to severely damage three Italian battleships. The Japanese would incorporate the lessons of Taranto in their own carrier-launched air attack on Pearl Harbor a little over one year later.

After General Metaxas's death on 29 January 1941, the new Greek government agreed to the stationing of British ground forces in the country. The arrival of British (mainly Australian and New Zealand) troops posed a potential threat to German plans for the invasion of Russia. The Germans' right flank would be vulnerable to an attack from the south. Also, the vital oil fields and refineries at Ploeşti, Romania, were now exposed to attacks from British airplanes stationed in Greece.

To eliminate these dangers before the attack on Russia, and to rescue the Italians freezing in the Albanian mountains, Hitler decided to invade Greece. Prior to this, the Germans sought to make arrangements with Greece's Bulgarian and Yugoslav neighbors, both of which were already in German economic thrall. Once again, Bulgaria proved willing to accommodate the Germans, becoming a signatory of the Tripartite Pact on 1 March 1941.

Initially, the Yugoslavs seemed disposed to follow their Bulgarian neighbors into subservience to the Germans. A Yugoslav delegation signed the Tripartite Pact on 25 March 1941. Two days later a pro-British cabal of mainly Serbian Yugoslav air force and army officers overthrew the government, encouraged by the British. The new government's proclamation of allegiance to the Tripartite Pact did not assuage Hitler, who quickly decided to destroy the country. To that end, the Germans attacked Greece through Yugoslavia.

On 6 April the Luftwaffe bombed Belgrade, initiating Operation Maritsa. That same day German soldiers, together with Hungarian and Italian units, attacked Yugoslavia. The Yugoslav armed forces collapsed along ethnic lines: while Serbian units attempted to resist the invaders, some Croat soldiers refused to obey orders. German units entered Belgrade on 13 April, and within a week the Yugoslav government had signed an armistice. Yugoslavia ceased to exist as a state. The Germans and Italians divided Slovenia, the Italians took Dalmatia, Bulgaria reclaimed Macedonia, the Hungarians took the region between the Danube and Tisza rivers and two other areas, and Italian-controlled Albania took Kosovo. Two theoretically independent states made up most of the remainder of Yugoslavia: Serbia, restricted approximately to its pre-1878 borders, and the new state of Croatia, which included Bosnia.

The Germans, whose losses were very light in the fighting against Yugoslavia, continued to press their attacks against Greece. These had begun the same day as the invasion of Yugoslavia. The fighting in Greece was more intense. German forces invading from Bulgaria quickly broke through Greek lines in Macedonia and headed south. A hastily arranged defense at Thermopylae failed to hold the German advance for long. The Royal Navy carried out another Dunkirk-style evacuation of British soldiers before the Germans arrived in Athens on 27 April.

Many of the British and Greek troops evacuated from Greece arrived in Crete to assist in its defense. Crete commanded the Aegean Sea as well as the eastern Mediterranean; it also served as a forward defense position for the Suez Canal and a potential air base from which to bomb Ploeşti. The defenders had reason for confidence. The Germans had no navy in the Mediterranean. The Italian navy had suffered several setbacks over the previous year, most recently a serious defeat at the hands of the Royal Navy off Cape Matapan on 28 March, losing three cruisers and two destroyers. On 20 May, however, the Germans undertook an airborne assault on Crete. Although they were outnumbered, the Germans managed to consolidate their landing zones quickly. Their control of the air, with planes using Greek bases, negated the power of the Royal Navy.

The British staged another evacuation on 30 May, conceding Crete to the Germans. The Battle of Crete represented the greatest success for airborne soldiers in the war.[10] The victory was Pyrrhic, however. German losses were so high, more than 7,000 dead, that they would not undertake another major airborne operation.

The victors divided Greece into zones of occupation. Germany took southern Macedonia, Athens, eastern Crete and several other Aegean islands, and the border zone with Turkey. Bulgaria took western Thrace and eastern Macedonia, and Italy took the rest.

Operation Maritsa was probably unnecessary. All of southeastern Europe, including Greece and Yugoslavia, were already in the German economic sphere. Their governments were well disposed toward the Third Reich. Mussolini's blunder in Greece, however, brought British forces back to the continent, where they posed threats to the Romanian oil fields and to the German invasion of Russia. The Germans invaded Greece to eliminate this threat and rapidly brought all of southeastern Europe under their control.

The German renewal of the European war initially met with outstanding success. In less than two years German power swept over Europe. Polish, Danish, Norwegian, Dutch, Belgian, French, and British armed forces succumbed to superior German tactics and equipment. Mussolini's attempt to conduct a separate war led to defeat and to the total subordination of Italian efforts to the Germans. The defeat of the Yugoslavs and Greeks added southeastern Europe to the German realm. This gave the Germans complete control of continental Europe. Even neutral Spain, Sweden, and Switzerland acknowledged the extent of German power. The cost in terms of men and material had been heavy. Nevertheless, considerable reserves of both remained. In June 1941 the Germans dominated Europe to a degree matched only by the French in the summer of 1812 on the eve of their thrust into Russia.

Chapter 9

GERMAN-RUSSIAN WAR

The realization of lebensraum in eastern Europe and especially in Soviet Russia had always been an important goal of Hitler's foreign policy. The defeat of France in the summer of 1940 made the realization of this goal possible. Even though Great Britain remained in the war, plans for the invasion of Soviet Russia, code-named Operation Barbarossa, began in the fall of 1940. In an echo of Napoleonic reasoning, Hitler thought that the defeat of Soviet Russia might encourage the British to come to terms. The Germans were confident of success. After all, they had defeated Russia during the previous war, even with most of their resources engaged on the western front. The Germans also knew that great discontent existed in Soviet Russia. Non-Russian nationalities such as the Ukrainians and the recently annexed Baltic peoples resented Russification, the peasants hated communist collectivization, and much of the population feared the Stalinist terror. "We have only to kick in the door," Hitler observed, "and the whole rotten structure will collapse."[1] The Germans, however, had no intention of rectifying the injustices behind this discontent. Hitler anticipated a war of conquest, not one of liberation. As Europe entered the fifth decade of the century, the Long War entered its most intense and bloody phase.

Initial planning for the invasion of Soviet Russia began in the summer of 1940. On 18 December 1940 the German army received the directive for Operation Barbarossa and started planning in earnest. The Germans intended to invade along three axes. In the north, they would head for Leningrad, the old imperial capital and the birthplace of the Soviet state. In the center, the target would be Moscow, the medieval capital and the administrative and transportation hub of Soviet Russia.

In the south, the goal was Ukraine, where foodstuffs and raw materials were abundant. The Germans did not intend to conquer and occupy all the vast territories of Soviet Russia. They would stop at a line drawn from Archangel, on the White Sea in the north, to Astrakhan, where the Volga flows into the Caspian Sea. The areas east of this line were of little interest to the Nazis. The exploitation of the peoples and resources of Soviet Russia would enable Germany to dominate Europe indefinitely. The promise of lebensraum would be realized, and the Third Reich would endure for a thousand years.

During the spring of 1941 the Germans assembled massive forces in eastern Europe in preparation for the invasion. They received assistance from several quarters. In the north, the Finns prepared for a "Continuation War" against Soviet Russia. They did not seek a direct alliance with Hitler. Rather, they considered their efforts to regain the territories they had lost during the Winter War to be separate from the German campaign against Soviet Russia. In fact, the Finns were an important but independent ally of Germany in the attack. But once they attained their limited objectives, they had little interest in proceeding further.

In the south, the Romanians sent more soldiers to participate in the attack on Russia than any other German ally. Marshal Ion Antonescu (1882–1946) wanted to regain the territories lost to Soviet Russia the previous year. He also wanted to retain the good graces of the Germans in order to press for a further revision of the division of Transylvania contained in the Second Vienna Award. A Romanian failure to enthusiastically support the attack on Russia risked a shift in German goodwill toward Hungary.

The Hungarians sent a corps to participate in the invasion. Although they had no territorial aspirations to Soviet lands, they too wanted to remain in Hitler's good graces. The Second Vienna Award had satisfied neither Hungary nor Romania, and they competed for Hitler's favor in hopes of its revision. Both Hungary and Romania sent units to Russia, but they also retained important forces at home in case the Transylvania issue led to the outbreak of hostilities between them.

A corps of two divisions from the Slovak army also participated in the invasion. The Slovaks had already joined in the German attack on Poland. Like the Hungarians, the Slovaks aspired to no Soviet territory, and their presence was indicative of Slovakia's subservience to Germany.

Finally, Benito Mussolini, not wishing to be left behind, sent an Expeditionary Corps consisting of three divisions; additional Italian units would follow the next year. National units from Spain and Croatia later participated in the campaign. Except for the Finns and possibly the Romanians, these soldiers added little to the German war effort. They were not well equipped, well led, or well motivated. Their presence did, however, allow the Germans to depict the war for lebensraum in terms of a crusade against communism and for European civilization, once the war in the east began to falter.

After the stunning German victories during the summer of 1940, Stalin understood that his calculations of the previous year had gone awry. He had increased Soviet security with the direct annexation of the Baltic states and the Romanian territories of Bessarabia and northern Bukovina, but Russia was alone on the continent in terms of dealing with its nominal ally, Nazi Germany. The Russians generally attempted to accommodate the Germans with the delivery of raw materials. On 19 April the Russians signed an important agreement with the Japanese, their recent enemies. This nonaggression pact provided some security in the Far East, allowing the Soviets to focus their attention on Europe. Of course, even with the pact, they could not entirely neglect the areas in eastern Mongolia and northern Manchuria where they had recently fought the Japanese.

German preparations for war in eastern Europe did not escape Russian notice. Stalin did not, however, want to provide the Germans with any pretext for attack.[2] The Red Army was not ready for war, and any delay in the German attack could only help the Russians. Soviet and foreign intelligence sources, including American and British, warned the Russians of the pending onslaught. As the immediacy of the attack became apparent in the spring of 1941, the Russians struggled to meet the challenges of the growing danger in the west.

The attack began in the early-morning hours of 22 June. The Germans achieved tactical surprise everywhere. German air raids destroyed much of the Russian air force on the ground. Russian communications soon broke down. Although Red Army soldiers often resisted the invaders fiercely, the German offensive soon overwhelmed the forward units, which had lost contact with headquarters.

In the north, the Germans advanced rapidly into the Baltic states. After a year of direct Soviet rule, many Lithuanians, Latvians, and

Estonians welcomed the Germans as the lesser of two evils. After all, the Germans had been in most of these areas from 1915 to 1919. One Lithuanian later explained, "The Germans and Russians both treated us brutally. The Germans did not care whether we liked it or not, but the Russians expected us to like it."[3] The Germans were in Vilnius on 23 June and in Riga by 1 July; on 27 July Tallinn fell. The Baltic peoples hoped for the restoration of independence or at least some kind of self-government under the Germans. One year of Soviet occupation had erased memories of the German attempts to annex these regions in 1917–1920. In their hope for independence, the Baltic peoples were disappointed. The Germans had no interest in promoting Baltic nationalism.

By the middle of September the Germans had advanced to the suburbs of Leningrad, which they brought under siege. The Finns cut off the northern approaches to the city as they quickly retook their pre-1940 borders. The Finns also occupied some areas north of Lake Ladoga and advanced as far as Petrozavodsk on the Leningrad-Murmansk railroad, but they refused to go farther. They had no interest in moving beyond their old frontier in the Karelian Isthmus and entering Leningrad itself. Rather than risk fighting in the streets of the birthplace of the Russian Revolution, the Germans preferred to impose a siege. By October the Russians' only route to and from Leningrad was across Lake Ladoga. With the onset of the winter of 1941–1942 came starvation. The population was reduced to eating dogs, cats, and wallpaper paste. Cannibalism also appeared that winter. Although the Russians managed to establish a lifeline over the ice and water of Lake Ladoga, the blockade of Leningrad lasted until January 1944. Of the three million inhabitants on the eve of the war, roughly one-third lived, one-third evacuated, and one-third died.

In the center, German armies also advanced rapidly. Minsk fell on 28 June, although Russian soldiers in the old fortress at Brest-Litovsk held out for more than a month. In a pincers movement in August the Germans succeeded in killing or capturing 475,000 Red Army soldiers between Minsk and Smolensk in a huge *kesselschlact*, or caldron battle. In this *kesselschlact*, German blitzkrieg units surrounded Red Army forces while standard infantry troops marched to the battlefield. These forces crushed the Russians against the armor, cleaned up stragglers, and isolated areas of resistance. After this huge victory the commander of Army Group Center expected to proceed to Moscow. Some German generals later claimed that had Army Group Center done so, the Soviet capital would have fallen by October, and victory in Operation Barbarossa and the Second World War itself would have been assured. After the victory at Smolensk, however, the German command ordered Army Group Center to halt. One armored detachment went north to assist in the siege of Leningrad; the other went south.

The advance of Army Group South initially lagged behind that of Army Group North and Army Group Center. Rainy spring weather in southeastern Europe had impeded the positioning of German formations in Romania, and many Romanian units were not ready on 22 June. Army Group South soon made up for lost time, however. The Ukrainians, especially in areas recently annexed by the Soviet Union from Poland, often welcomed the German invaders. These western Ukrainians hoped the Germans would establish some kind of Ukrainian state. The Germans, however, had come not as liberators but as conquerors, determined to obtain lebensraum. They soon quashed any manifestations of Ukrainian nationalism.

From the outset, German and Romanian units in the south encountered strong Soviet Russian resistance. Stalin was especially determined to defend Kiev. There, in September, the Germans achieved what was probably their greatest victory in the Russian campaign if not the entire war. In the area around Kiev, they carried out another caldron battle in which they captured more than 665,000 Red Army soldiers. Stalin's refusal to allow a withdrawal from exposed positions was an important factor in the Soviet disaster. The number of dead remains unclear. Kiev itself fell on 19 September. After this victory the Germans occupied most of the rest of Ukraine.

Meanwhile, in southern Ukraine, Romanian forces advanced beyond Bessarabia along the Black Sea coast to Odessa, where they undertook a costly siege. The Russians held out there until 16 October, at which time the Soviet navy evacuated the remaining soldiers to the Crimea. The Romanians took over the territory between the Dniester and Bug rivers, which they named Transnistria. This included their hard-won prize Odessa, which they renamed Antonescu after the Romanian dictator. The Germans intended Transnistria to be compensation for the areas of Transylvania the Romanians had lost to Hungary in the Second Vienna Award of 1940. German and Romanian forces then broke into the Crimea and brought the large Soviet Russian naval base at Sevastopol under siege.

After the huge German victory at Kiev, the armored units returned to Army Group Center, and the advance on Moscow resumed. Another important German success occurred at Vyazma and Bryansk in October. There, German units surrounded and destroyed another 660,000 Soviet Russian soldiers. Moscow appeared about to fall. On 19 October Stalin was close to leaving the capital. Some foreign legations left for Kuibyshev on the Volga. The autumn rains, however, brought about the *rasputitsa,* the "time without roads." The muddy roads forced the Germans to halt, and they had to wait for a hard freeze on 7 November before they could renew their offensive on Moscow, dubbed Operation Typhoon. The Germans experienced logistical problems caused by distance and by the lack of adequate locomotives and railcars. The Russian broad-gauge (five-foot) railroad did not mesh with the standard European gauge of four feet, eight and a half inches. The retreating Russians had taken care to remove or destroy as much motive power and rolling stock as possible, greatly increasing German logistical problems.

At the twenty-fourth anniversary celebration of the October Revolution, held on 6 November 1941, Stalin invoked not only Lenin but also leading Russian figures of the past, including novelist Leo Tolstoy (1828–1910), composer P. I. Tchaikovsky (1840–1893), and such military heroes as Alexander Nevski (1220?–1263), Dmitri Donskoi (1350–1389), and Alexander Suvorov (1729–1800). This oration, which became known as the "Holy Russia Speech," demonstrated that communist ideology was insufficient to motivate the Russian people to resist the German invasion. In this dire situation, with German units bearing down on Moscow, Stalin resorted to a direct appeal to Russian nationalism.

At the German high command, the leaders of the three fronts decided at a conference at Orsha on 13 November that they had little choice but to continue their offensive, even though their soldiers were still clad in summer uniforms and often had only cold meals to eat. They lacked the ability to dig in where they were, out in the open in wintertime Russia. They also lacked the will to retreat at this point.

The cold and exhausted Germans reached the outskirts of Moscow at

EASTERN EUROPE
WORLD WAR II

SWEDEN

FINLAND

0   150   300
miles

Helsinki

Leningrad

Tallinn

ESTONIA

Baltic *Sea*

Riga

Rzhev   Moscow

Vyazma

S O V I E T

U N I O N

Smolensk

EAST
PRUSSIA

Minsk

GENERAL
GOVERNMENT

Warsaw

Kursk

Kiev   Kharkov

Stalingrad

SLOVAKIA

Rostov

Budapest

HUNGARY

Odessa

CROATIA   Belgrade

ROMANIA

Sevastopol

Bucharest

SERBIA

Sofia

Black   Sea

BULGARIA

Istanbul

ALB   Salonika

GREECE

T U R K E Y

Athens

	International boundary
- - - -	Front–December, 1941
⊔⊔⊔⊔⊔	Front–November, 1942
— · —	Front–July, 1943
•–•–•–	Front–June, 1944
•••••••	Front–February, 1945

the beginning of December. The Red Army counterattacked on the night of 5–6 December, throwing the Germans back from the city. Directing the counterattack before Moscow was General Georgi Zhukov (1896–1974), the victor at Khalkin Gol along the Mongolian-Manchurian border in 1939. During this Russian counterattack, Hitler assumed command of the German army and ordered it to hold. Nevertheless, the Russians forced the Germans back from the approaches to Moscow. Only the spring thaw and a renewal of the *rasputitsa* brought the Russian counteroffensive to a halt. The Battle of Moscow was the critical battle of the renewed war and perhaps the single most important battle of the entire Long War. The German failure to take the Soviet capital meant another year of fighting in Russia. Blitzkrieg had failed. In a conflict of resources, as in 1914–1918, the Germans would be less likely to prevail. The goal of lebensraum slipped away in the snows around Moscow.

The Russian counterattack made some other gains elsewhere. In the north, the Red Army succeeded in slightly loosening the German stranglehold on Leningrad by retaking the railroad station at Tikhvin. This enabled rail traffic to resume to the shores of frozen Lake Ladoga. The Russians also encircled a large German force around Demyansk. In the south, the Russians recaptured Rostov on Don, the gateway to the Caucasus. Also, in an effort to relieve the siege of Sevastopol, they crossed the narrow Strait of Kerch and attacked German and Romanian units on the eastern end of the Crimean Peninsula. They also landed farther west at Feodosiya. The Germans and Romanians fell back, evacuating the Kerch Peninsula.

To make matters worse for the Germans, in a show of solidarity with his Japanese allies, Hitler declared war on the United States on 9 December. This ensured that vast American resources would sooner or later appear on the eastern front. The Germans had no sure means to counter the combination of American material and Russian manpower.

Some fighting continued through the spring thaw, but in late spring 1942 both sides were ready to resume the offensive. The Red Army struck first, with an ambitious attempt to capture the industrial city of Kharkov in northeastern Ukraine, on 12 May 1942. The Germans, who were preparing their own offensive in this area, contained the Russian attacks and destroyed the Russian forces by the end of the month.

In the Crimea, the Germans and Romanians resumed offensive operations in May. First, they cleared the Russian beachheads in the eastern part of the peninsula. Then, using massed heavy artillery, they renewed their assault on Sevastopol. The Russian forces trapped there resisted fiercely, but in the absence of any relief effort, they had to surrender on 4 July 1942. The operation was costly for both sides. Given their limited resources and their plans to undertake another big offensive in the south, the Germans might have done better just to maintain the siege until the lack of food and munitions caused the eventual surrender of Sevastopol.

After their successes at Kharkov and in the Crimea, the Germans were ready to resume the initiative in the east. Because of the huge losses sustained in the first year of the war, they were unable to advance on all three Russian fronts. In the north, Leningrad remained under siege. In the center, Moscow had eluded the German grasp the previous winter. An offensive in the south offered the most advantage. If the Germans could retake Rostov on Don and break through into the land bridge between the Black and Caspian seas, they could strike at the vitally important oil fields and refinery complexes around Baku. The seizure of this area would simultaneously provide the Germans with petroleum resources and deprive the Red Army of the same. This strategy made sense economically. Strategically, however, it risked overextension of the southern forces and offered an exposed left flank to the Red Army. The German high command divided Army Group South into two parts. Group A was to advance along the eastern shore of the Black Sea to the Caucasus and then on to Baku. Group B, including the German Sixth Army, received the assignment to move to Astrakhan at the mouth of the Volga River. To accomplish this, they had to protect their left flank. Astride the left flank along the Volga River was the city of Stalingrad. The Germans would have to take or at least block Stalingrad to accomplish their goals in the south.

The Germans' southern offensive began on 28 June in the vicinity of the city of Kursk. The Germans headed east toward Voronezh on the Don River and then turned south. They recaptured Rostov on Don on 23 July and reached the lower Don near Stalingrad that same day. Less than a month later, on 19 August, the Germans arrived at the Volga River and at Stalingrad. Soldiers from Group A moved along the Black Sea coast as far as Tapse and came up against the Caucasus. One detachment climbed Europe's highest mountain, Mount Elbrus, on 21 August. This feat provided dramatic photos for German propaganda.

In this desperate situation, Stalin issued Order No. 227 on 28 July, which established the slogan "Not one step back." Retreat was forbidden. Special rear units joined regular security troops in enforcing this order. As German forces approached the Volga, the Red Army dug in.

When the Wehrmacht neared Stalingrad, the Luftwaffe bombed the city into rubble. The ruined city provided the Russian defenders with excellent cover from which to attack the German armor. Blitzkrieg fighting was not suitable in cities, and the Germans soon became bogged down in the streets and buildings of Stalingrad. Hitler's determination to take the city on the Volga bearing the name of his adversary was matched by Stalin's determination to defend his city. Fighting in the ruins of the city raged throughout the autumn. Stalingrad became a Verdun on the Volga. German and Russian commanders fed men and machines into the furnace of war. Germans stripped their flanks of units and sent them into the city. The Romanian Third Army took up positions on the left flank. However, Russian forces remained at some points on both sides of the Don River. On the right flank, the Romanian Fourth Army faced the open steppe south of Stalingrad. Farther north, the Italian Eighth Army and the Hungarian Second Army held the line. The Italians acted as a buffer between the Hungarians and Romanians, who would have preferred to fight each other over Transylvania instead of confronting the Russians. The utilization of these minimally equipped, trained, and motivated soldiers indicated the extent to which the German effort in Russia had become overextended.

By the beginning of November the Germans had reduced the Russian footholds in the city to three small areas. The Russians could reinforce and resupply these footholds only at night. Even then, these operations were under heavy German fire. The preservation of these west bank positions became vital to Russian plans for a massive counteroffensive that would strike both Army Group Center and Army Group South. In the center, Operation Mars was intended to strike against the German-held salient at Rzhev, which stuck out like a fist toward Moscow. In the south, Operation Uranus was supposed to hit the Romanian-held flanks of the German position at Stalingrad and surround the German forces fighting there. The Russians planned to follow up with Operations Jupiter and Saturn, which were intended to surround Army Groups Center and South and win the war in 1943.

Operation Mars began on 25 November. The Russians continued

their attacks in the area of Rzhev until late December but made little headway against the German defenses and sustained heavy casualties. The Germans also suffered high losses. Although the Russian attacks ended with the turn of the year, German control of the Rzhev salient was fatally weakened. Within three months the Germans had to evacuate Rzhev as well as a smaller salient to the north at Demyansk.

Meanwhile, in the south the Red Army enjoyed a stunning success. On 19 November, with the Red Army forces in Stalingrad barely hanging on, the Russians launched a massive offensive on the flanks. They crashed through the Romanian Third Army in the north and the Romanian Fourth Army in the south.[4] These two Russian thrusts then met at Kalach on the Don River, less than fifty miles west of Stalingrad. Surviving Romanian units from the Third Army retreated westward past the Chir River; some units from the Fourth Army retreated into Stalingrad itself, while others move to the northwest. The Red Army trapped almost 300,000 German and Romanian soldiers in the Stalingrad pocket. The Russians had accomplished a *kesselschlacht*, which the Germans had used so successfully against them in 1941. At this point, the surrounded forces might have been able to break out of the Russian trap, but Hitler ordered them to remain where they were. He relied on assurances from Air Marshal Hermann Göring (1893–1946) that the Luftwaffe could supply Stalingrad from the air, just as it had done in Demyansk the previous winter. Also, the German army began to prepare for Operation Winter Storm, in which a relief force was to attack from the south and break into Stalingrad.

Operation Winter Storm, commanded by General von Manstein, began on 12 December.[5] Initially, it met with some success. However, stiffening Russian defenses south of Stalingrad, as well as Russian attacks along the Don north of Stalingrad against the Italian Eighth Army beginning on 16 December, forced the German relief offensive to halt some thirty miles short of its goal. Manstein's efforts narrowed the territory the Germans controlled north of the Black Sea. Meanwhile, the German attempt to supply Stalingrad by air failed. One-third of the German air detachment was lost to weather, Russian fighter planes, and antiaircraft fire. By the end of December, German relief efforts were over. The German and Romanian soldiers within the Stalingrad pocket were doomed.

Russian attacks farther up the Don in the vicinity of Voronezh in January 1943 destroyed the Hungarian Second Army. Also, by this time, the Italian Eighth Army had disintegrated.[6] The loss of these armies compounded the disaster for the Germans. The soldiers within the Stalingrad pocked continued to hold out while Group A evacuated the areas it had occupied north of the Caucasus. Finally, on 31 January 1943, the remaining German and Romanian forces in Stalingrad surrendered. The Germans and Romanians lost almost 300,000 men killed, missing, or captured and as much as one-quarter of the equipment of the German army. The Germans could not make up these losses in manpower, having been unable to find sufficient replacements for casualties since back in August 1942. Although Stalingrad is often perceived as the turning point of the German-Russian war, German plans had already gone seriously awry with their failure to take Moscow the previous year and rapidly conclude the campaign against Soviet Russia.

Even after such catastrophic losses, German armies remained in force deep within Russia. After briefly losing Kharkov in February 1943, they retook it on 13 March. The victory at Kharkov was the last major offensive success for the Germans on the eastern front. On the same day the Germans returned to Kharkov, Hitler issued a directive for Operation Citadel. The success of the Russian winter offensives had left a large salient protruding into the German lines around the city of Kursk. Operation Citadel envisioned attacks north from the direction of Orel and south from the direction of Kharkov toward Kursk, pinching off the salient and trapping significant Russian forces there. Success would also shorten the German lines.

The Germans had lost so much manpower and equipment that they could no longer achieve anything more than local numerical superiority against Russian forces. They hoped to compensate for their lack of numbers with superior military machinery. Three new weapons that had been under development were readied for deployment in the offensive. One of these formidable weapons was the Panther medium tank, intended to counter the successful Russian T-34 medium tank. The second was the heavy Tiger I tank, and the third was the Elephant self-propelled antitank gun. So desperate were the Germans to regain the initiative on the eastern front that these fighting vehicles were rushed into production and sent to the east without the usual testing and breaking-in periods. They would be tested on the field of battle. For Operation Citadel, the Germans also made a major effort to achieve local air superiority.

The Russians anticipated the German offensive around Kursk and spent much of the spring and early summer of 1943 preparing deep defensive positions north and south of the city. Massive amounts of machines and manpower arrived to meet the anticipated German onslaught.

The Germans began their attacks on 4 July.[7] Initially, they achieved local successes, advancing from the north and the south. The Russian defenses, however, took their toll as the Germans advanced. Russian antitank guns and mines proved effective against the German machines. Also, the new German weapons frequently broke down and demonstrated other vulnerabilities. One major problem was the lack of a machine gun to protect against infantry forces on the massive but slow Elephant gun. Also, summer thunderstorms and rains slowed the German advance. Another problem for the Germans developed hundreds of miles away. On 10 July 1943 Anglo-American forces landed in Sicily. Three days later Hitler ordered the termination of Operation Citadel. Initiative in the east passed to the Red Army for the remainder of the war.

The Germans had expended their last resources in the Kursk offensive. Because of their heavy losses, the Germans reverted to a defensive strategy in the east, attempting to contain the Russians with World War I western front–type defenses. These soon proved to be incapable of stopping the Russian counteroffensive that followed the cessation of the Kursk operation. Two days after the termination of Operation Citadel, the Russians began their counteroffensive and swept the exhausted German forces away. On 5 August the Russians took Orel, on 23 August they were back in Kharkov; on 6 November, despite a strong German counterattack, they entered Kiev, the site of their huge defeat two years earlier.

The Russians continued their offensives the next year, without taking the customary pause for the *rasputitsa*. In January 1944 they finally succeeded in breaking the Wehrmacht's grip on Leningrad. The Red Army then slowly began to push the Germans back toward the Baltic countries. In the spring and summer of 1944 the Russians initiated several caldron battles, demonstrating once again that they had mastered the strategy used so successfully against them in 1941 by the Germans. The Russian General Staff had learned to envelop the German flanks and surround the center. The Russians succeeded in surrounding large German forces in Cherkassy, Ukraine, in January 1944.[8] By the end of February the Cherkassy pocket had ceased to exist, and more than 70,000 German troops were eliminated. The Russians trapped a smaller number of Germans at Tarnopol, Ukraine, in March. Hitler's reluctance to condone evacuations contributed to the German defensive defeats. Had the fighting not continued to be so brutal and desperate on the eastern front, the Russian General Staff might have saluted their German captives by repeating the gesture of Tsar Peter I (1672–1725) after the Battle of Poltava in 1709, when he toasted the captured Swedish generals as "his teachers."

Another major German defeat occurred in the Crimea during the spring of 1944. Even after the Russians had recaptured Odessa on 10 April and isolated the Crimea, Hitler hoped to retain this strategic region to protect the vital Romanian oil fields. The German and Romanian defenders of the Crimea could not hold off the Russians, but unlike two years earlier, Sevastopol did not become the scene of a prolonged siege. By 14 May the Germans and Romanians completed their evacuation of the Crimea.

The summer of 1944 brought the Germans no respite. On 22 June the Red Army initiated Operation Bagration, named after General Peter Bagration (1765–1812), a Russian-Georgian hero of the fighting against Napoleon in 1812. It was intended to mark the third anniversary of the German attack on Russia, as well as coincide with the American and British landings in Normandy. The result was the greatest cauldron battle of the entire war.[9] The Russians quickly broke through the northern and southern flanks of Army Group Center in Byelorussia and then moved to eliminate large numbers of surrounded Germans. This is often described as a "modern Cannae" because the Russian forces enveloped the German flanks in general imitation of Hannibal's (247–182 BCE) classic victory over the Romans in 216 BCE. This was the greatest Russian victory in the war.

By the summer of 1944 most of the remaining Luftwaffe units were desperately attempting to counteract the American and British air offensive over Germany. The lack of air support in Byelorussia was especially devastating for German units attempting to break out of the Russian trap. The Russian air force constantly harassed them. The Russians returned to Minsk on 3 July, after an absence of three years. Vilnius fell on 13 July. By the end of the summer Army Group Center had lost more than 400,000 men. Byelorussia was the greatest German defeat of the war. By August the Russians were at the gates of Warsaw. A Russian thrust reached the Baltic Sea near Memel on 9 October, cutting off Army Group North's route of retreat. By that time Tallinn had already fallen on 22 September, and the Russians returned to Riga on 13 October. The remnants of Army Group North retreated to the Courland Peninsula, where they held out until the end of the war. Rather than attempting to evacuate this force by sea, Hitler chose to leave it in place, in part so the Germans could retain control of the Baltic Sea. Defeat after defeat in the eastern front battles of 1944 confirmed the verdict of Kursk and destroyed the Werhmacht's remaining reserves of manpower and material.

Germany's two important eastern front allies also felt the Russian wrath in 1944. In the north, a Russian offensive in the Karelian Isthmus in June pushed the Finns back from their 1939 frontiers and once again out of Viipuri. At the same time, the Russians rapidly retook the territories north of Lake Ladoga that the Finns had occupied in 1941. With all the territories taken in the Continuation War lost, and with their German allies facing certain defeat, the Finns withdrew from the war. On 25 August they signed an agreement with the Russians, under which the Finnish army pushed the remaining German forces in the far north out of their country.

Meanwhile, in the south, the Romanians also had to confront the reality of defeat. Russian forces broke through German and Romanian defenses along the Dniester River beginning on 20 August and moved into pre-1940 Romania. On 23 August young King Michael, together with some army officers, arrested General Antonescu. Two days later, Romania declared war on Germany, and Romanian and Russian troops fought together to expel the Germans from Romania. For the Germans, the loss of Romania also meant the loss of the vital Ploeşti oil fields and refining complexes.

The loss of Romania made Bulgaria's adherence to the German alliance problematic. When Russian forces appeared on the north shore of the Danube, the Bulgarians hastened to surrender, unimpeded by the fact that they had never declared war on Russia and had not participated in the eastern campaign. The Red Army met only cheers and flowers in Bulgaria when it crossed the Danube on 8 September 1944. The Bulgarians also joined the war against Germany, and Bulgarian forces then occupying Macedonia helped the Russians and Yugoslav partisan forces push the Germans out of Serbia.

Other German eastern European allies sought to deal with the defeat of their patron. As the Russians approached the Carpathians in August 1944, elements of the Slovak army, together with communist sympathizers and even some prisoners of war, revolted against the Germans. Some help was parachuted in from Russia, but it was insufficient to save the Slovak national insurrection, and the Red Army was still too far away to provide direct aid. By October the Germans and those Slovaks still loyal to them had suppressed the revolt. After the war, this insurrection permitted the Slovaks to point out that despite their initial subservience to Hitler, they had revolted. Their Czech partners, however, could make no such claim.

Admiral Miklós Horthy, the regent of Hungary, likewise sought a way for his country to leave the war. The Germans had occupied Hungary in the spring of 1944 in an effort to ensure loyalty. In October, after Horthy announced an armistice, Germans forces arrested him and replaced him with a fascist Arrow Cross government headed by Ferenc Szálasi (1897–1946). This new government was determined to stay with the Germans until the bitter end.

The bitter end occurred in December 1944, when a Russian offensive trapped a considerable German and Hungarian force in Budapest. The Red Army and Yugoslav Partisans had liberated Belgrade on 20 October. The Russians then headed north into the Hungarian plain. Other Russian units, together with forces from the newly turned Romanian allies, crossed the Carpathians into Hungary. By Christmas 1944 the Red Army had surrounded Budapest on both sides of the Danube and brought the Hungarian capital under siege.[10] While Arrow Cross elements instituted a reign of terror in the city, Soviet forces pounded its German and Hungarian defenders. Between January and March 1945 Hitler undertook three major attacks to relieve the city, but to no avail. The Germans wanted not only to retain Budapest and the small western Hungarian oil fields but also to protect the approaches to Vienna. Nevertheless, Pest (on the east side of the Danube) fell on 18 January 1945. A last-minute attempt by surviving German and Hungarian forces to break out of Buda (on the west side of the Danube) ended in disaster. Budapest finally had to surrender after horrendous fighting on 13 February 1945. For the second time in slightly more than twenty-five years, Romanian troops occupied the Hungarian capital.

Meanwhile, in Poland, the Red Army resumed its offensive. After halting in the fall of 1944 at the gates of Warsaw, the Russians had taken some time to rest and regroup. This halt had tragic consequences for the Polish nationalist uprising in Warsaw. When the Russian offensive resumed on 12 January 1945, its main objective was obvious: the German capital of Berlin. The Russians quickly smashed through the German defenses based on the Vistula River. Secondary Russian forces turned north to the Baltic, where the German navy made a desperate effort to evacuate German refugees from the old eastern Baltic Hanseatic cities and East Prussia. Russian submarines operating in the Baltic exacted a terrible toll through the sinking of refugee ships, including the *Wilhelm Gustloff* on 30 January, the *General von Steuben* on 12 February, and the *Goya* on 16 April.[11] Around 15,000 lives were lost on these three ships, about half of those on the *Goya*. Millions of other Germans from the eastern regions, some of them unfortunate refugees from failed Nazi settlement schemes, fled westward before the onslaught of the Red Army.

By the beginning of April 1945 the Russians had advanced to the Oder and Neisse rivers, along what would become the eastern border of postwar East Germany. The Russians crossed the Oder River on 12 April and four days later began the final assault on the German capital.[12] Stalin seems to have encouraged a competition between General Zhukov, commander of the first Byelorussian front, and General Ivan Konev (1897–1973), commander of the first Ukrainian front, over which would be the first to take Berlin. This would hasten the capture of the city and enhance the glory of the successful general. Fighting began in the suburbs on 19 April, and by 25 April the Red Army had surrounded the German capital. Intense fighting occurred throughout Berlin. Hitler killed himself in his underground bunker on 29 April. Three days later, on 2 May, Berlin surrendered. The Russians, together with a Russian-established Polish army, lost more than 350,000 men in the taking of the city. The number of German soldiers and civilians who died probably exceeded 500,000.

Fighting between German and Russian forces continued in the western regions of Czechoslovakia. The Germans had controlled these areas as the Protectorate of Bohemia and Moravia since 1939. What was left of Army Group Center came under Russian attack as elements of Konev's Ukrainian front began to move on Prague on 5 May. The Russians assisted in a spontaneous anti-German uprising by the inhabitants of Prague, who sought to mitigate their previous loyalties by turning on their German masters. Also aiding the Czechs were elements of General Andrei Vlasov's

(1900–1946) Russian Liberation Army. There was no repeat of Warsaw or Budapest in Prague. The Russians enjoyed good relations with the Czech government in exile. Russian forces reached Prague on 9 May and cleaned up the remaining German resistance.

The Russians defeated the Germans, but at a tremendous cost. At least ten million Russian soldiers died, along with as many civilians.[13] Four years of fighting devastated the most productive areas of the country, from the western frontier to Leningrad, Moscow, and Stalingrad. Buildings, bridges, rail lines, and other infrastructure were destroyed. Livestock was gone. Both sides practiced scorched-earth policies in retreat. All these disasters were inflicted on a people who had barely begun to recover from the previous catastrophes of war, revolution, civil war, and collectivization. Losses in Byelorussia, the scene of intense fighting in 1941 and 1944 and of guerrilla war and retribution during the entire German occupation, were especially severe. Needless to say, the large Jewish communities there perished because of German racial policies.

The Germans also sustained enormous losses. They suffered at least five million dead, the vast majority of those in fighting against Russia. Germany's allies also sustained large numbers of casualties. Romania's losses in the war against Russia amounted to almost 400,000, and another 100,000 Romanian soldiers died fighting on the side of the Russians. Thus Romania lost about the same number of soldiers in the war as did the United States. Hungarian military and civilian losses were also heavy.

The Russians received help from abroad, especially from the United States. The Americans extended the Lend-Lease Act to Russia in November 1941; however, significant amounts of war material did not appear in Russia until after Stalingrad. Thereafter, American supplies poured into Russia, primarily through Iran in the south and the arctic port of Murmansk in the north. Even though Russian soldiers might drive jeeps and eat Spam, they gave their lives to defeat the Wehrmacht.

The other important assistance rendered to the Russians by their allies was the bombing campaign over Germany. Beginning in 1942 the American and British bombing raids over German cities forced the Luftwaffe to concentrate its forces on the defense of Germany. This eliminated the air cover that had protected German forces and harassed Russian forces since the beginning of the war. Thereafter, the Germans would enjoy only local air superiority.

Both sides inflicted horrible atrocities on civilian populations. One particularly brutal and horrific aspect of the fighting in the east was its urban component. Cities such as Berlin, Budapest, Kharkov, Stalingrad, and Warsaw endured total destruction as the German and Russian armies and their modern military machines clashed in the streets. The huge number of civilian casualties in Soviet Russia is a testament to the barbaric rule of the Germans. The Russians repaid the Germans in kind. With so much of the German male population either dead or in Allied prisoner of war camps, the Red Army exacted much of its vengeance on the German female population. The Red Army engaged in a deliberate policy of mass rape and did not confine this atrocity to German women. Many females in Russian-occupied areas, whether German, Hungarian, Polish, Romanian, or Yugoslav, were violated by Red Army soldiers.

Ideology overlying nationalism sustained both sides. Nazi ideology was extreme nationalism. Soviet Russian ideology became more nationalistic as the war continued. Significantly, at the conclusion of the war, Stalin thanked the Russian people for their efforts, ignoring the efforts of non-Russian peoples and tacitly acknowledging that many Ukrainians, Byelorussians, Lithuanians, and others had supported the German invaders.

The dynamics of the Russian victory were complicated. The Germans overestimated their own capabilities and underestimated those of their opponents. The Russians demonstrated an ability to learn from previous mistakes and had much greater population resources than the Germans.

The German-Russian conflict was the most intense and most destructive phase of the entire twentieth century. Once again, a force from the periphery determined the outcome of fighting in Europe. In the previous round of fighting, American material and later fresh American forces broke the stalemate and ensured an entente victory. In the renewed fighting, the effectiveness of Russian arms and the ability and willingness of the Soviet peoples to sustain huge casualties to defeat the invading German and allied armies were the decisive elements in the war's outcome.

Chapter 10

AMERICAN INTERVENTION, 1940–1945

The renewal of the twentieth-century European conflict did not initially attract a great deal of interest in the United States. The country was in the grip of the Depression. Many Americans, disappointed by the failed settlement of the previous war, were determined to avoid further involvement in European affairs. In addition, some Americans, among them the aviation hero Charles Lindbergh (1902–1974) and ambassador to Great Britain Joseph Kennedy (1888–1969), evinced some sympathy for the new regime in Germany. These factors underlay a strong sense of isolationism in the United States. The spread of Japanese power in Asia dominated the attention of those Americans who retained an interest in international issues. In 1935, 1936, and 1937 Congress passed a series of neutrality acts. If a war broke out in Europe or Asia, these acts prohibited American participation in arms sales, required the sale of nonmilitary commodities to be on a cash basis, and forbade American citizens to travel on the ships of belligerents.

Although he signed these neutrality acts, President Franklin Delano Roosevelt (1882–1945) did not share this pervasive sense of isolationism. He recognized the potential danger the rise of Nazi Germany posed for Europe and for the United States. Nevertheless, upon the renewal of war in Europe in 1939, he initially followed a policy of neutrality. On 4 November 1939 Roosevelt obtained a new neutrality act from Congress that allowed the purchase of arms on a cash basis, which was intended to benefit the British and French. The German victories in the spring of 1940 brought Europe under Nazi domination, with only Britain still holding out. The British determination to resist the Germans, convincingly demonstrated by their destruction of the French fleet at Oran, made an impression on

Roosevelt and American policy makers. They recognized that if conflicts between American and German interests led to war, American forces would need a forward base from which to operate against the Germans. Since virtually all of continental Europe was under German control, that base had to be the island of Britain. After the summer of 1940, American policy incrementally moved toward confrontation with Germany.

The first step toward war occurred in August 1940. As a result of a meeting between Roosevelt and Canadian Prime Minister Mackenzie King (1874–1950) in Ogdensburg, New York, the American and Canadian governments began to cooperate in matters of defense. With Britain under direct German threat, the Americans and Canadians undertook joint responsibility to defend the North American continent.

The next month the Americans concluded the so-called Destroyer Deal with Great Britain. Responding to a British initiative of the previous spring, President Roosevelt agreed on 2 September 1940 to lend the Royal Navy fifty destroyers in return for a promise that these warships would not be surrendered or scuttled and for a ninety-nine-year lease on bases in the British West Indies, including the Bahamas, Jamaica, St. Lucia, Trinidad, Antigua, and British Guiana, as well as in Bermuda and Newfoundland. The destroyers enabled the British to increase protection for convoys bringing war materials from North America to Britain. The Caribbean bases enabled the Americans to increase the security for the eastern approaches of the Panama Canal.

In March 1941, with the Germans on the verge of attacking Yugoslavia and Greece, the U.S. government finalized plans for material aid to Great Britain, including military materials, oil, and other items, as well as services. It also provided for the transportation of war materials to Britain. The United States provided this service to the British without collateral and with no immediate expectation of repayment (that system had, after all, failed during the previous war). The lend-lease system was really a subsidy: the U.S. government paid the British government to fight the war against Nazi Germany. The United States also provided a giant subvention for Great Britain, which had the important domestic benefit of aiding its recovery from the Great Depression. As a major source of material aid to Britain, and with the commitment to deliver those supplies, the United States was on a collision course with Germany. The U.S. government extended the lend-lease program to Russia in November 1941 and later to other belligerents in the war against the Axis Powers.

The logic of intervention demanded that the Americans establish security for the North Atlantic routes to Britain. Greenland, the world's largest island, lay near sea-lanes in the North Atlantic. Greenland was nominally a Danish colony, but after the German occupation of Denmark, the Danish administration in Greenland renounced the connection to Copenhagen. In April 1941 the U.S. government signed an agreement with the Free Denmark movement, accepting responsibility for security of the island and obtaining the right to establish air bases there. The American occupation of Greenland was never complete. German meteorological units operated weather stations in eastern Greenland throughout the war. Nevertheless, the American occupation of Greenland helped ensure control of the vital sea-lanes between North America and Europe.

American control expanded eastward toward Europe when American forces landed in Iceland. Iceland had been part of the Danish realm since 1380. When Germany overran Denmark in April 1940, Iceland declared its temporary independence. The next month British soldiers landed in Iceland, and Canadians arrived later to prevent a German occupation. In July 1941 American soldiers replaced these British and Canadian troops so that they could be used elsewhere. Iceland made its independence permanent in 1944.

American forces entered the arena of conflict in the Battle of the Atlantic in 1941. The obligation to deliver war supplies under the lend-lease agreements ensured that the U.S. Navy would clash with German submarines. The Germans had begun U-boat patrols in the Atlantic in 1939, but their efforts intensified after the fall of France in the summer of 1940. By that time the Germans had acquired submarine bases in France and Norway that provided them with easy access to the North Atlantic and the waters around Britain. The use of surface ships to interdict convoys ended, for the most part, after the British fleet sank the German battleship *Bismarck* in the Atlantic Ocean west of Brittany on 27 May 1941. German U-boat attacks on convoys escorted by American warships made combat between the two inevitable.

The first real clash occurred on 4 September 1941 when a U-boat attacked the destroyer USS *Greer* in the North Atlantic.[1] No damage ensued, but as a result of this incident, President Roosevelt ordered the U.S.

Navy to shoot on sight, officially sanctioning attacks on German and Italian submarines in the Atlantic. At the same time, British warships were authorized to utilize American ports for repair. A more serious incident happened on 31 October when a U-boat torpedoed the U.S. destroyer *Reuben James*, killing 115 sailors. These were the first American casualties in the renewed war against Germany. For all practical purposes, the United States was at war against Germany in the Atlantic Ocean in the fall of 1941.

The Germans declared war on the United States in support of their Japanese ally on 11 December 1941.[2] Because a condition of war already existed between Germany and the United States in the Atlantic Ocean, Hitler had little to lose by making it official. In 1942 the Battle of the Atlantic expanded and intensified. Convoys began to sail from North America to the Russian ports of Archangel and Murmansk. At the same time, German U-boats expanded their range of operations to the American East Coast. Initially, the Americans were unprepared to deal with these challenges, but the implementation of escorted convoys along the East Coast alleviated this problem. At the same time, transatlantic convoys came under attack by a new German tactic. Groups of U-boats, called "wolf packs," attacked convoys, seeking vulnerable ships such as tankers and forcing the escorting vessels to disperse their efforts.

The Battle of the Atlantic continued until the end of the war. By the middle of 1943, however, the Americans, British, and Canadians defeated the U-boat menace and secured the Atlantic sea-lanes between North America and Europe. Several factors were important in this success. One was the use of air cover, provided by planes taking off from land bases or from escorting aircraft carriers, to protect convoys from U-boats. Bases in Canada, Iceland, and Britain were instrumental in maintaining regular air patrols. Another was the use of intelligence, first gained from the Enigma machines obtained by the Polish Secret Service in the 1920s. A third was the development of sonar (*sound navigation ranging*), which enabled warships to detect submerged U-boats. Probably the single most important factor in the defeat of the Germans in the Battle of the Atlantic, however, was the tremendous productive capacity of American industry. War materials and foodstuffs lost to U-boats were readily replaced from the almost inexhaustible American storage depots. Even the Liberty ships carrying these cargoes to Europe were produced quickly and in great quantities.

First launched in September 1941, these ships carried war material, men, and petroleum, oil, and lubricants. In a publicity stunt, one Liberty ship was built in less than five days from the laying of the keel to its launch.

Once again the Germans had failed to protect the outer reaches of the continent. The Allied victory in the Battle of the Atlantic ensured a steady flow of men and materials for the war in Europe. It was a more costly victory than that over the U-boats twenty years earlier, but no less decisive for the outcome of the war.

Even before the victory at sea, the Americans were taking steps to intervene in the war taking place in European skies. In the summer of 1942 the U.S. Eighth Air Force began to undertake offensive action against German targets on the fringes of continental Europe. Royal Air Force (RAF) squadrons had been bombing the enemy since 1940, but attacking targets during the day with unescorted bombers had led to such heavy losses of men and machines that by the end of 1941 the RAF had stopped daylight raids. In 1942, immediately before the arrival of the American air force at British bases, the RAF adopted a strategy of bombing at night, usually sending large numbers of bombers to attack a single target. With this so-called area bombing, accuracy was not a major issue. The purpose was to dump as much ordnance as possible on the target. Also, the British expected that the inevitably high number of civilian casualties resulting from this indiscriminate bombing would break German morale. In this expectation, the British were just as wrong as the Germans had been when they attempted the same thing during the Battle of Britain in the fall of 1940.

The Americans adopted a policy of strategic bombing. Like the British, they used unescorted bombers. Unlike the British, they attacked specific targets from high altitudes during the day. In doing so, they sought greater accuracy against targets vital to the German war effort, such as oil refineries, ball bearing plants, and airplane factories. In following this strategy, they risked the same heavy losses that had deterred the RAF earlier in the war.

The Americans and British undertook a combined air offensive starting in January 1943. The British achieved some notable successes. In May 1943, using a specially designed bomb, they destroyed two dams in the Ruhr area, flooding a considerable area. In July 1943 the RAF dropped incendiary bombs on Hamburg, igniting a firestorm that killed around

45,000 people, mainly civilians. The Americans had fewer obvious victories and suffered increasing casualties as the Germans shifted much of the
Luftwaffe from the eastern front to home skies for defensive purposes. In
raids on 17 August and 14 October on ball bearing plants in the area of
Schweinfurt, losses were so high, over 15 percent, that the Americans had
to suspend strategic bombing raids over Germany. The bombing of targets
in German-occupied Europe continued from British bases and from bases
in Italy. In particular, the oil-refining installations around the Romanian
town of Ploeşti were the target of bombing raids launched from North
Africa and later from Italy. On 1 August 1943 a large American raid destroyed much of Ploeşti's refining capacity, but at the cost of 54 bombers
out of a total of 178. Production for the German war effort continued at
Ploeşti until the arrival of the Red Army in August 1944.

Strategic bombing of Germany resumed in February 1944. At that
time, the Americans introduced the P-51 "Mustang," a fighter plane with
a range that allowed it to escort bombers all the way to Germany and back,
owing to the extra fuel capacity in its drop tanks. During "Big Week,"
a major resumption of the air offensive against German aircraft plants
beginning on 20 February 1944, the P-51 made its first major appearance. Although the Americans lost many bombers, the German aircraft
industry was devastated, and large numbers of German fighter pilots were
lost. The Luftwaffe did not recover from these losses. The defection of
Romania from the German alliance in August 1944 and the Red Army's
subsequent occupation of the Ploeşti oil-refining complex deprived the
Luftwaffe of its major source of fuel, thus ending its ability to interdict
the oncoming American and Russian invasions. The British continued
their strategy of area bombing and dropped incendiaries on many German cities. Most notoriously, on 13 February 1945, RAF bombers caused
a firestorm in Dresden that destroyed much of the city and killed between
25,000 and 35,000 people.[3]

The air war against Germany had mixed results. The bombing seriously
disrupted German industrial production. In particular, it kept the railroad
systems of Germany and occupied Europe in a state of continual disorder.
Marshaling yards, terminals, and repair facilities were favorite targets of
the bombers. The bombing campaign had important consequences for
the eastern front. It drew the Luftwaffe back to German skies to defend
against the bombing. This left German supply columns and rear forma-

tions as well as frontline troops exposed to continual harassment from the Russian air force. Also, the trained fighter pilots lost while defending against the air invasion were irreplaceable, virtually ending Germany's presence in the European skies. Not even the introduction of a jet fighter, the Messerschmidt 262 "Swallow," in 1944 could save the Luftwaffe.

Despite the bombing campaigns, German industrial production actually rose in 1944. German civilian morale did not crack, even after the horrors of firebombing. Nevertheless, the American and British air effort was an important aspect of the defeat of Nazi Germany. Around 50,000 American airmen and a like number of British died in this effort. The number of Germans killed in the skies and on the ground as a result of the bombing was as high as 750,000. German cities and the German transportation infrastructure were destroyed. Undoubtedly, the bombing campaign was a significant aspect of the victory over Germany.

The American land assault on German-controlled Europe took a little longer to mount than the American effort in 1917 and 1918. Unlike then, the Americans had no continental embarkation point. They had to establish their forward bases in Britain and then fight their way onto the European continent. Both American and British staffs quickly excluded an early assault directly across the English Channel on German-held France because of the Germans' strength and the difficulties of mounting an amphibious assault. The British, who had experience fighting the Germans, were especially opposed to a cross-Channel attack. They favored softer targets located in the Mediterranean region, where British sea power would be more effective and German land power less so.

With British forces already heavily engaged in fighting in Egypt, the Americans began their attack on Europe by first establishing control of western North Africa. American landings in the French colonies of Morocco and Algeria and an advance eastward would squeeze German and Italian forces between the Americans and the British units that were slowly moving westward after their victory at El Alamein in August 1942. American forces, supplemented by some British units, landed at Casablanca, Port Lyautey, and Sali in French Morocco and at Algiers and Oran in Algeria on 8 November. At the time, the pro-German Vichy government controlled these two French possessions. The Americans had hoped that the Vichy soldiers would not resist American landings, but these hopes were not realized. Serious fighting ensued at Casablanca.

Within three days of the landings, the Vichy commander in Morocco and Algeria, Admiral Jean François Darlan (1881–1942), agreed to a cease-fire. In response, Hitler ordered the German occupation of Vichy France and sent additional units to the French possession Tunisia. He was determined to defend Europe in North Africa, and Tunisia was especially important: from there, American and British units could cross the Mediterranean to Italy via the stepping-stone of Sicily. Unfortunately for the Germans, when they moved into the Vichy areas, the Vichy fleet in Toulon scuttled itself. It would have been a valuable asset for the Germans in maintaining their forces in Tunisia.

The first major clash between the Americans and Germans occurred in Tunisia in 1943. The German commander, General Erwin Rommel (1891–1944), launched a spoiling offensive against American forces at Kasserine Pass on 19 February. By 21 February veteran German troops routed the inexperienced Americans. This was the first land battle between American and German soldiers since 1918. The Kasserine defeat was only temporary. Because of their superior logistics and greater numbers, the Americans soon regained the initiative and resumed their advance into Tunisia.

In May 1943 the Americans and British trapped a large German and Italian force on the Bon Peninsula in Tunisia. British control of the Mediterranean made supply of this force increasingly difficult. When it surrendered on 13 May, the Americans and British took 238,000 prisoners.[4] Hitler's decision to send additional soldiers to Tunisia in November proved to be a poor one. The extent of Germany's losses in this defeat was reflected in the name applied to it: "Tunisgrad." These men and equipment would have been better utilized defending Europe in Europe, where they would not have encountered the difficulties of maintaining supply routes across the Mediterranean in the face of enemy control.

The conquest of Tunisia positioned American and British forces to undertake an assault on the European continent. They were poised to follow the British strategy first displayed at Gallipoli in 1915 of hitting the enemy's "soft underbelly." The British possession of Malta in the Mediterranean, in between Libya and Sicily, made an assault on Italy very attractive. Despite an Axis siege and an intense German and Italian bombing campaign begun in 1940, the British had maintained control of Malta. This enabled them to interdict German and Italian efforts to supply their forces in North Africa. The most important immediate target to acquire before an attack on the Italian mainland was Sicily.

Prior to the invasion of Sicily, a British force seized Pantelleria, a small Italian-held island between Tunisia and Sicily. Its airfield posed a threat to the pending invasion. The extent of the demoralization of the Italian armed forces was manifest in the negligible resistance they offered the invaders. The British force landing on the island sustained no casualties.

The invasion of Sicily began on 10 July 1943.[5] This was the first major joint American and British land operation of the war in Europe. Inevitably, some frictions ensued, but their consequences were minor. The Americans landed on the southwestern coast, and the British, under General Bernard Montgomery (1887–1976), the victor of El Alamein, landed on the east coast near Syracuse. Two German divisions offered strong resistance, but the Italian forces were less inclined to fight. The Americans swept through the western part of the island and converged on Messina from the west, while the British raced toward Messina from the south. The invasion of Sicily not only threatened the German position in the Mediterranean; it also distracted Hitler from the colossal Battle of Kursk, then raging in central Russia. The German command had to divert men and equipment intended for Kursk to meet the Italian emergency.

As fighting continued in Sicily, a cabal in Rome consisting of senior army officers, some fascist leaders, and King Victor Emmanuel III overthrew and imprisoned Mussolini. The Italian war effort had utterly failed. The Italian forces committed to North Africa had been killed or captured in Tunisia. An Italian army sent to the eastern front had met disaster on the Don in December 1942. Italian troops in Yugoslavia were increasingly bogged down in a complicated guerrilla war. By August 1943 most Italians realized that the war was lost. With their strategic position imperiled, the Germans prepared to evacuate Sicily. On 16 August they pulled their remaining forces off the island at Messina, just as American units dashed into the city.

For the first time in more than twenty years, Mussolini was not in charge in Rome. The new Italian government began desultory negotiations with the Allies. Meanwhile, the Germans rushed reinforcements into Italy. By the time the Allies and the Italian government announced an armistice on 8 September, the Germans had at least sixteen divisions in Italy. These units had two objectives. The first was to disarm and intern the Italian armed forces, and in this action, they were overwhelmingly successful. Aided by confusion, demoralization, and a total breakdown of command among the Italian military, the Germans quickly eliminated them as an effective fighting force. The Italian government's haste in fleeing Rome also facilitated German efforts to neutralize the Italian military. The Germans captured more than 650,000 Italian solders and interned many of them in prisoner of war camps in Germany. Others became forced laborers there.

The other German objective in Italy was to force the Allies to fight all the way up the Italian peninsula. The topography of Italy offered excellent opportunities for defensive purposes. A chain of mountains, the Apennines, ran up the calf of the Italian boot. A number of fast-flowing streams ran off the Apennines to the east into the Adriatic and to the west into the Tyrrhenian Sea. The Germans intended to use these natural advantages to retard an Allied advance up the peninsula. As long as the Allies were fighting in Italy, the men and material engaged there would be unavailable for a major Allied assault elsewhere in German-controlled Europe. Nor could a campaign in Italy be decisive for the Allies. Even if they succeeded in clearing the Germans out of Italy, the Allies were unlikely to surmount the barrier of the Alps and get into Germany.

Even before the announcement of the Italian armistice, Allied units landed on the Italian mainland. Elements of the British Eighth Army landed on the toe of the peninsula at Reggio di Calabria on 3 September and at Bagnarra the next day. Other British troops seized the Italian naval base at Taranto on 9 September. These landings marked the return of the British to the European mainland after leaving in defeat in a naval evacuation from Greece in May 1941.

The landings that began at Salerno on 8 September were carried out by the U.S. Fifth Army. The Germans fiercely resisted the landings at Salerno and almost succeeded in driving the Americans back into the sea. American superiority in men and equipment prevailed, however, and by 28 September 1943 the Americans entered Naples. A daring German raid freed Mussolini from his mountaintop confinement. With German support he then established the Italian Social Republic, also known as the Saló Republic because of its location in that northern Italian city. The fascist Saló Republic ostensibly controlled northern Italy until the end of the war.

For the American-led forces, further advancement up the Italian peninsula was slow. The Germans established an excellent defensive position northwest of Naples anchored around (but not in) the medieval monastery at Monte Cassino. They called this position the Gustav Line. After the Allies bombed the monastery, the Germans moved into the ruins, which provided excellent defensive positions and actually strengthened the Germans' ability to withstand Allied attacks. In an effort to get around the Gustav Line and take Rome, the Americans and British undertook a landing at Anzio, a small Tyrrhenian port about thirty miles south of Rome, on 22 January 1944. After disembarking, the Allied force met little opposition, but it failed to move out from the landing zone. The Germans rushed reinforcements to the area and contained the slow-moving Allied units. Heavy losses forced the Allies into a defensive stance. Only on 25 May 1944, after extensive strengthening, were the Allied forces able to break out and accomplish their original mission.

Farther south, after many attacks, Allied units were finally able to breach the Gustav Line. Monte Cassino fell to an assault by Polish forces on 17 May. The Allied troops then met up with those at Anzio, and the combined force entered Rome on 5 June 1944.

After the capture of Rome, the Italian theater assumed secondary importance. The establishment of new fronts in Normandy and in southern France received priority. In Italy, Allied forces continued to move slowly northward through the summer of 1944. In the autumn they encountered another strong German defensive position north of Florence, called the Gothic Line, and halted there until the final month of the war. Only in April 1945 did they break out into the Po Valley. Italian partisans captured Mussolini as he attempted to flee to Switzerland and executed him on 28 April.

Two days after the liberation of Rome from the Germans, Allied forces undertook the long-anticipated cross-Channel attack on German-occupied France. The Allied command, under General Dwight D. Eisenhower (1890–1969), had assembled a force of more than 130,000 American, British, Canadian, Free French, and Polish soldiers for the initial assault. The landings, which came to be known as D-day, began early on the morning of 6 June 1944. This operation, dubbed Overlord, had been envisioned since the Casablanca conference of January 1943 and had been in planning since February 1944. The Allies attempted to fool the Germans into thinking that the landings would occur at the narrowest part of the Channel at Calais. German Atlantic wall defenses, under construction since 1942 and strengthened by Field Marshal Rommel, the commander in the west, represented serious obstacles to any Allied attempt to land on the European continent. The landings took place in Normandy, between Le Havre and the Cherbourg Peninsula. The Allied air forces, operating from English airfields, and French resistance operations hampered the German effort to interdict the landings. The massive Russian offensive in Byelorussia launched on 22 June, Operation Bagration, effectively prevented the Germans from shifting any forces from the east to contain the Normandy landings.

The landings in Normandy marked the return of British forces to France, not far from where the Germans had ignominiously expelled them four years earlier. The British atoned for Dunkirk in Normandy. As much as possible, given the overwhelming strength of their American allies, the British maintained a separate force in Europe with separate objectives. Particularly important in preserving this separate British identity were Britain's intelligent and capable leaders, Prime Minister Winston Churchill and General Bernard Montgomery.

The initial landings incurred heavy casualties—more than 10,000 killed, wounded, and missing on the Allied side. Nevertheless, they succeeded in establishing a sustained Allied presence on the continent of Europe. Tough fighting continued in Normandy through most of the summer. Only in August did the Allies succeed in breaking out of the confines of Normandy.[6] In doing so, they trapped a considerable number of German forces in a pocket south of Falaise. Most of these German units were destroyed, but some managed to escape, and Allied forces pursued them to the north and east. Free French troops entered Paris on 25 August 1944. A small American force moved west into Brittany and cleared the Germans out. Some Germans held out in the Breton ports of Saint-Nazaire and Lorient until the end of the war. German occupation forces also remained in the Channel Islands until the end.

On 15 August 1944 the U.S. Seventh Army landed at several locations in the French Riviera. This operation, called Operation Anvil/Dragoon, encountered only light German resistance.[7] This force took Marseilles on

25 August and then moved rapidly to the north. In September these units linked up with General George Patton's (1885–1945) Third Army moving east from Normandy.

Throughout the autumn of 1944 American units moved eastward toward Germany. After entering German territory in September, American forces became bogged down in the difficult terrain of the Huertgen Forest south of Aachen. Fighting continued there for months. Only at the beginning of December did the Americans break out of the forest.

Meanwhile, British and Canadian units advanced northeasterly into Belgium. American and Polish airborne troops, in conjunction with British units, attempted to move into the Netherlands and gain a foothold across the Rhine at Arnhem in September 1944. This effort, called Operation Market Garden, encountered bad weather and determined German resistance. As a result, the operation failed and the Allied forces withdrew into Belgium.

The British continued to move into Belgium and the southern Netherlands. They were especially determined to take V (for *vergeltung,* or "vengeance") weapons launch sites located there. The V-1s were pilotless jet planes with affixed warheads. Often called "buzz bombs," these rained down on London beginning on 13 June 1944. Because they were relatively slow and flew at a low arc, they were vulnerable to interdiction by fighter planes patrolling the English Channel. The V-2s, however, were ballistic missiles that flew at a high arc and were impossible to shoot down. They began to hit London in September 1944. The Germans also used V-1s and V-2s to attack the Belgian port of Antwerp after it fell to the Allies on 4 September 1944.[8]

The advance of the British and Canadians into the Low Countries and the Americans' drive east toward the Rhine left a thinly held gap in the Ardennes forest between the two axes of advance. Hitler and his commanders, who had launched their Sickle's Cut through this same region four and a half years earlier, perceived an opportunity in this gap. They could exploit the weak Allied positions in the Ardennes by attacking through them with the same objective as in 1940: the English Channel. This time, the precise point was farther north, at Antwerp. After its liberation, Antwerp had become a major supply point for the Allied forces, and its capture would deal the Allies a severe logistical setback. At the same time, the Germans hoped to trap the more northerly of the two

Allied advances and force its evacuation. This would give them time to deal with the oncoming Soviet advance in the east.

A relative lull in the fighting occurred in the east during the fall of 1944, as the Red Army sought to address logistical problems. This allowed the Germans to shift mechanized forces and much of their remaining air force to the west for their counteroffensive. A major Allied intelligence failure enabled the Germans to do so and to make further preparations undetected. The onset of bad weather protected the attacking Germans from the Allied air forces.

With these advantages, the Germans launched their counterattack on 16 December. Surprise enabled them to make significant initial gains toward their goal.[9] The Americans held out, however, at the important junction at Bastogne. This position, which was almost surrounded by the oncoming Germans, gave the engagement its name: the Battle of the Bulge.

The return of clear weather enabled the Americans to respond to this final German initiative on the western front. Some units, most notably General Patton's Third Army, altered their line of advance and moved to the north to relieve the troops beset at Bastogne. By this time the Germans had exhausted their limited reserves of men, machines, and petroleum, oil, and lubricants. By the middle of January the German counteroffensive had ended. A renewal of the Soviet offensive on the eastern front on 12 January commanded the attention and the dwindling resources of the Germans.

After the Ardennes counteroffensive, the Americans resumed their advance into Germany and moved rapidly into the Rhineland. The German failure to destroy a railroad bridge at Remagen enabled the Americans to cross the Rhine on 7 March. In the north, the Allied advance across the Rhine trapped a large German force in the Ruhr pocket. When it surrendered on 17 April its commander, General Walther Model (1891–1945), committed suicide. With the Ruhr in Allied hands, the Germans lost their last major industrial area.

The Allied commander, General Eisenhower, communicated to the Russians on 31 March that the Americans would advance only as far as the Elbe River. Even though Berlin was more or less open to the Americans, Eisenhower preferred to let the Russians take it. Any army assaulting the German capital would incur heavy casualties fighting the

Nazi fanatics. Also, the huge Russian casualties imparted a moral weight to a Russian attack on the German capital. American and Russian troops met at Torgau on the Elbe on 25 April.

Meanwhile, other American units broke into southern Germany and western Austria. Units that had moved eastward into Pilsen (Plzeň), Czechoslovakia, pulled back after a subsequent American-Russian agreement. British and Canadian forces advanced into northern Germany and reached Lübeck on 2 May. The Germans surrendered to American and British forces on 7 May 1945 and to the Russians the next day. The war in Europe was over.

The American effort in the war against German-controlled Europe was of vital importance for the defeat of Nazi Germany. As during the previous round of fighting, the Americans provided strong material support for the war against Germany. This wealth was critical not only for the success of American arms but also for the British and Russian victories. American supplies streamed across the North Atlantic and poured into British and Russian ports.

The Anglo-American bombing of Germany also played an important role in the defeat of Nazi Germany. It destroyed the German transportation infrastructure and much of Germany's industrial production base, and it drew the German air force away from the eastern front. The lack of an effective German air force in the east was of immense value to the Russians.

The effect of the Anglo-American ground assault on the continent was also important to the downfall of Nazi Germany. The landings in Italy could not produce a decisive defeat. The landings in Normandy, however, led to the rapid collapse of German power in western Europe. Russian advances in the east commanded the attention of the majority of German forces, making them an important aspect of Anglo-American success in the second phase of the conflict.

Chapter 11

COLLABORATION, NEUTRALITY, RESISTANCE, AND GENOCIDE

At the onset of the second European war, the Germans had begun to dominate eastern European economics. After their victories in eastern and western Europe in the first year of the war, the Germans exercised an unprecedented control over all of Europe. Never in European history had any one power dominated the continent to such an extent. In this way, Nazi Germany surpassed even Napoleonic France. German domination of Europe increased after the June 1941 invasion of Soviet Russia, when large areas of that country came under the direct rule of German civilian or military authorities. The year 1942 marked the acme of German control of Europe. After the defeat at Stalingrad, the proportion of Europe under direct or indirect German rule steadily diminished. It did not entirely disappear, however, until the end of the war.

Collaboration

In addition to direct rule and military and economic alliances, the Germans maintained control through the collaboration of individuals residing in countries overrun by German armies. The Germans annexed parts of the sovereign states of Czechoslovakia, France, Lithuania, Poland, and Yugoslavia. They established alliances with Bulgaria, Croatia, Denmark, Hungary, Italy, Romania, Slovakia, and Spain. Notable collaborationist regimes emerged in France, Greece, Norway, and Serbia. Finally, individuals from all over Europe assisted and supported the Germans' control of Europe by various means, often by serving in German-sponsored military formations. The largest number of these individuals came from Soviet Russia.

Hitler's Greater Germany expanded considerably beyond the Weimar frontiers and even beyond those of the Second Reich. To the Weimar frontiers Hitler had appended Saarland, Austria, Sudetenland, Eupen and Malmedy, Alsace-Lorraine, Luxembourg, Danzig, Memel, and parts of western Poland and northern Slovenia. These areas had been part of the old ninth-century German Confederation, which the Greater German Reich came to resemble geographically. Non-Germans in these annexed areas were subject to Germanization through educational and cultural policies. Non-German males were liable for service in the German military or in the German labor corps. The Czech regions of Bohemia and Moravia constituted a German protectorate. The central area of the former Polish state became the general government, which was essentially a reservation for the Poles. Whereas lower- and midlevel Czech bureaucratic func-tionaries helped manage the protectorate, administration of the general government was the exclusive purview of the Germans; Poles assisted at only the most rudimentary level. This situation was due to the attitudes and inclinations of both the Germans and the Poles. The Germans did not seek Polish participation in political or military affairs; nor did the Poles express any desire to assist the Germans. In general, Czechs and Poles did not have to serve in German military formations. Authorities established similar arrangements in the occupied eastern territories of Ukraine and Ostland, which included the Baltic states and most of Byelorussia. The Germans exploited these areas for raw materials, foodstuffs, and slave labor. Inhabitants of other areas annexed to Greater Germany, such as Alsace-Lorraine and Luxembourg, did serve in the Wehrmacht.

With most of the male population of Greater Germany involved in the military and part of the female population already working, men and women from all over Europe labored under various degrees of coercion to perform much of the heavy work required by a wartime economy. Workers from western Europe received better treatment than workers from eastern Europe and the Soviet Union. The latter, called *Ostarbeiteren*, often lived and worked in slave conditions.[1] The internationalization of the German labor force prefigured the *Gastarbeiteren*, or "guest workers," who were so important to the West German economy during the Cold War.

Alliances helped the Germans maintain their military and economic control of Europe and furthered their war aims. Ironically, Germany's largest European ally was the least useful for German aims. Italy, which had signed an alliance with Germany in 1937, pursued a separate policy of aggrandizement until 1941. This policy brought little benefit to either Italy or Germany. The Italians had few economic resources to offer the German war effort. In the autumn of 1940 the Italians embarked on unsuccessful military adventures in Greece and Egypt. In both cases the Germans had to expend their own resources to rescue their feckless ally. After the virtual subordination of Italian policy to Germany following defeats in the Balkans and North Africa, the Italians contributed an army to the German campaign against Soviet Russia. The Red Army destroyed this Italian Eighth Army on the Don in December 1942. By 1943 the Italians were so demoralized that they did little to defend their homeland against the Anglo-American invasion.

Far more important for the realization of German war aims was Romania. Marshal Ion Antonescu sent more military personnel to Russia than any other German ally. The Romanians sustained heavy casualties in taking Odessa in October 1941, and two Romanian armies, the Third and the Fourth, were destroyed at Stalingrad. Romania had abundant food resources that helped feed the German Reich. Most important to the German war effort were the petroleum production facilities around Ploeşti. Without the active assistance of the Romanians, the German campaign against Soviet Russia and the German domination of Europe would have been much more difficult.

Other smaller allies, including Croatia, Hungary, and Slovakia, facilitated German economic and military endeavors. All three contributed food and raw materials to Germany, sent troops to Russia, and made sacrifices for the German war effort. The murderous policies of the Croatian Ustaše contributed to the horrendous fighting that raged throughout Yugoslavia.[2] A Croatian infantry brigade was lost at Stalingrad, and the Hungarian Second Army was annihilated in January 1943 at Voronezh. Much of the Hungarian army fought with the Germans through the fall of Budapest, and Slovak military units participated in the invasion of Poland and served in Russia and Italy. The German alliance resulted in heavy losses and much destruction in all three countries, particularly Hungary.

The Bulgarians, under the leadership of King Boris III, had a much easier experience in the Second World War than in their previous twentieth-century wars. As in the First World War, Bulgarian raw materials and foodstuffs supported the German war effort. Bulgarian troops performed occupation duties not only in annexed areas of Greek and

Yugoslav Macedonia but also in other regions of these two countries. The Bulgarians did not, however, declare war on Soviet Russia; nor did Bulgarian volunteers participate in the campaign there. In partial compensation for their failure to engage the Russians, the Bulgarians did declare war on the United States—something they had not done in the First World War. Bulgarian policy did not change appreciably after the premature death of Tsar Boris in 1943. Nevertheless, the outcome of the Second World War was the same as that of the Balkan Wars and the First World War for Bulgaria, which lost Macedonia for the third time in the twentieth century.

Finland also made an important military contribution to the campaign against Soviet Russia. Although the Finns explained their efforts as a "parallel war" or "Continuation War," they cooperated closely with the Germans in the northern regions. Nevertheless, General Mannerheim always maintained a certain distance from the Germans. The Finns' importance to the German war effort, their remoteness from Germany, and their military prowess enabled them to maintain a relatively independent attitude toward their German allies.

Germany's allies ranged from democratic Finland to clerical, authoritarian Slovakia to the Romanian military dictatorship to the murderous state of Croatia. All sustained strong economic and military ties to the Greater German Reich, and all sought and facilitated German victory against Soviet Russia.[3] However, as small eastern European countries caught between Nazi Germany and Soviet Russia, few had any illusions about the course of the war. By the end of 1944 most of these former allies had turned on the Germans. The Russians required Romanians, Bulgarians, and Finns to fight against the Germans as a condition of armistice. Even the Slovaks undertook a national uprising against the Germans in the autumn of 1944 as the Red Army approached the Carpathians. This uprising failed, but it provided many Slovaks with an enhanced sense of nationhood. Hungary's Admiral Horthy attempted to break his ties to the Nazis in 1944, but German units occupied his country on 19 March 1944. When Horthy's government sought an armistice with the Russians, the Germans removed it on 15 October 1944 and installed a fanatical, fascist Arrow Cross regime in its place. This government, as well as that of Ante Pavelić in Croatia, remained with the Germans until the end of the war.

Collaborationist governments in states conquered by the Wehrmacht also facilitated German control over Europe. The archetype for these German stooges was Vikdun Quisling (1887–1945) in Norway. His Norwegian Fascist National Union Party enjoyed little support in Norway; nevertheless, Quisling assisted the invading Germans, and they appointed him head of a pro-Nazi government in Oslo. His name became synonymous with pro-German traitors in Europe during the Second World War and subsequently with traitors in general. This government supported German war aims just like Germany's eastern allies. Norwegian volunteers served in the *Schutzstaffel* (SS) Viking formation.

The most important Quisling regime in western Europe was in France. There, the aged "hero of Verdun," General Henri-Philippe Pétain, acted as a German ally. In June 1940, as the newly appointed prime minister, Pétain sought an armistice with Germany as the French armies collapsed. He then became the head of state (*Chef d'Etat*) in a new government located in the central French town of Vichy, which was not directly occupied by the German army. Pétain assisted the Germans in the deportation of Jews and in securing French labor for Germany. His government in Vichy replaced the old republican slogan of "Liberty, Equality, Fraternity" with "Work, Family, and Country." This change revealed the chasm in French politics that extended back to the revolution of 1789. After the Anglo-American landings in North Africa, German forces occupied all of France. Pétain and his government continued to assist the Germans until the end of 1944, when the Anglo-American victory in France ended the German occupation. Pétain claimed that he acted from motives of patriotism. His sometime subordinate Pierre Laval (1883–1945) displayed a behavior toward the Germans that easily transcended patriotism and wallowed in cravenness.

Quisling regimes also existed in Greece and Serbia. As in France, both were headed by military men. The commander of the Greek army in Macedonia, General Georgios Tsolakoglou (1886–1948), negotiated an armistice with the invading Germans and established a pro-German regime in Athens. He was later replaced by civilian politicians. In Serbia the elderly General Milan Nedić (1878–1946) headed a Quisling regime. A variety of formations, including Serbian fascists and Russian Cossacks, upheld the Nedić government. Nedić and his followers were uneasy with the German connection but detested the communist resistance.

The Danish government maintained continuity with its prewar counterpart. The German invasion had been so rapid that neither Danish monarch Christian X (1870–1947) nor members of the Danish government had been able to escape to form a government in exile. A pro-German coalition emerged to govern the country. The Germans, for their part, behaved with restraint. They treated Denmark as a showcase for their new order in Europe. The Danish government signed an alliance agreement with Germany in November 1941. Not until August 1943, when signs of Danish disquiet became overt after the German defeats at Stalingrad and Kursk, did the Germans assume direct administration of the country.

In the Low Countries the German military administered Belgium, while a German administrator governed the Netherlands. The Nazis regarded these two states as potential provinces of the Greater German Reich. In both countries they found willing collaborators who assisted their rule and served in their military and police formations. Notable among these was the Dutch Nazi Anton Mussert (1894–1946) and the Walloon Leon Degerelle (1906–1994). Flemish separatists received favorable treatment from the German authorities in Belgium, as they had during the previous German occupation. As before, this movement found little support among the Flemish population.

Europeans of many nationalities participated in the German war effort in military uniform. The Germans impressed soldiers into their military formations from all the areas annexed directly to the Greater German Reich. In addition, volunteers from all over Europe acting on a variety of motivations served in the German ranks. Initially, the Germans resisted the inclusion of foreign nationals in their own combat forces. Recruitment of such volunteers, however, became increasingly desirable after heavy losses in the campaign in the east began to erode German strength. After the defeat at Moscow, the Germans increasingly strove to depict their efforts against Soviet Russia as having a Pan-European character. They purported to be leading Europe against communism.

Most prominent among these foreign soldiers in the ranks of the Wehrmacht were Soviet citizens, called *Hilfswilligers* (auxiliaries) or, familiarly, *Hiwis*. They became increasingly apparent in the German ranks after the June 1941 invasion of Soviet Russia. Many Soviet citizens, alienated from the Moscow regime because of Stalinist policies or nationalist aspirations, greeted the Germans as liberators. This widespread hostility to the Soviet government, especially in the Baltic areas and Ukraine, offered the invaders a tremendous advantage in the attempt to realize their goal. However, the Nazis invaded the Soviet Union not as liberators but as conquerors, squandering much of the initial goodwill they received. Nevertheless, many Soviet citizens sought opportunities to support the Germans. The appalling conditions in German prisoner of war camps caused many captured Soviet soldiers to seek food and shelter among the Hiwis. As German losses increased, Hiwis, in defiance of Hitler's wishes and with the implicit agreement of local commanders in the field, often served in combat capacities, either in Hiwi units or intermingled in German formations. These soldiers were frequently used in antipartisan efforts in the east. As many as 800,000 Hiwis served in the German Wehrmacht during the war. Exact numbers are impossible to ascertain due to the surreptitious nature of their status in the German ranks. The Germans rarely trusted these soldiers and often treated them with casual brutality. If captured by the Red Army, the Hiwis' fate was likewise grim. Those unfortunates were often shot on the spot.

Both the SS (the Nazi ideological army) and the Wehrmacht established national formations from among the European nationalities. As noted earlier, the SS recruited the Viking division in Denmark and Norway. It established the Charlemagne division for French volunteers and formed divisions for almost all other German-controlled European nations, with the notable exceptions of Czechoslovakia and Poland. There were even attempts to establish British and Indian SS formations from among prisoners of war. German authorities raised formations of Baltic peoples and Ukrainians from among the numerous anti-Soviet elements in these populations. Even as the Germans retreated after 1943, they enlisted Baltic peoples in their formations. For many Estonians, Latvians, and Lithuanians, Nazi brutality was preferable to Soviet terror, and they sought only to prevent a Russian reoccupation of their countries. Others, chiefly the SS auxiliary formations of Latvians, Lithuanians, and Ukrainians, played a particularly heinous role in implementing Nazi extermination policies in eastern Europe.

The Germans established several Russian formations in the east. One of the most important of these was the Russian Liberation Army (ROA), led by the captured Red Army General A. A. Vlasov (1900–1946).[4] Vlasov, a promising young Soviet officer, had participated heroically in the defense of Moscow and had been captured after a failed offensive in July

1942, south of Leningrad. Because of his disgust at the Stalinist war effort, he offered his services to his captors and attempted to raise an ROA from among the Soviet prisoners of war. Because of Nazi racial policies and Hitler's personal opposition, the ROA never realized its potential as an anti-Soviet instrument. It saw combat only at the end of the war, but by then, it had long since lost any hope of effective action. Deployed in April 1945, some ROA units even joined the Czech resistance and participated in the liberation of Prague. This did not save them. ROA soldiers, including General Vlasov himself, surrendered to Anglo-American forces and were turned over to the Red Army, which meted out punishment appropriate to traitors. Many were executed, including Vlasov.

Neutrality

Most of the European neutrals cooperated with the Germans to some degree. Much of this cooperation was based on opportunism, and it emphasized the unprecedented German control of Europe. The most pro-German neutral regime in Europe was Francisco Franco's Spain. Franco had benefited from German and Italian assistance during the Spanish civil war. The Spanish Nationalist regime aided the Germans with material deliveries and with information derived from espionage and other sources. They also sent a military formation, the so-called Blue Division composed of anticommunist volunteers, to participate in the campaign against Soviet Russia. It served with Army Group North in the fighting around Leningrad. However, Franco dodged Hitler's attempt on 23 October 1940 to enlist Spain in the war. His price for direct participation on the German side included Gibraltar, French Morocco, and territory in French West Africa, which was more than Hitler was willing to pay. After the Anglo-American invasion of Italy in September 1943, most of the Blue Division returned home. Spain prospered by supplying the Germans with raw materials, but ultimately, it was insufficiently recovered from the civil war to be much of an asset to the Axis cause.

The neutral positions of Sweden and Switzerland were somewhat similar. Both were surrounded by Axis-controlled territory, and both sought to preserve their neutrality with well-equipped militaries. The Swedes permitted the Germans transit rights across their territory between Norway and Finland until the turn of the war in 1943. The Swiss permitted the transit of nonmilitary materials between Germany and Italy. Both sought economic advantages in German-controlled Europe. The Swedes sold high-grade Kiruna iron ore to the Germans throughout the war. The Swiss provided a safe location for many German financial stockpiles and transactions. Finally, both Sweden and Switzerland provided havens for those fleeing German-controlled Europe. The Swedes accepted most of the Danish Jews in 1943; the Swiss allowed some Jews in and excluded others.

The authoritarian regime of Antonio Salazar (1889–1970) in Portugal was conflicted. Ideologically, Salazar inclined toward clerical fascism. Portugal, however, was historically pro-British and had participated in the First World War on the Allied side. Also, Portugal's position at the southwestern corner of Europe permitted little or no contact with the fascist center. In the Second World War Portugal was neutral, but after October 1943 it permitted the Allies to establish air bases in the Azores. These bases were especially important as landing strips for the Americans to ferry airplanes from North America to Britain and North Africa.

An independent state since 1922, Ireland (Eire) by geographic necessity maintained a neutrality that was tilted toward the British. The Royal Air Force and Royal Navy regularly violated Irish airspace and waters. Airmen from both sides who landed or crashed in Ireland were interned. The Irish government could demonstrate its disconcertion only by maintaining diplomatic relations with the Axis Powers and by the defiant anti-British gesture of Irish President Eamon de Valera (1882–1975), who personally visited the German legation to express his condolences upon the death of Hitler. Significantly, de Valera had made no such gesture on the earlier death of Franklin Roosevelt.

Unlike in the First World War, the Turks showed little inclination to become involved in the fighting in Europe. In the summer of 1939 the Ankara government concluded security arrangements with both the British and the French. The German victories of 1939 and 1940 and the German invasion of Yugoslavia and Greece in 1941 forced a reconsideration of the situation. In June 1941 the Turkish government signed a treaty of friendship with its World War I German ally. Nevertheless, the Turks resisted German efforts to lure them into the war against Russia. Only at the end of the war, in order to join the new United Nations, did the Turks abandon their neutral status and declare war on Germany.

Resistance

German control of Europe encountered resistance wherever it was implemented. Nationalism provided the main ideological bases for opposition to the Germans throughout Europe. Communist-led organizations also resisted German occupation, but only after the Germans attacked Soviet Russia on 22 June 1941.

In western Europe the German occupation authorities were, at least initially, relatively restrained in their treatment of the civilian populations. Also, opportunities for large-scale pitched battles were limited because of the high level of urban development and the lack of geographic features that favored concealment. With the exception of Denmark, the states overrun in western Europe all maintained governments in exile and military units in Britain. From there, efforts were coordinated with resistance groups to obtain intelligence and conduct sabotage. Resistance organizations in western Europe were also important in finding and concealing downed Allied airmen.

The western European resistance movements had a mixed record of success. Norwegian resistance in particular participated in some spectacular operations, including the raids on the Lofoten Islands in March and December 1941 and the sabotage of the heavy-water plant at Rjukan in February 1943. In contrast, German security forces succeeded in compromising Dutch resistance organizations by 1941, regularly interdicting agents coming from Britain. This seriously hampered Allied intelligence effectiveness in northwestern Europe.

The most important western European resistance organization was the Free French, which maintained forces in France as well as forces fighting with the Allies. This organization, led by General Charles de Gaulle (1890–1970), represented the pro-Allied alternative to the Vichy government. His prickly personality proved to be an asset in his efforts to restore France to the position of an Allied power. The participation of Free French troops in the North African campaign, in Italy, and in the landings in Normandy and southern France greatly facilitated this effort. De Gaulle's Free French forces were the first Allied troops to enter and liberate Paris.

In eastern Europe the situation for resistance to German authority was much more fluid. There, the Germans did not hesitate to implement brutal racial policies against peoples they regarded as inherently inferior. Also, the great size and varied topography of eastern Europe afforded ample opportunities for anti-German forces to shelter and hide. German efforts to send young people from local populations to the Reich as slave laborers greatly increased resistance efforts throughout eastern Europe.

No country in Europe suffered more at the hands of the Nazis in terms of population and material losses than Poland did. The Poles made no compromise with the Nazis and resisted them from the beginning of the occupation. A well-organized Polish government in exile, based in London after June 1940, directed Polish resistance efforts. Within occupied Poland a virtual underground state existed, which included schools, newspapers, and communications. The most important underground institution was the *Armia Krajowa* (Home Army), a military force that conducted intelligence and sabotage operations and collected weapons and munitions while awaiting the right time to strike against the occupation. It rose in Warsaw against the Germans in August 1944 as the Red Army approached from the east. The Red Army's failure to help the Armia Krajowa contributed to its defeat in October 1944. As had occurred five years earlier, the Germans and Russians had acted to smash Poland (albeit separately in 1944). Other Polish resistance organizations, ranging in ideology from the extreme Right to communism, were active, especially in eastern regions.

The most extensive resistance organization developed in Soviet Russia. The rapid advance of the German armies in the summer of 1941 left large numbers of Soviet soldiers behind German lines. These soldiers prepared the initial recruits for partisan units when brutal German occupation policies provided the incentive. After the German reverse outside Moscow demonstrated that the Wehrmacht was not invincible, partisan units coalesced in the marshes and forests of Byelorussia, Russia, and Ukraine. German efforts to impress young people into labor in the Reich increased the number of partisans. These partisan units received their direction from Soviet authorities in Moscow. They cut rail and telegraph lines and harassed rear units. Especially important to the Soviet war effort were their actions to terrorize collaborators and their families to preserve the idea of Soviet power behind the German lines. Partisan-controlled areas, which grew larger through 1942 and 1943, became known as the "Little Land," whereas the "Great Land" consisted of the Soviet-controlled area behind the Russian lines. As the Red Army swept westward, it incorporated many partisan units into its ranks.

Nationalist resistance to the Germans and later the Russians developed in the Baltic countries and Ukraine. Disappointed by the Germans' failure to sanction Baltic and Ukrainian independence, armed groups of Estonians, Latvians, Lithuanians, and Ukrainians harassed the Germans and their collaborators. In Ukraine these units often grew out of elements of the prewar Organization of Ukrainian Nationalists (OUN). Founded in 1929, the OUN struggled to preserve the concept of Ukrainian statehood against Polish and Soviet oppression. The OUN initially cooperated with the Nazi invasion of Soviet Russia. The Germans, however, refused to recognize the OUN's proclamation of an independent Ukraine in L'vov on 30 June 1941 and imprisoned much of its leadership. Another group of Ukrainian nationalists came to be known as the Ukrainian Insurgent Army (UPA) in 1943. The UPA engaged in a multisided war against the Germans, the Soviets, and Polish nationalist forces in western Ukraine.[5] Among their greatest successes was the killing of Soviet General Nikolai Vatutin (1901–1944). As the Germans retreated from these regions and the Soviets returned, the opposition to foreign rule grew more desperate. Some Estonian, Latvian, and Ukrainian nationalist partisans continued their struggles against Soviet authorities into the early 1950s.

Some of the most chaotic and horrific fighting of the entire war occurred in Yugoslavia. A plethora of armed units emerged after the collapse of the Yugoslav state and its division into Bulgarian, German, Hungarian, and Italian zones of occupation and the nominally independent states of Croatia and Serbia. Two resistance organizations soon emerged. The first to do so was the mainly Serbian Četniks, led by a Royal Yugoslav Army colonel, Dragoljub (Draža) Mihailović (1893–1946).[6] After the Germans invaded Soviet Russia in June 1941 the multinational Partisans arose, led by the leader of the Yugoslav Communist Party, Josef Broz, known as Tito (1892–1980). Whereas Mihailović represented a return to the values of prewar Yugoslavia, Tito offered a vision of a nonnationalist Yugoslavia. Soon a multisided civil war developed as the Četniks and Partisans fought against the foreign invaders and their collaborators and against each other. At times both the Četniks and the Partisans cooperated with the occupation forces. All sides perpetrated atrocities. The fascist Ustaši regime in

Croatia particularly distinguished itself in this regard. As many as one million Yugoslavs died, often at the hands of other Yugoslavs. The major arena of this complex conflict was Bosnia. Initially, the British government supported the Četnik forces with money and advisers. As the war progressed, however, the British realized that the Partisans were far more interested in fighting the Axis forces in Yugoslavia than were the Četniks, so they shifted their support accordingly. This withdrawal of British support forced the Četniks to rely on the Germans for logistical and strategic support. By the end of the war the Partisans prevailed, driving out the invaders with the help of the Red Army and massacring many of their domestic opponents. The Partisans also benefited from significant American and British material aid. Tito's forces captured, tried, and executed Mihailović in 1946. Because of their victory over foreign and domestic opponents, the Yugoslav Partisans were the most successful resistance movement in the Second World War.

The situation in Yugoslavia was replicated to some degree in neighboring Albania and Greece. In Albania, the Italians initially enjoyed some success because of their annexation of Kosovo and western Macedonia to Albania, thus creating a Greater Albania, albeit under Italian rule. German forces replaced the Italians after the overthrow of Mussolini in July 1943. A nationalist opposition movement, the *Balli Kombëtar* (National Front), rose in opposition. At the same time, the Communist Partisan movement formed under the leadership of Enver Hoxha (1908–1983), with the help of the Yugoslav Partisans. As in Yugoslavia, a multisided war developed. After the retreat of the Germans in the fall of 1944 the Partisans were able to overcome Balli Kombëtar forces and take control of the entire country.

A three-sided struggle also ensued in Greece. There, German and Italian occupation forces and their collaborators fought against the communist-inspired and -led National People's Liberation Army (ELAS) and the smaller National Republican Greek League (EDAS). After EDAS was eliminated as an effective force in 1944, ELAS and its political arm, the National Liberation Front (EAM), came to dominate the antioccupation movement. After the German withdrawal from Greece in October 1944, a small British contingent arrived in Athens. Fighting broke out in December 1944 between ELAS and the British, who found support among the former collaborationist police. This fighting was the first combat of the Cold War—the third phase of the Long War. It ended in a January 1945 armistice but began again in 1946 in a renewed Greek civil war.

Despite the establishment of a Czechoslovak government in exile in London, the existence of an anti-German network with connections to high-level Czech administrators, and individual acts of public martyrdom, few instances of overt resistance occurred in the Czech lands. In an effort to stimulate anti-German resistance, the Czech government in exile parachuted two agents into the country. These individuals wounded Reinhard Heydrich (1904–1942) on 27 May 1942, and he died a week later. Heydrich, second in command of the SS and the viceroy (*Reichsprotektor*) of Bohemia and Moravia, was the highest-ranking German official to fall as a result of a resistance effort during the war. In partial retribution, the Germans leveled the Czech village of Lidiče and massacred the male population. They sent the female population to concentration camps and dispersed the children. This action at Lidiče became symbolic of the brutality of German rule in eastern Europe. In fact, there were thousands of Lidičes throughout German-occupied Europe, but especially in eastern Europe.

Resistance to Hitler's rule also developed within Germany, with communist, Christian, and nationalist bases. One communist effort consisted of an espionage organization, the so-called Red Orchestra (*Rote Kapelle*), whose members included men in the Luftwaffe. Before the *Abwehr* (German military intelligence) destroyed it in August 1942, the Red Orchestra imparted much valuable information to the Soviets. Another form of resistance came from a group of students in Munich known as the White Rose. A brother and sister, Hans (1918–1943) and Sophie (1921–1943) Scholl, distributed anti-Nazi pamphlets in 1942. Upon their betrayal, they were executed.

A far larger and more important resistance group was a loosely organized amalgamation of conservatives, socialists, and military officers. At its core were a number of military and intelligence officers, ostensibly led by former chief of the General Staff Ludwig Beck (1880–1944), who had resigned his position in 1938 because of his opposition to Hitler's plans for war against Czechoslovakia. In fact, the group was motivated by deputy commander of the Abwehr, Major General Hans Oster (1888–1945), who in turn benefited from the protection of the chief of the Abwehr, Admiral Wilhelm Canaris (1887–1945). These people were not opposed to the German domination of Europe, but they detested how the Nazi regime intended to accomplish it. After several false starts, this group implemented a plot to kill Hitler, reach an accommodation with the Anglo-Americans, and resist the oncoming Russians. On 20 July 1944, as German forces were reeling in Normandy and Byelorussia, decorated veteran Lieutenant Colonel Claus von Stauffenberg (1907–1944) planted a bomb in Hitler's East Prussian command bunker and flew back to Berlin to install the new government headed by General Beck.[7] Though wounded, Hitler did not die in the explosion. He succeeded in rallying his supporters, and they killed or imprisoned most of the principals involved in the plot. Nazi rule continued for another nine months. Even if their goal of continuing the fight against the Russians with Anglo-American concurrence was not realistic, the plotters of 20 July represented an attempt to restore decency to Germany. Had they succeeded, the war might have ended nine months sooner. Innumerable German lives, German cities, and German infrastructure might have been saved as a result. Conversely, these plotters struck at the German leadership at a time when the country was in peril. In retrospect, the former interpretation has loomed much more important than the latter.

The Soviets attempted to establish their own counterpart to the ROA and the other German-sponsored formations in the east. Using German prisoners of war captured at Stalingrad and elsewhere on the eastern front, the Soviets created a League of German Officers and, for enlisted men, a National Committee for a Free Germany. Although they succeeded in gaining the backing of some high-ranking officers captured at Stalingrad, including Field Marshal Paulus, these organizations never enjoyed much support among German prisoners, and they never reached the level of becoming military formations. They were managed mainly by German communist émigrés such as Walter Ulbricht (1893–1973), later the head of the German Democratic Republic. They were established for propaganda purposes and represented the Soviets' attempt to create an alternative government for Germany. This would have been useful if relations with the Americans and British ever deteriorated to the point that the Soviets might want to sign a separate peace with such a government. By the time of the Yalta Conference in February 1945, these two formations had lost their usefulness to Soviet authorities. They were not formally disbanded, however, until after the war.

Genocide

Hitler and the Nazis always maintained a social Darwinist perspective on their German nationalism. They regarded the peoples of Europe as composing a racial hierarchy, with Germanic peoples at the pinnacle and Slavs and Jews at the bottom. During their brief control of Europe from 1939 to 1945, the Nazis acted on their racist ideology. In particular, they tried to alter the ethnic composition of Europe by mass murder, directing their efforts against Slavs, Roma (Gypsies), and, above all, Jews. After 1941 the Germans devoted a considerable amount of military effort toward the elimination of European peoples they regarded as racially inferior and unfit to remain in their new Europe.

The imposition of genocide in Europe consisted of three steps. The initial goal was not genocide; however, the practices and policies directed against Jews and others led to this horrific end. The process began when the Nazis came to power in 1933. German civil authorities increasingly ignored Nazi-inspired violence against Jews. Hitler also ordered that legal measures be taken against the German Jewish population. By 1934 German Jews, who numbered only about 500,000, lost their government jobs. Only Jews who were World War I veterans or Jewish families who had lost relatives in the war received exemptions. The next year the Nazi state enacted a number of legal sanctions directed at German Jews. These so-called Nuremberg (Nürnberg) Laws effectively deprived German Jews of their citizenship rights. Among these was the Law for the Protection of German Blood and Honor, which forbade marriage and sex between Germans and Jews.

During the 1936 Berlin Olympics the Nazi government relaxed its anti-Jewish measures in response to threats of boycott from abroad. In 1938, however, the de-legalization process increased. On 7 November 1938 a young Polish Jew assassinated a German diplomat in Paris, and the Nazis decided to use this murder as an excuse to organize a mass reprisal against German Jews. On 12 November, as police and firemen stood aside, Nazis burned and looted Jewish homes, businesses, and synagogues, and they murdered or imprisoned a number of Jews. This pogrom became known as *Kristallnacht* (Crystal Night) because of the large amounts of broken glass that resulted from the attacks on Jewish establishments. Eventually, Jews were forbidden access to public schools, universities, theaters, movies, and other public places.

The second phase began with the outbreak of war in September 1939. By this time, around half the German Jewish population had emigrated, but the war made further emigration extremely difficult. The conquest of Poland brought a large Jewish population under German control, since most Polish cities contained large Jewish populations living in distinct quarters, or ghettos. The Germans walled up these Jewish ghettos, creating large urban concentration camps. The amount of food and material permitted into the ghettos was limited. By the beginning of 1940 each inhabitant of the Warsaw ghetto received around 500 calories per day. As a result, Jewish populations in Warsaw, Lublin, Lodz, Krakow, and other cities began to experience disease and starvation. Some of the remaining German Jews were shipped east to Poland, adding to the misery of the ghettos. The Nazis briefly toyed with the idea of sending Jews to some remote location, such as Madagascar, but nothing came of this absurd idea.

With the German attack on Soviet Russia on 22 June 1941, the extermination process began. Following behind the frontline troops were special SS *Einsatzgruppen* (Action Groups). These units, often supplemented by local Baltic and Ukrainian volunteers, began the process of mass murder. When they entered towns and villages they rounded up the local Jewish populations, marched them to ravines or other suitable locations outside of town, and murdered them. At a site outside of Kiev known as Babi Yar, *Einsatzgruppen* and Ukrainian auxiliaries murdered around 35,000 Jews on 29 and 30 September 1941.[8]

By the autumn of 1941 the extermination process began to falter. The Nazis required a more efficient means of murder.[9] Beginning in 1938 Nazi authorities had used gas chambers to murder thousands of Germans deemed "useless eaters"—those who were retarded or epileptic or had major physical or mental problems. Although a public outcry had ostensibly ended the program in 1939, it actually continued under the cover of war.[10] That autumn the Germans began to adapt gas chambers for the destruction of the European Jews. Extermination camps were established at Auschwitz, Belżec, Chelmno, Majdanek, Sobibor, and Treblinka. A conference of officials from the German government and the SS that met at Wannsee on 20 January 1942 confirmed that these death factories were already in operation.[11] The Nazis emptied the Polish ghettos by sending their freezing and starving inhabitants to the death factories. Meanwhile, the *Einsatzgruppen* continued their deadly work in the rural areas of eastern Poland.

Even before the Nazis had emptied the Polish ghettos, they began to cast around Europe to implement their racist policies. Jews from all over were fed into the maw of the death factories. Although brave individuals in many places, including Germany, tried to help the Jews, few authorities resisted the German summons to deliver up the Jews. Except for the Finns and Bulgarians, Hitler's eastern allies, including the Hungarians, Romanians, and Slovaks, behaved brutally toward the Jews. Bulgarians, Danes, and Finns refused to send their Jewish populations to be "resettled" in the east. The Danes tried to send their Jews to neutral Sweden. Also, in the areas it occupied in France, Yugoslavia, and Greece, the Italian army generally protected the Jews. After the surrender of Italy and the dispersal of the Italian army, the Jews lost that protection.

Nazi racial policies were not limited to European Jews. Roma were also subject to extermination.[12] Czech and Polish intelligentsia, professors, teachers, priests, lawyers, and even Olympic champions were murdered. Soviet prisoners of war died in huge numbers in German captivity. The Nazis shot them, starved them, and gassed them in the chambers of Auschwitz. More than three million of the six million under German control died.

Even after the war turned against Germany, the Nazis continued their extermination policies. They devoted human, material, and transportation resources to the process, even though these might have been utilized for the military effort. Extermination was, in fact, a part of the German war effort. The Nazis fought the war not only to gain control of Europe but also to murder portions of its population.

Hitlerian Germany's control of Europe was brief, lasting approximately as long as that of Napoleonic France. It was, however, much more thorough and brutal. Like Napoleon, Hitler established a precedent for the economic and political unity of the continent. Like Napoleon, Hitler was not unwelcome in many places, at least initially. Unlike Napoleon, Hitler sought the extermination of many of the inhabitants of Europe. In the end, most Europeans neither supported nor opposed Hitlerian domination. They merely sought to stay out of the way and survive the conflict.

During this conflict, eastern Europe played a primary role in Nazi Germany's attempt to dominate the continent. The main source of support for the German domination came from eastern Europe. The major arena of armed opposition to German domination of Europe was also in the east. In part because of this support and in spite of this opposition, the main location of Nazi-inspired genocide was also in eastern Europe.

Chapter 12

ORIGINS OF THE COLD WAR

The origins of the settlement of the Second World War began during the actual fighting. This settlement is inseparable from the beginning of the Cold War, the third phase of the twentieth-century European conflict. The Cold War began as the Second World War concluded and prevented a formal resolution of that war for some time.

German war aims were fairly straightforward, though they tending toward the fantastical. The Germans wanted to dominate Europe economically and politically as far as the Ural Mountains. This involved the defeat of France in western Europe and the conquest of Soviet Russia for the acquisition of lebensraum in eastern Europe. This lebensraum was partly economic, intended to ensure that Germany would never have to endure economic travails because of a British blockage. It was also partly political: Hitler wanted to ensure German domination of Europe for a thousand years.

Mussolini sought the realization of a new Roman Empire in the Mediterranean region. Germany's eastern European subordinates were mainly interested in realizing their national objectives, usually at their neighbors' or one another's expense. Both the Finns and the Romanians wanted to regain and expand territories previously ceded to Soviet Russia.

The Allied objectives were more problematic. Britain and France initially went to war to protect Poland, but after the first month of the conflict, the German-Russian victory over Poland made this goal unrealistic. German successes throughout Europe in 1940 further obscured Allied war aims. For Britain, the sole remaining enemy of German expansion plans, simple survival became paramount in the face of German domination of the European continent.

Stalin had two major objectives. One was ideological: he sought to preserve and spread his version of accelerated Marxist Leninism. The other was political: he wanted Soviet power to survive. These two objectives combined in his domestic program. In 1928, upon assuming power, he had imposed on Soviet Russia a policy of development through his Five-Year Plans for industrialization and the collectivization of agriculture, enforced by terror. These efforts succeeded in industrializing Russia, but at the cost of millions of lives lost through starvation, impression into labor gangs, or deliberate brutality. The human costs of Stalin's dictatorship were well known in Europe and the United States. Both his ideology and his politics were abhorred everywhere. For many Europeans, Stalin's alignment with Hitler in 1939 simplified the European political conflict to one of democracy versus dictatorship, civility versus brutality, and good versus evil.

The German attack on Soviet Russia on 22 June 1941 offered Britain some respite at last. An arrangement with Soviet Russia provided Britain with a means to expand its isolated and thus far largely unsuccessful struggle against Nazi Germany. Overcoming considerable qualms about the Stalin dictatorship and its previous relationship with Germany, British Prime Minister Winston S. Churchill proposed an arrangement to the Soviets soon after the German invasion. This Anglo-Soviet alliance further complicated the issue of war aims. Soviet Russia had, after all, participated in the invasion and division of Poland, Britain's first ally.

The Anglo-Soviet alliance caused the British prime minister profound unease. He had long been an opponent of Soviet communism and was aware of the horrific Stalinist excesses of the 1930s. Britain had entered the war to protect Poland from German and Russian invasion, yet from September 1939 to June 1941, half of Britain's ally was under Soviet rule. To allay his suspicions about his Soviet ally, Churchill sought assurances from the United States. In August 1941 Churchill sailed across the North Atlantic on the battleship *Prince of Wales* to meet with President Franklin D. Roosevelt in Placentia Bay off the coast of Newfoundland. During that meeting, which lasted from 9 to 12 August, they agreed to the Atlantic Charter. This document established eight basic principles of the war effort, including no territorial aggrandizement, no territorial changes without the consent of the affected populations, people's right to choose their own form of government, economic agreements for all nations, the end of Nazi tyranny, freedom of the seas, and the end of the use of force. The Atlantic Charter was a less specific version of Woodrow Wilson's Fourteen Points. Like the Fourteen Points, it envisioned an idealistic resolution of the war. Churchill and Roosevelt intended this idealism to offset Stalin's totalitarian regime, just as Wilson had hoped his Fourteen Points would diminish the appeal of Lenin's political programs. The Soviets subsequently agreed to the Atlantic Charter; however, this turned out to be more a demonstration of Soviet desperation at this stage of the war than a firm commitment to the ideals of the charter. Even though the Americans were not yet participants in the war, Roosevelt committed his country to the distant peace process. The American failure to remain engaged in the peace process after the First World War had contributed to the failure of the Paris settlement. Although the Atlantic Charter did not specify a world body, its points were incorporated into the Declaration of United Nations of 1 January 1942 as a statement of Allied war aims. Great Britain, Soviet Russia, the United States, and twenty-two other nations agreed to the provisions of the charter. Thereafter, members of the anti-German, -Italian, and -Japanese coalition referred to themselves as the United Nations.

A year passed before the next major effort by the United Nations to determine the course of the war. After British and American troops had secured Vichy-governed Morocco and Algeria in November 1942, Churchill and Roosevelt met from 14 to 24 January 1943 at Casablanca. Stalin, the third member of this grand coalition, could not attend because of the demands of the Stalingrad battle, which was then in its final stages. The Americans, who had wanted a landing in France in 1943, agreed to Churchill's proposal for a landing in Italy. The British prime minister recognized Mussolini's state as a soft target that could draw German resources away from the eastern front. Fighting in Italy, however, was unlikely to force Germany out of the war. Churchill and Roosevelt also agreed to the principle of unconditional surrender. Unlike in 1918, the Germans would not be permitted to claim that they had not really lost the war. The demand for unconditional surrender also eliminated the possibility of a negotiated peace and ensured that the war would continue to its bloody conclusion. Stalin later agreed to both these stipulations.

The next important wartime conference occurred the following November in the Iranian capital of Tehran. By this time the Russians had not only defeated the Germans at Stalingrad but also stopped the German offensive at Kursk in the summer of 1943. The Russians assumed the initiative on the eastern front, and by autumn a Soviet counteroffensive was pushing the Germans westward. Churchill and Roosevelt met Stalin for the first time at Tehran. This meeting, which lasted from 28 November to 1 December, occurred in the shadow of an event that had taken place the previous April involving the Poles.

For some time, the Polish government in exile in London had expressed concerns about Polish soldiers captured by the Russians during the 1939 campaign. By 1943 most Polish enlisted personnel in Soviet custody had been accounted for, and the majority of them had chosen to leave Russia in the Polish forces organized and commanded by General Władysław Anders (1892–1970). Few were interested in the Polish units organized by the Soviets under the command of Lieutenant Colonel Zygmunt Berling (1896–1980). The fate of the captured Polish officers, however, remained a mystery. Then in April 1943 the German government announced the discovery of a mass grave outside Smolensk at a location known as Katyń forest.[1] An investigation quickly determined that the grave contained the bodies of nearly 4,500 Polish officers. Their hands had been tied behind their backs, and they had all been shot in the head. The time of the murders appeared to be May 1940, while the Poles had been in Russian custody. The news from Katyń and the realization by the Polish government in exile that an additional 10,000 Polish officers in Soviet custody remained unaccounted for caused a break in relations between the London Poles and Moscow.

Churchill and Roosevelt chose to believe the Russian denials of involvement in the Katyń incident. Although these Russian assurances were less than convincing, the Americans and British could hardly incriminate their ally that, thus far, had done the major part of the fighting and incurred the greatest casualties in the struggle against Nazi Germany. Despite this situation, the Americans and British agreed to the Soviet demand that the eastern border of Poland follow the Curzon Line, a border proposed by British Foreign Secretary Lord George Curzon (1859–1925) in 1919 that roughly conformed to the ethnic frontier. This decision effectively erased the gains achieved by the Poles at the 1921 Treaty of Riga after their success in the Russo-Polish War. The Polish government in London did not accept this decision but was powerless to prevent it. The only other major decision resulting from the meeting in Tehran was the agreement to undertake the Normandy landings simultaneously with a major offensive on the eastern front.

Before the next major conference, another dramatic event involving Poland further undermined the wartime alliance. On 26 July 1944, in the aftermath of the successful Byelorussian offensive and the appearance of the Red Army on mostly ethnic Polish territory, the Soviets established a Polish government in Lublin. Soviet interests clearly dominated this government. At the same time, the Red Army approached Warsaw. In response, Polish underground forces known as the Home Army prepared to seize control from the Germans before the arrival of the Russians. To the Home Army, both the Germans and the Russians were enemies. The Warsaw uprising began on 1 August.[2] The insurgents captured much of the city but soon faced a determined German counterattack. The Russians, ensconced across the Vistula River, did little to assist the Home Army. The Americans and British requested landing rights on Russian-held airfields east of Warsaw, but the Russians refused, ostensibly because they could not provide security. American and British aircrews attempted to drop supplies to aid the insurgents, but the long round-trip from Italian airfields required large amounts of fuel and limited the supplies that each plane could carry. Consequently, the air supply effort was of limited value. Some units from Berling's army attempted to cross the Vistula to aid the insurgents, but without success. By October the Home Army forces were exhausted. The survivors surrendered on 2 October, five years to the day after the last Polish units had surrendered to the Germans in 1939.

The failure of the Warsaw uprising of 1944 exacerbated relations between the Americans and the Russians. Soon after the surrender of the Home Army, Churchill, who had resented the Poles' preemptive actions, went to Moscow to meet with Stalin. Seeking to establish some control for the Americans and British as the Red Army moved beyond Russia's western borders, Churchill proposed a division of influence in eastern Europe. He wrote the following on a piece of paper: "Romania, USSR 90%, Others (USA and UK) 10%; Greece, USSR 10%, Others 90%; Yugoslavia, USSR 50%, Others 50%; Hungary, USSR 50%, Others

50%; and Bulgaria, USSR 75%, Others 25%."[3] Stalin indicated his assent with a checkmark on the paper. This cynical division of power in eastern Europe had little practical significance. The Red Army was already in the countries indicated by Churchill; the Americans and British had no forces there, except for Greece. Greece, with its Mediterranean location, was most important to the British, and British troops landed there in October. Only the Russians were in a position to determine the real course of events in the other countries.

In fact, the Americans and British had little real interest in the fate of eastern Europe. Most of the peoples living there were obscure to American policy makers and only slightly less so to the British. Cooperation with the Nazis had compromised many eastern European governments. Others, such as the Poles, were exhausted by their resistance of the Nazi occupation. In any event, the Americans and British had no intention of intervening militarily to prevent the Soviet takeover of eastern Europe. Instead, the Americans would express outrage from afar. This had the effect of consolidating the American presence in western Europe. Expressions of indignation without further action would mark American policy toward eastern Europe throughout most of the Cold War.

The next major meeting of the wartime Allies occurred in Yalta on 4 to 11 February 1945. Churchill and Roosevelt joined Stalin in old tsarist vacation quarters on the Crimean coast to acknowledge the Russian contribution to the pending victory against Nazi Germany. They decided to divide Austria and Germany and their respective capitals, Vienna and Berlin, into occupation zones after the war. Initially, Britain, Soviet Russia, and the United States were the only occupation powers. Later, the British and Americans included France as an occupying power, with the concurrence of the Russians. The Russians stipulated, however, that the French occupation zones should be carved out of American and British territory. The Soviets also agreed to enter the war against Japan two to three months after the end of the war in Europe. The Americans were eager for the Soviets to tie down Japanese forces in Manchuria before undertaking an invasion of the Japanese home islands. The three leaders also agreed that the Polish governments in London and Lublin should merge. The London government had been the legitimate continuation of the pre–September 1939 Polish government, so the bestowal of legitimacy on the Russian-controlled Lublin government was a significant concession. This new legitimacy indicated that the Americans and British recognized Russia's particular interest in Poland. It was also a means for the Russians to obtain much of the same concessions in Poland from their American and British allies as they had obtained from their German ally in 1939. The Americans and British could do little to contest this Russian interest, since the Russians had made the greatest contributions in terms of men and material toward the defeat of Nazi Germany and had actually occupied Poland.[4] Removing the Russians from Poland would require a military effort by their erstwhile allies. In addition, the territories they had taken from Poland east of the Curzon Line were inhabited mainly by Byelorussians and Ukrainians who, in theory, joined their conationals in the neighboring Soviet republics.

The Declaration on Liberated Europe signed at Yalta by Churchill, Roosevelt, and Stalin provided some cover for the two Western leaders. This document committed the Allies to the establishment of democratic governments and the maintenance of the principles of the Atlantic Charter in the countries freed from Nazi domination. The blatant Soviet failure to uphold this declaration only aggravated the tensions between the Russians and the Americans. By this time, any illusions the Americans might have had that Soviet Russia would become less totalitarian and more open as a result of the war were gone.

One final meeting of the leaders of the now victorious Allies occurred after the surrender of Nazi Germany. From 17 July to 2 August Stalin met with new president Harry S. Truman and Churchill in the Berlin suburb of Postdam, the location of the old Prussian and German military infrastructure. Halfway through the conference, Clement R. Attlee (1883–1967) replaced Churchill when the Labour Party won an election and took control of Parliament. The meeting confirmed the Oder-Neisse river line as the western frontier of Poland. It achieved little else. Truman was a determined opponent of Soviet communism. Also, the successful test of the nuclear bomb in New Mexico raised the possibility of a quick end to the war without the heavy American casualties that would be incurred during an invasion of Japan. This development made the participation of Soviet Russia in the war against Japan unnecessary and undesirable from the American perspective. Thanks to an extensive espionage effort, the Soviets knew about the American success. This contributed to Soviet unease. As a result, no major agreement came out of the Potsdam conference.

The war had inflicted huge human and material losses on Soviet Russia. At least twenty-five million people had died. Soviet territory from Leningrad, Moscow, and Stalingrad to the western borders was in ruins. American military losses had been much lighter (around 300,000 dead), and the continental United States had suffered no damage at all. The difference in power between the United States and Soviet Russia at the end of the war led Stalin to assume that the Americans would act on their advantage. After all, his previous ally, Hitler, had turned against him. Mutual suspicions between the United States and Soviet Russia had been growing throughout the war.

After Potsdam this reciprocal mistrust became open hostility, and for the next forty-five years Soviet Russia and the United States assumed hostile attitudes toward each other. This hostility divided Europe in two as the European nations took sides. Mutual fear of nuclear holocaust, however, limited the possibility of another "hot" war. European conflict proceeded directly from the expenditure of millions of tons of ordnance into a confrontation in which military hardware was not fired. This was the Cold War.

One institution resulting from the Second World War linked both sides in the Cold War: the United Nations. Its goals were based on the January 1942 Declaration of United Nations, which was essentially the formal basis for the anti-Nazi alliance. The Dumbarton Oaks conference of 1944 resulted in formal institutional details, and initial meetings of the United Nations took place in the spring of 1945 in San Francisco. This organization, with a more inclusive membership than its predecessor the League of Nations, was led by a Security Council consisting of the four victorious members of the anti-Nazi coalition—Britain, France, Soviet Russia, and the United States—plus Chiang Kai-shek's (1887–1975) Nationalist China. It also had a modest military enforcement arm. The United Nations, however, would not play a major role in Europe during the Cold War.

The wartime alliance managed one final cooperative action after Potsdam: the war crimes trials of the surviving Nazi leadership in Nuremberg, Germany. The main portion of these proceedings occurred from October

1945 to November 1946 and involved twenty-three former Nazi leaders. Of these, thirteen were sentenced to death, seven received terms of imprisonment up to life, and three were acquitted. One of the condemned, Martin Bormann (1900–1945), Hitler's chief of staff, received his sentence in absentia.[5] Additional trials of lesser Nazi functionaries continued at Nuremberg until 1949. These actions were undertaken to document the extent of Nazi crimes against humanity and to establish the principle of legitimate orders. Many of the perpetrators excused their crimes by insisting that they had been following legal orders, but after Nuremberg, that was not a legitimate defense for crimes against humanity. Individual states held additional trials for participants in Nazi war crimes in every remaining decade of the century, but by no means did all the perpetrators receive the justice they deserved. Some Germans complained about "victors' justice" and noted that the Soviets too were guilty of hideous crimes, such as the Katyń massacre. These issues failed to undermine the importance of the Nuremberg war crimes trials. These proceedings served as a template for future trials, notably the actions taken against the Croatian, Muslim, and Serbian leadership in the aftermath of the Bosnian war.

Victory in the war had brought Soviet Russia farther into Europe. The annexation of the Finnish port of Petsamo; the Baltic states; eastern Poland; the northern portion of East Prussia from Germany, where the old Prussian capital of Konigsberg was renamed Kaliningrad; Carpatho-Ukraine (Ruthenia), formerly attached to Czechoslovakia; and northern Bukovina and Bessarabia from Romania had greatly improved the Russians' strategic situation. The Russian advance into Europe ensured a strong, sustained presence and put the Red Army in a position to overrun the remainder of the continent. This was not lost on the Americans and their western European allies.

By 1946 the Soviets had established control over almost all the states lying between Russia and Germany. Stalinization began in all these countries soon after the entry of the Red Army. This process involved the establishment of a security service, seizure of control of the media and educational institutions, the co-option or elimination of opposition, and the nationalization of enterprise. The Byelorussian and Ukrainian parts of Poland and the Baltic states Estonia, Latvia, and Lithuania had already undergone this procedure in 1939 and 1940 when they had first been annexed by Soviet Russia. With the return of the Red Army in 1944, the process merely took up where it had left off in 1941. In the other eastern European states, Sovietization began in 1944 and 1945. Overtly pro-Soviet regimes appeared Poland in 1945, in Bulgaria and Romania in 1946, and in Hungary in 1947. The traditional pro-Russian sentiment in Bulgaria and the restoration of Dobrudzha, annexed from Romania in 1940, facilitated the imposition of Soviet control in Bulgaria by 1946. The remains of the Romanian army cooperated with the Red Army in 1944 in the hope of regaining most of Transylvania. Czechoslovakia maintained a parliamentary democracy until 1948, largely because the Soviets believed a Stalinist regime might come to power through free elections. When this opportunity passed in 1948, in part because of Czech interest in the Marshall Plan, the Czech Communist Party mounted a coup d'etat to seize power. The still unexplained suicide or murder of Foreign Minister Jan Masaryk (1886–1948), son of the founder of Czechoslovakia, marked the transition to Soviet control. In Yugoslavia and Albania pro-Soviet regimes came to power through the efforts of the Communist Partisan movement led by Tito. Armed opposition to the Soviet regimes arose in the "Forest Brotherhoods" of the Baltic states and through remnants of the Home Army in Poland, the Organization of Ukrainian Nationalists and Ukrainian Insurgent Army, and the Četniks in Yugoslavia. Many of these bands fought until the early 1950s, hoping that the Cold War might ignite and provide them with the opportunity to liberate their countries from Russian rule. The Americans maintained limited contact with some of these fighters, but only as a means to harass the Soviets. They never had any real intention of rolling the Soviets back from eastern Europe.

The fate of the German populations of eastern Europe was harsh. Whether or not they had supported the Nazis, Germans were forced to leave areas they had settled as early as the Middle Ages. Czech authorities expelled the Germans from Sudetenland in 1945. The Poles drove the remaining Germans out of East Prussia and Silesia. Many Germans also had to leave Hungary and Yugoslavia. During the mass expulsions as many as fourteen million ethnic Germans were forced out of eastern Europe, with perhaps two million dying as a result.[6]

Nevertheless, the heavy-handed Soviet methods created genuine alarm among the Americans and their western European allies. Anticommunist figures such as Nikola Petkov (1893–1947) in Bulgaria, Dragoljub Mihailović in Yugoslavia, and various Home Army figures in Poland were subjected to sham trials and extreme penalties.[7] These trials and subsequent executions emphasized to American and western European sensibilities the brutality of the Soviet dictatorship.

Only one former Soviet enemy and German ally in eastern Europe escaped this process. Even though Soviet military forces held a base at Porkkala near Helsinki, Finnish democracy and capitalism remained intact. Finland did not join most of the international organizations established by the Soviets. The only neutral and democratic country to share a European border with the Soviet Union, Finland provided its communist neighbor with a window to the West and demonstrated that Western-style democracy was not incompatible with Soviet proximity.

Winston Churchill took note of the Sovietization of eastern Europe in a speech at Westminster College in Fulton, Missouri, on 5 March 1946. He stated that an "Iron Curtain" extending from Stettin in the Baltic Sea to Trieste in the Adriatic divided Europe into two hostile camps. The term stuck as a way to describe the physical as well as psychological division of Europe that endured for the next forty-five years.

The establishment of Soviet power in eastern Europe evoked a serious but belated response from the Americans. Anxious to strengthen the governments in the American zone of western Europe against a possible Red Army advance, as well as to prevent electoral success by the communist parties in France and Italy, the Americans instituted both a military and an economic response intended to contain the Soviets. Essentially, the Americans adopted a policy intended to confine the Soviet presence in Europe to those areas in the east that were already occupied by the Red Army and undergoing the process of Stalinization. This American policy became known as containment. An influential article appearing in the July 1947 issue of the journal *Foreign Affairs* embodied the clearest statement of this policy. It was written by American diplomat George F. Kennan (1904–2005), who had considerable experience in Soviet affairs, and published under the pseudonym "Mr. X." After 1947 the basic parameters of the United States' policy for Europe were established, and that policy would be followed throughout the Cold War.

The military response, announced in a speech by President Truman on 12 March 1947, became known as the Truman Doctrine. This program offered American military aid to countries threatened by the Soviets. In particular, it was directed at Greece and Turkey. Both countries, cut off from western Europe, had come under Soviet pressure.

After being expelled by the Germans in 1941, the British returned to Greece in 1944, bringing with them the Greek government in exile. Immediately, fighting began between the British and their Greek allies, some of whom had collaborated with the German occupation, and the communist-led resistance forces the National Liberation Front and National People's Liberation Army, which had fought the Germans. The fighting temporarily ceased in 1945 but resumed the next year. By 1947 the British no longer had the military or material ability to maintain the Greek government. Under the Truman Doctrine, the Americans replaced the British in Greece. American military aid and the subsequent loss of the communists' Yugoslav sanctuary in 1948, after the Yugoslav-Soviet split, enabled Greek government forces to overcome the communist-led rebels by 1949.

Turkey had declared war on Germany only on 23 February 1945, largely to become eligible to attend the United Nations conference in San Francisco and to deflect increasing Soviet pressure on its sovereignty and territory. Stalin demanded the return of Kars and Ardahan in eastern Anatolia, territories the Turks had seized after the collapse of Russia in 1918. The Russians also wanted to have a role in the defense of the straits. The Truman Doctrine provided the Turkish government with military aid and even U.S. military forces that enabled it to deflect the Soviet threat.

The other program initiated by the Americans in 1947 to contain the Soviets was the Marshall Plan.[8] Secretary of State George Marshall (1880–1959) announced in a speech on 5 June 1947 that economic aid was available to all European countries that needed help rebuilding after the war. Although Czechoslovakia and Poland showed some initial interest, the Soviets and their eastern European satellites rejected the Marshall Plan. Acceptance of American economic aid could have suborned the Soviet and eastern European economies, including that of Finland, to the much stronger U.S. economy. Stalin preferred to use the Soviet model to rebuild without outside assistance. Other European countries, including neutral Sweden and Switzerland, but not fascist-leaning Spain, received large amounts of U.S. economic aid. American generosity had a Cold War dimension, but it also had a domestic agenda. After the war, millions of discharged servicemen were seeking employment. The Marshall Plan ensured that American industrial productivity would approach wartime levels so that jobs would be available for veterans. In all these endeavors, it succeeded.

In 1947 Germany's wartime allies Bulgaria, Finland, Italy, and Romania all signed peace treaties with the victorious Allies. No treaties were possible with Croatia and Slovakia because the Allies considered these states to be illegitimate and defunct. These treaties allowed the Italians to integrate into western Europe more fully and permitted the Soviets to formalize their control over their former enemies in eastern Europe. After the conclusion of the treaties, the Allied Control Commissions left these countries.

Few territorial changes resulted from these treaties. Bulgaria suffered no territorial losses, since Russian favor allowed it to retain southern Dobrudzha. The Finns lost the arctic port of Petsamo and the major city of Viipuri (Vyborg) to Soviet Russia. Hungary gave up a bit of territory south of Bratislava to Czechoslovakia. The Italians lost the Istrian Peninsula, the Adriatic island Lastovo (Lagosta) and several other islets, and the Dalmatian port of Zara to Yugoslavia. They also ceded the Dodecanese, islands in the Aegean seized from the Ottoman Empire during the Italo-Turkish War of 1911, to Greece. Finally, the Italians ceded the island of Sazan (Saseno) to Albania. Romania had to acknowledge the loss of Bessarabia and northern Bukovina, first surrendered to Soviet Russia in 1940 but reoccupied during the war.

The conclusion of peace treaties with Germany's former allies brought renewed emphasis to the question of Germany itself. In 1947 the permanent division of Germany became more certain as parts of the country began to unify. That year, first the British and then the French announced that they could no longer afford the costs of maintaining governments in their occupation zones, so the United States incorporated those zones within its own. By the beginning of 1948 American authorities introduced a single currency in the three zones of western Germany. To the Soviets, this administrative simplification appeared to be preliminary to the establishment of a united German state under the aegis of the United States, and they reacted with some alarm. Russia had, after all, lost the First World War to a Germany fighting on two fronts, and Soviet Russia had only barely—and at an extremely high cost—defeated the Germans in the recent war. Now the most powerful nation in the world seemed to be restoring Germany.

Determined that any new U.S.-protected German state would not control the historic capital of Germany, the Soviets, in a classic case of passive aggression, announced on 12 May 1948 that the road and rail lines leading from the western sections of Germany to Berlin would be shut down for repairs. Although they did not want to see a united Germany directed against them, the Russians did not seek an armed conflict with the Americans. The Americans chose not to respond with military force. Instead, they mounted a massive logistical effort in the skies over Germany. Beginning in June 1948 American and some British cargo planes landed around the clock at the three Berlin airfields to deliver the food, fuel, and materials necessary to sustain the inhabitants of the American, British, and French sectors of Berlin.[9] Soviet fighter planes often harassed these cargo planes, but the Soviet pilots did not fire on them. This Berlin airlift lasted for more than a year, until September 1949. To demonstrate the United States' vast logistical capacities, the airlift provided not only the materials necessary for Berlin to survive and rebuild but also frivolities such as nylons and candy. The Soviets unceremoniously announced on 12 May 1949 that the road and rail lines into Berlin had been reopened, ending their futile effort to starve the Americans out of the city. The Soviets also felt less threatened by the American presence in Berlin after their successful development of a nuclear bomb, which underwent final testing in August 1949. With their own nuclear weapon, the Soviets could respond to an American atomic attack with a short-range attack of their own. The equalization of nuclear capacity contributed toward the temporary stabilization of Europe.

In the aftermath of the Berlin crisis, several new political and economic institutions formalized the division of Europe. On 4 April 1949 twelve western European and North American countries (Belgium, Britain, Canada, Denmark, France, Greece, Italy, Luxembourg, Norway, Portugal, Turkey, and the United States) established a military alliance, the North Atlantic Treaty Organization (NATO).[10] The purpose of this endeavor, according to a widely circulated quip, was to keep the Americans in, the Russians out, and the Germans down. NATO committed the

United States to the defense of western Europe. It was the military basis for the containment policy. It also ensured that the German issue would be managed within a framework that included the western Europeans and the Americans. This provided considerable reassurance for nations such as Belgium, Britain, and France, which had exhausted themselves by fighting Germany twice within a thirty-year period.

Many of the European colonial powers were no longer able to maintain their presence abroad. The British left India in 1947 and Palestine the next year. Both areas exploded into violence. The Dutch departed the East Indies in 1949 after vainly attempting to restore their rule in 1945. The French fought the communist, nationalist Vietminh in Vietnam and clung to their increasingly restive possessions in North Africa. NATO declined to become involved in any of these issues directly but did provide protection in Europe and equipment, training, and weapons used in the struggles to maintain a European presence abroad.

The Soviets did not respond immediately to NATO. Initially, they imposed reciprocal military relations with each of their eastern European satellites. Only in 1955, after the establishment of a West German military force and the admission of West Germany to NATO, did the Soviets institute an all-inclusive eastern European military alliance—the Warsaw Pact. This agreement, signed in Warsaw on 15 May 1955, included Albania, Bulgaria, Czechoslovakia, Hungary, Poland, Romania, and Soviet Russia. The German Democratic Republic (East Germany) joined the next year. Strict Soviet control over the military forces of its satellites belied the eastern European focus indicated by the location of the signing of this pact.

As the Americans were establishing the NATO military alliance, the Soviets were consolidating their control of eastern Europe with an economic association. The Council for Mutual Economic Assistance (COMECON) was designed to coordinate the planned autarkic economies of eastern Europe and Soviet Russia. The initial members were Albania, Bulgaria, Czechoslovakia, Hungary, Poland, Romania, and Soviet Russia. East Germany joined in 1950. Later, Yugoslavia and Finland made special arrangements but never achieved official membership. COMECON expanded outside of Europe with the addition of Mongolia in 1962, Cuba in 1972, and finally Vietnam in 1978. Because of

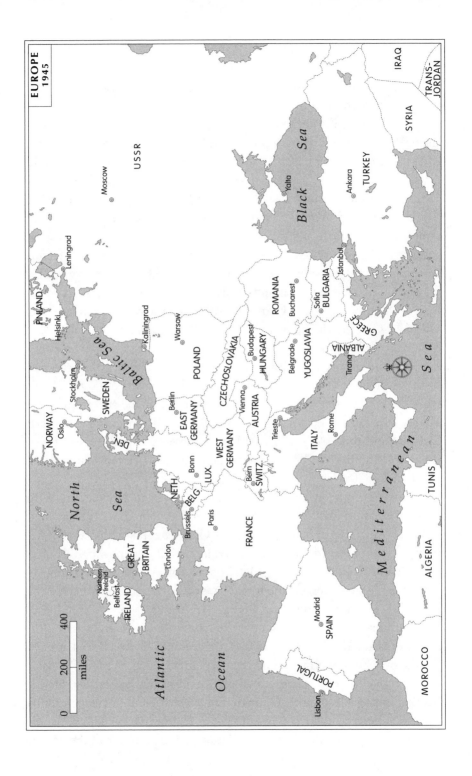

EUROPE
1945

an imbalance of economic and political power, the Soviets dominated COMECON from its inception.

The western European economic alliance progressed through incremental steps, beginning with the establishment of the Benelux economic union of Belgium, the Netherlands, and Luxembourg in 1948 and the establishment of the European Coal and Steel Community in 1951. The latter organization integrated the coal and steel industries of Benelux, France, Italy, and West Germany to increase production, reduce redundancies, and ensure reciprocal cooperation among its members for postwar reconstruction. It also ensured that the members could not manufacture weapons to use against one another. The 1957 Treaty of Rome created the European Economic Community (EEC), which included the six members of the Coal and Steel Community. Unlike the Soviet domination of COMECON, the United States did not seek a dominant role in the EEC. Whereas the EEC provided an institutional framework for the economic development of western Europe, COMECON established the economic basis for Soviet control of eastern Europe. The benefits of COMECON were not entirely one sided, however. Raw material and fuel from Soviet Russia were bartered through COMECON for eastern European manufactured and processed goods. Although these eastern European goods were often inferior, the Soviet raw material and fuel grew in value into the 1960s and 1970s.

Another consequence of the Berlin crisis was an acceleration of the process of consolidating the three western German zones into a single political unit. The Federal Republic of Germany, known as West Germany, was proclaimed on 23 May 1949; its capital was the relatively quiet Rhineland city of Bonn. On 7 October the Soviet zone of Germany became the German Democratic Republic, or East Germany; its capital was located in Pankow, a suburb of Berlin.[11] In March 1952 Stalin proposed the reunification of Germany upon the condition of neutralization. The Americans and many West Germans perceived this to be a Soviet attempt to take over all of Germany, and the idea quickly died. With the division of Germany into two states, a final resolution of the Second World War became impossible. Neither German state would accept full responsibility for the actions of their Nazi predecessor. Neither German state would cooperate with the other to seek a solution to the problems of the Second

World War because of the Cold War. Thus, the Second World War neatly segued into the Cold War without an interim like the twenty years that separated the First and Second World Wars.

The defeat of Nazi Germany and the onset of the Cold War reversed the European power structure. The central European military and economic power that had been lost and then restored by Germany was exhausted by defeat. Likewise, both the western and eastern peripheries were exhausted by five decades of conflict. As a consequence, outside forces intruded. A reinvigorated Russia, motivated by the horrors of the Nazi invasion and the harsh discipline of its own totalitarian dictatorship, divided Europe between itself and the United States, with the latter assuming a position of global responsibility. Only Ireland, Spain, Sweden, and Switzerland remained outside this division, although for practical purposes, they were part of the western zone of Europe. This division recalled the partition of Europe into Catholic and Orthodox areas or, later, into Catholic and Protestant regions. The Cold War, however, imposed a much more comprehensive partition on Europe. As in those previous divisions, ideology played an important role, but the reasons for division always extended beyond mere ideology. Here, considerations of power politics were a strong factor. Yet almost from the moment the separation occurred, the beginnings of the end of the Cold War were taking place in eastern Europe—the same location where the previous twentieth-century European conflicts had begun.

Chapter 13

EUROPE DIVIDED

Soon after the establishment of Soviet hegemony in eastern Europe, Soviet control there began to erode. To a considerable degree, the Cold War had developed out of the American reaction to the Soviet takeover of eastern Europe during and immediately after the Second World War. Yet the Soviets' control of eastern Europe began to unravel even before the institutions to maintain their presence were in place. Yugoslavia, initially a stronghold for the Soviets, slipped out of Soviet hands as early as 1948. This event helped precipitate an opportunity for the Cold War to end during the 1950s.

After the victory of the communist-backed Partisans over foreign and domestic enemies during the Second World War, Yugoslavia became one of the staunchest Soviet clients in eastern Europe. Partisan leader Tito established the Federal Republic of Yugoslavia as a means to avoid the nationalist conflicts that had plagued the state between the world wars. In place of the prewar Serbian-dominated state, the 1946 Constitution established six federal states—Serbia, Croatia, Slovenia, Bosnia-Hercegovina, Macedonia, and Montenegro—with Kosovo and Vojvodina as autonomous regions within Serbia. Tito's initial foreign polices were aggressive. In addition to the territories Yugoslavia had received from Italy after the war, including Istria, Zara, and a few Adriatic islands, Tito sought the Adriatic port city of Trieste. Located at the northeastern corner of the Adriatic, Trieste had been the chief port of the old Austro-Hungarian Empire. The city and its hinterland also contained a large Slovene population. Tito raised claims to southern Carinthia, a region contested by the first iteration of the Yugoslav state after the First World War. He also tried to establish a Balkan federation consisting of Albania, Bulgaria, and

Yugoslavia. For a time, this Balkan federation appeared to be quite feasible. Bulgaria's communist government initially indicated some interest in the idea, and the Yugoslavs already controlled Albania.

Tito's international policies produced some friction with the West. The Partisans came close to fighting the New Zealand soldiers occupying Trieste in April 1945. In August 1946 the Yugoslavs forced down one U.S. transport plane and shot down another flying over Yugoslav airspace from Vienna to Rome. The entire crew of the latter plane died. These incidents exacerbated relations with the United States. In addition, Tito's ambition to establish a Balkan federation and his reluctance to permit the intrusive instruments of Soviet power to establish themselves in Yugoslavia drew Stalin's ire. The dispute between Stalin and Tito escalated until 28 June 1948, when the Soviets portentously ended their relations with Yugoslavia. This proved to be a Soviet miscalculation. Stalin reportedly stated that he would move his little finger and eliminate Tito, but this did not happen. Most of the domestic opposition to Tito had been eliminated by the war, and he was popular among many elements of the Yugoslav population. Any Soviet move against Yugoslavia also risked Cold War complications. A military effort to remove Tito might have provoked a Western intrusion into Yugoslavia. Thus, the Soviets launched no attack on Tito; they did, however, subject the leadership of their other eastern European satellites to increased scrutiny. Show trials eliminated the communist leadership suspected of "Titoist" tendencies in every country. Koci Xoxe (1911–1949) in Albania, Traicho Kostov (1897–1949) in Bulgaria, Vladimir Klementis (1902–1952) in Czechoslovakia, and László Rajk (1909–1949) in Hungary were among those ostensibly loyal communists who were executed. Władysław Gomułka (1905–1982) in Poland and Vasile Luca (1898–1954) in Romania received terms of imprisonment. Occurring so soon after the elimination of noncommunist leadership in eastern Europe, these trials tied the regimes there even more firmly to the Soviet system.

Undoubtedly, the Americans demonstrated some interest in defending Tito. At the same time, the Soviets were reluctant to engage the Americans in such an unpromising theater of war as Yugoslavia. In any event, by 1950 Tito's Yugoslavia began to receive discreet economic and military aid from the United States. In 1949 Tito closed Yugoslavia's borders to the insurgents in the Greek civil war, which helped bring an end to the communist-led insurgency. In 1954 the Trieste dispute was resolved when Yugoslavia obtained the largely Slovene suburbs while Italy retained the old city center. Also in 1954 Yugoslavia joined an ephemeral Balkan Pact, also known as the Treaty of Bled, with Greece and Turkey. This arrangement soon collapsed due to Greek-Turkish disputes over the island of Cyprus. The instability of the Balkan Pact led Tito to accept Soviet overtures the next year to resolve the 1948 split. Although Soviet-Yugoslav relations improved, Tito maintained his independent stance.

The Soviet-Yugoslav split enabled Tito's Albanian satellite to enact a similar split of its own. Albania's communist government, led by Enver Hoxha (1908–1986), had been in thrall to Tito ever since help from his Partisans had enabled it to come to power during the war. When Stalin broke off relations with Tito, so did Hoxha, and Albania switched its allegiance from Yugoslavia to Soviet Russia. In breaking with Yugoslavia, Hoxha replicated the policy of King Zog in the 1920s. After attaining power in 1924 with Yugoslav support, Zog later changed his orientation from Yugoslavia to Italy. Attempts in the early 1950s by American and British intelligence to detach isolated Albania from the Soviet bloc ended in failure, largely due to the actions of H. A. R. "Kim" Philby (1912–1988), a British intelligence operative working for the Soviets. He betrayed Western agents sent into Albania and ensured the survival of the Hoxha regime.

Stalin's death on 5 March 1953 brought to a close the initial phase of the Cold War. The Soviet state's failure to develop a regular protocol for political succession resulted in a two-year period during which leadership there was unclear. During this time disorder broke out in eastern Europe, largely directed at the harsh and drab existence imposed by the Soviet political and economic models. Strikes occurred in Plzeň, Czechoslovakia, and in Poland. The most dramatic anti-Soviet actions were riots in East Berlin and disquiet elsewhere in East Germany. Soviet tanks had to suppress the Berlin riots. These acts were the first overt manifestations of discontent in eastern Europe since the imposition of Soviet rule.

Various figures from Stalin's coterie competed for leadership. A general consensus among Stalin's successors soon eliminated the odious head of the KGB Lavrenti Beria (1899–1953), who was imprisoned and shot. Georgi Malenkov (1902–1988) and Nikita Khrushchev (1894–1971), two of Stalin's henchmen, vied for leadership for the next two years. By 1955

Khrushchev had secured control of the Soviet Union, but his power was not absolute. It depended on a shifting alliance of the top functionaries of the Politburo. No one wanted to return to the structure of Stalin's rule. Nevertheless, having attained a paramount position, Khrushchev was determined to overcome the colossal destruction the war had caused in the Soviet Union and to begin realizing the ideals of Marxist Leninism. To attain both these goals, he understood that he had to reach an accommodation with the United States to end the Cold War.

After he secured power, Khrushchev acted on his agenda, undertaking three initiatives in 1995. First, he visited Tito in Belgrade to try to resolve the Soviet-Yugoslav split. The tone of the visit was collegial. Khrushchev hoped that Tito would rejoin the eastern bloc. Although Tito was careful to preserve his independence, relations between the Soviet Union and Yugoslavia improved. With the Balkan Pact becoming increasingly unreliable because of the Greek-Turkish dispute, friendlier relations with the Soviets were important to Tito. The détente with Yugoslavia also indicated to restive eastern European countries that the era of Stalinist control was over and that a little nationalist latitude was now possible.

Second, Soviet forces withdrew from the Porkkala naval base near Helsinki, Finland. Soviet troops had been on Finnish territory since the September 1944 armistice between the two countries. Finland thereafter became a model neighbor. It was the Soviet Union's only European connection, except for Norway, not under direct Soviet control. Finland maintained a capitalist economy, a functioning democracy, and a neutral foreign policy. It became a go-between zone for East and West.

Khrushchev's third initiative concerned neutral Austria. At Yalta the Allies had divided Austria, like Germany, into American, British, French, and Soviet zones of occupation. Vienna, like Berlin, had likewise been divided into four zones. After signing the Austrian State Treaty of 15 May 1955, the four occupying powers withdrew their forces from Austria. The Republic of Austria became fully independent as a neutral state, joining neither NATO nor the new Warsaw Pact. The treaty also forbade unification with Germany. Undoubtedly, Khrushchev hoped that a similar arrangement might be procured for Germany, for he still pursued the old Stalinist policy of a unified neutral Germany in the center of Europe. This would have several advantages for Soviet Russia. With a united neutral Germany, traditional German military expertise would be out of contact with the Americans. The Soviet buffer zone would extend farther west into Europe. Also, American forces already in Europe and reinforcements from across the Atlantic would have to deploy west of the Rhine. This gave them only a narrow band of territory in the Low Countries and France to hold in case of a Soviet attack.

None of these initiatives softened the American stance toward Soviet Russia. The Americans were still coping with triumph of communism in China, the aftermath of the Korean War, and the domestic fear of communism exploited by Senator Joseph McCarthy (1908–1957) and others. Then on 25 February 1956 Khrushchev gave a "secret" speech to the Twentieth Congress of the Communist Party in which he specified his program. He made three main points. First, he denounced Stalin as a cruel and irrational tyrant whose excesses had almost cost Soviet Russia the war against Nazi Germany. Stalin, he said, had engaged in a "cult of personality" and self-aggrandizement (though Khrushchev had served Stalin loyally while the old Georgian was alive). Second, he emphasized the end of the dispute with Tito. Khrushchev's statement that "there are many roads to Communism" was intended to address one of the causes of the Cold War and to relax relations with eastern Europe. Third, Khrushchev spoke of the need for "peaceful coexistence." He wanted an end to the Cold War.[1] The content of the "secret" speech soon became widely known throughout Europe, which may well have been Khrushchev's intention. The Americans failed to respond.

The West soon tested Khrushchev's intentions. In the fall of 1956 both Poland and Hungary became restive. The Poles sought their own Tito in Gomułka. After serving three years in prison as a Titoist, Gomułka had been released in 1954. Many Poles, both communist and noncommunist, hoped that he could lead Poland more independently, as Tito had done in Yugoslavia. Similar agitation developed in Hungary around Imre Nagy (1896–1958), another Titoist who had been imprisoned. After a dramatic visit to Warsaw, during which the Poles indicated they might be willing to fight to maintain their choice of leadership, Khrushchev confirmed Gomułka in office. This "Polish October" appeared to be a victory for Polish nationalist communism. It also seemed to be a success for Khrushchev's "many roads" policy.

Events in Hungary, however, spun out of control. On 30 October, in an effort to stabilize the country, Nagy proclaimed a democratic govern ment and took an independent international stance.[2] This went further than anything Tito had done. Khrushchev had to uphold Soviet power or risk losing all of eastern Europe. Four days later the Red Army, which had left Budapest earlier, returned to suppress the Nagy government. As many as 20,000 Hungarians were killed, and around 200,000 fled to the west. Nagy sought sanctuary in the Yugoslav embassy, but he was turned over to the Soviets under murky circumstances and executed two years later. Concession in Poland and suppression in Hungary made strategic sense for the Soviets, if only because of the relative numbers involved. Poland, with thirty-five million people mostly opposed to Soviet control of their country, would have put up a much bigger fight than the ten mil lion Hungarians.

The events in eastern Europe in the autumn of 1956 confirmed to the Eisenhower administration that Khrushchev could not be trusted. The U.S. government had done nothing to help the Hungarians, yet it remained distant from Khrushchev. That year, 1956, represented the last time the eastern Europeans could have adopted the Soviet system volun tarily. Had the "Polish Tito" succeeded, Soviet control over eastern Europe might have gradually become entrenched. Gomułka, however, proved to be a disappointment to most Poles. After a brief relaxation of Soviet-style strictures, such liberalizations ceased, and he became just another Soviet stooge. Titoism's promise to establish independent communist regimes in eastern Europe was not fulfilled due to Soviet opposition and American apathy.

Having failed to secure a neutral united Germany in the heart of Eu rope, Khrushchev attempted a different means to achieve the same end. On 2 October 1957 Polish Foreign Minister Adam Rapacki (1909–1970) proposed that central Europe, including both East and West Germany, Poland, and Czechoslovakia, become a nuclear-free zone, with provisions for other European countries to join. All nuclear weapons would be with drawn to the periphery of Europe. This plan offered the Soviets many of the same strategic advantages of a neutral united Germany, in the guise of a Polish initiative. Not unexpectedly, the Americans rejected the proposal in 1958. Warsaw Pact forces outnumbered NATO troops in Europe and operated closer to their command structure and bases of supply than did

chief component lay across the Atlantic Ocean. NATO
ıclear weapons to even the odds in case of a Warsaw Pact

early 1950s developments in nuclear technology and delivery systems complicated Khrushchev's efforts to reach an accommodation with the Americans. In November 1952 the Americans succeeded in
exploding a hydrogen bomb. Based on nuclear fusion rather than nuclear
fission, hydrogen bombs were far more powerful than atomic bombs. In
August 1953 the Soviets announced that they too had detonated a hydrogen bomb. Delivery systems also became more sophisticated during this
time. Both the Americans and the Soviets possessed long-range bombers
that could threaten each other's cities, but the success of these bombers was
always problematic. In August 1957 the Soviets were the first to develop
an intercontinental ballistic missile (ICBM). Two months later, in October 1957, the Soviets compounded their technological accomplishments
by launching Sputnik, the first artificial earth satellite. The Americans,
lagging behind the Soviets for the first time, scrambled to match their
technological achievements. These Soviet successes made the Americans
even less open to an easing of Cold War tensions.

Undeterred, Khrushchev continued to pursue détente with the
Americans. In 1959 he and his wife, Nina (1900–1984), visited the United
States. The future of Europe was pursued in the cornfields of Iowa as the
Soviet leader toured the country. The visit produced much publicity but no
improvement in relations. Before President Eisenhower could reciprocate,
the Soviets shot down an American U-2 spy plane near Sverdlovsk, deep
in Soviet Russia, on 1 May 1960. This incident made Khrushchev furious,
especially when Eisenhower initially denied American culpability. As a
result, the Paris meeting between the American and Soviet leaders later
that month produced no easing of tensions.

For Khrushchev, the U-2 incident was final proof that the United
States had no interest in peaceful coexistence. East-West tension increased
in Europe, and once again, Berlin became the focus of this stress. East
Germany had been a problem for the Soviets ever since its establishment
in 1949, and the difficulty lay in the division of Berlin. American, British,
French, and Soviet troops maintained the quadrilateral division of the
city, yet the city itself remained open. Travel from East Germany into the

western zones of Berlin remained possible through the Soviet zone. The Iron Curtain had a crack. As a result, during the 1950s, tens of thousands of East Germans left the onerous Soviet zone for the western zones of Berlin. From there, West German authorities offered them transportation to West Germany, where jobs and housing awaited them. This offer was especially appealing to young people. The continuing exodus resulted in a net population loss for East Germany, with an aging population left behind. This ultimately undermined the Soviet position in Germany. With a neutral united Germany no longer an option, Khrushchev proposed to sign a peace treaty with East Germany, concluding the Second World War. Theoretically, this would force American, British, and French troops to leave Berlin.

Eisenhower's successor, John F. Kennedy (1917–1963), indicated that the Americans intended to retain their section of Berlin. In response, on 19 August 1961 East German authorities began to construct a physical barrier between their section of the city and the American, British, and French sections. The Berlin Wall effectively closed the tear in the Iron Curtain and resolved the East German demographic crisis without conflict. Young East Germans now had to make the best of their situation at home. East Germany stabilized and, within the framework of COMECON, prospered. The Americans, who did nothing to prevent the erection of the wall, obtained an easy propaganda victory. The Berlin Wall became symbolic of the repressive nature of the Soviets' control of eastern Europe, but in all its ugliness, it also helped reduce the tensions of the Cold War.

The end of the Berlin crisis of 1961 marked the beginning of a twenty-year period of relatively good relations between the Americans and the Soviets known as détente. The notable exception was the Cuban Missile Crisis, when these Cold War adversaries came close to unleashing nuclear weapons in 1962. However, the peaceful resolution of that crisis helped accelerate the process of détente in Europe. One consequence was that the United States reduced the number of missiles located in Turkey, on the south shore of the Black Sea, aimed at Soviet Russia.

Several important steps occurred in Europe during the period of détente that contributed to an easing of the Cold War. One of the most significant was the emergence of West Germany as an important European state. By the mid-1960s the West German economy was undergoing the *Wirtshaftwunder,* or economic miracle. American aid under the Marshall Plan and military security contributed to this boom. Tens of thousand of foreign guest workers toiled in West German enterprises in a much more humane version of the foreign workforce enslaved by the Third Reich. An early indication of this success was the incorporation of Saar into West Germany in 1957, based on the results of a referendum the previous year. The Treaty of Versailles had separated this coal-rich territory from Germany and placed it under French control. A referendum had restored it to Germany in 1935, but after the Second World War the territory entered a customs union with France and had an autonomous government. The success of the German economic revival rendered this association unnecessary for most of the population. The reincorporation of Saarland was the first important indicator of Germany's return to the international arena.

Drawing on this economic success, West German Chancellor Willy Brandt (1913–1992) began a policy of conciliation with eastern Europe when he took office in 1969. This became known as *Ostpolitik,* or eastern policy.[3] Brandt signed treaties with Czechoslovakia, Poland, and Soviet Russia in 1970, recognizing the border and population changes resulting from the Second World War. During a visit to Warsaw in 1970 he fell to his knees in front of a memorial to the Warsaw ghetto uprising in a stunning acknowledgment of German guilt.

The most important aspect of Brandt's eastern policy was the search for an accommodation with East Germany. By the late 1960s the chances of German reunification through war were virtually nonexistent. Obviously, any war in central Europe would likely destroy both Germanys. Brandt's vision was one of "two states in one nation." Brandt visited East Germany in 1970, and his efforts culminated in the Basic Treaty of December 1972, under which the two German states recognized each other. This treaty represented the West Germans' repudiation of the Halstein Doctrine, under which West Germany had refused to maintain diplomatic relations with any country that recognized East Germany—Soviet Russia excepted. In 1973 both Germanys joined the United Nations. Subsequent agreements gave the East Germans access to the Common Market. East German goods could be sold in the West and earn valuable Western currency, and West German goods could be sold in East Germany. The East

German government stopped jamming West German radio and television broadcasts and eventually printed West German television schedules in East German publications. As a result, although East Germany remained a military and political satellite of Soviet Russia, it became a cultural and economic dependency of West Germany.

Another important success of détente was the Helsinki Accords. In August 1975 representatives of all the European countries except Albania, plus the North Atlantic allies Canada and the United States, approved two important agreements in the Finnish capital. The first was the so-called Final Act, which stipulated that the border changes resulting from the Second World War were permanent. This gave general recognition to Soviet Russia's advance into Europe and Poland's shift west, as well as the division of Germany.

The second important agreement at Helsinki addressed another aspect of the Cold War conflict: human rights. The Soviets insisted that human rights involved the right to housing, the right to a job, the right to education, and the right to affordable nourishment. In contrast, the Americans insisted that human rights embodied the concepts contained in the Bill of Rights, including freedom of assembly, freedom of speech, and freedom of religion. At Helsinki, the Soviets conceded the American definition in order to get the agreement on permanent borders.[4] The Soviet acknowledgment of freedom as a human right resulted in the formation of Helsinki Watch Committees throughout eastern Europe and in Soviet Russia itself. After Helsinki, however, Soviet authorities and their eastern European clients demonstrated no inclination to act on their assurances. This undermined Soviet claims regarding the legitimacy of their ideology and their control of eastern Europe. The Helsinki Accords were an important step toward the end of Soviet rule in eastern Europe.

All of Europe benefited from the Helsinki Accords. They reinforced much of Brandt's *Ostpolitik* and his efforts to ease tensions between the West and the East. They were also a success for the Soviets, representing the de facto end of the Second World War and an international recognition of their gains in Europe. Finally, the Helsinki Accords were a success for the Americans, since the Soviets acknowledged the validity of the American position on human rights.

Both sides in the Cold War had important reasons to seek good relations during the détente era. One major reason was that both western and eastern Europe had become restive under the control of the periphery. France, an important American ally since the American Revolution, increasingly sought new foreign policy under the leadership of World War II hero Charles de Gaulle. De Gaulle wanted to restore some of the power and prestige France had lost from 1914 to 1940. In 1960 the French tested their first nuclear weapon. In 1966 de Gaulle took France out of the command structure of NATO to demonstrate his country's self-reliance and independence. Like Greece's later departure from NATO in 1974, this had little real effect on the cohesion of the alliance. De Gaulle also sought a greater sense of control through a 1963 treaty with West Germany intended to serve as a counterweight to Anglo-American influence in western Europe.

A similar situation occurred on the eastern side of the Iron Curtain. Before the Second World War the Romanian Communist Party had maintained a tenuous existence, largely because of conflicting Romanian and Russian claims to Bessarabia and because of Romania's peasant economy. The small Romanian Communist Party had come to power only in the wake of the invasion of the Red Army. In the early 1960s Romanian leader Gheorghe Gheorgiu-Dej (1901–1965) and then his successor Nicolae Ceauşescu (1918–1989) sought wider support for the Communist Party by adopting a nationalistic stance toward Soviet Russia. The Romanian Communist leadership deeply resented the COMECON policy of assigning specific economic endeavors to each member state. The Romanians were not satisfied with a mainly agricultural and raw material economy; they wanted to industrialize. This independent policy also had the benefit of attracting Western aid. After 1965 Romania ceased to participate in Warsaw Pact exercises. Ceauşescu also maintained a repressive domestic regime,[5] becoming, in effect, the Romanian Tito, albeit with a much more oppressive regime.

Romania's estrangement from the Warsaw Pact tied Bulgaria's communist regime even more closely to the Soviet system. The Bulgarians were surrounded by the dissident communist powers Romania and Yugoslavia and the NATO allies Greece and Turkey. Bulgaria had fought against all these neighboring countries at one time or another during the twentieth century. The Bulgarians considered themselves exposed and isolated at the Warsaw Pact's southern end. To rectify the Bulgarian sense of insecurity, the Soviet military established a barge operation to ferry Soviet soldiers and equipment across the Black Sea to the Bulgarian port of Varna if necessary.

In general, political disturbances in western Europe were far less serious than those in eastern Europe during the Cold War. Nationalist separatist movements relying on terrorist strategies emerged in several locations during the time of détente. The most important examples in the West occurred in the Basque regions of Spain and in Northern Ireland. Because of its initial ties to Nazi Germany and fascist Italy, Spain was not part of the Allied attempt to achieve a general European settlement in 1945. Cold War interests, however, led the Americans to make a military agreement with Spain in 1952, exchanging equipment for Spanish bases. This was the only European agreement the Americans undertook outside of NATO. Basque separatism in northern Spain remained strong even after the end of the civil war, and there were occasional outbreaks of discontent throughout this period. In 1959 the Basque independence movement became active, attacking police and other government targets.

The Irish Republican Army (IRA) in Northern Ireland pursued similar objectives with similar strategies. The IRA, which sought the unification of British-ruled Northern Ireland and the independent Irish Republic, had never completely disbanded after the Irish troubles of the early 1920s. Beginning in the 1970s, efforts by the Catholic minority in Northern Ireland to achieve greater social and economic rights led to hostile responses from the Protestant majority. This, in turn, provided the IRA with Catholic recruits for its attacks on Protestant and British government targets. The British government found itself between the two hostile factions and was attacked by both, though mainly by the IRA. Efforts to maintain order required a large contingent of British troops stationed in the troubled province.

Both the Basque and the Irish problems defied easy solutions. Force failed in both cases. Nor was the Spanish or the British government able to develop a viable political remedy. The British rejected the concept of joint sovereignty over Northern Ireland with the Irish Republic. The Spanish government resisted granting the Basque regions widespread autonomy. As a result, terrorist activities persisted throughout the 1970s and 1980s in Spain and Northern Ireland.

Problems arising from the process of decolonization caused remark-ably few problems among the western Europeans during the 1950s and 1960s. The British left India in 1947, and the Dutch departed the East Indies two years later. French defeats in Indochina in 1954 and Algeria in 1962 affected domestic politics but had few consequences for international relations. The ill-advised return of the British to Suez in 1956, with help from the French and Israelis, caused a brief rift in relations with the United States and provided the Soviets with some cover for their suppression of the Hungarian revolt, but it did not endanger the NATO alliance. Most decolonization efforts received international cooperation, especially the Belgians' botched departure from Congo in 1960 and 1961. By the mid-1960s the Europeans viewed the American endeavor in Southeast Asia with skepticism. Although they declined to participate in that venture, they remained committed to NATO. Portugal's attempts to use NATO to retain its colonial possessions failed, and the Portuguese withdrew from their African and Asian possessions in 1975, although they retained Macao until 1999.

Probably the most serious issue to arise among the NATO powers concerned the island of Cyprus. The British had taken over Cyprus from the Ottoman Empire in 1878 to protect the eastern Mediterranean ap-proaches to the Suez Canal. In 1915 the British had offered the island to Greece as an inducement to enter the war on the side of the Entente Powers, but to no avail. After the Second World War, Cypriote Greeks, about 80 percent of the population, sought unification with Greece. By the early 1950s a pro-Greek terrorist movement had become active against the British authorities as well as the Turkish minority. Turkey opposed unification on behalf of the Cypriote Turks, who constituted most of the remainder of the population. Independence for the island was based on a compromise power-sharing arrangement that satisfied few. In 1974 the unpopular Greek military dictatorship sought to gain some domestic sup-port by encouraging the overthrow of the compromise Cypriote govern-ment and the proclamation of union with Greece. This led to a massive Turkish invasion of Cyprus and the de facto partition of the island. The failure of union caused the downfall of the Greek military dictatorship and left the Greeks with about two-thirds of Cyprus and the Turks with the other one-third. In the aftermath of this fiasco, the new Greek government distanced itself from NATO, which it accused of Turkish favoritism. Greece rejoined the alliance in 1980.

On the eastern side of the Iron Curtain, disquiet began to grow in the 1960s. Somewhat surprisingly, the Soviets had managed to contain nationalist disputes among their Warsaw Pact allies. Occasionally, the Soviets would permit outbursts of Hungarian anger directed at Romania or indications of Bulgarian interest in Macedonia. Such nationalist exhibitions were often the means by which the Soviets finessed their control of eastern Europe. For instance, too great a display of Romanian independence could result in an intensification of awareness of the Hungarian minority in Transylvania. The relative absence of ethnic disputes in eastern Europe during the period of Russian domination is sometimes called the *Pax Sovietica*. Clearly, still-smoldering eastern European nationalist feelings helped facilitate Soviet control of the region.

Although interethnic disputes did not greatly hamper eastern Europe during the Cold War, national feelings there remained strong. Often these focused on and even challenged the Soviets themselves. At the beginning of the 1960s the Soviet alliance system suffered a significant loss. In 1961 Enver Hoxha, the Albanian communist leader who had broken with his Yugoslav overlords in 1948, took Albania out of the Warsaw Pact and COMECON. The Albanians compelled Soviet submarines to leave their Adriatic base at Vlorë. Albania's relatively isolated position made it impervious to any Warsaw Pact effort to restore Soviet control. A return to the Yugoslav orbit was out of the question for the paranoid Hoxha. Instead, he led Albania into an association with another opponent of Khrushchev's Soviet Union: Maoist China.[6] Although Hoxha emulated Chinese policies, including subjecting his underdeveloped country to a "Cultural Revolution," Albanians derived little benefit from their Chinese connection. In fact, the relationship with distant China only increased Albania's isolation in Europe and retarded its development. After the Chinese rapprochement with the United States, Hoxha, following his eccentric Albanian pattern, ended his country's connection with the world's largest nation. Although the Albanians flirted with Turkey and Libya, they found no additional patrons until the collapse of their communist regime in 1991.

A more serious problem for the Soviets arose in Czechoslovakia at the beginning of 1968. Influenced by the early humanistic writings of Karl Marx (1818–1883), a group of young communists came to power in Prague at the beginning of the year. Their leader was a Slovak communist and veteran of the 1944 uprising named Alexander Dubček (1921–1992). During the "Prague Spring" of 1968, this liberal communist government instituted a number of reforms easing restrictions on travel, speech, and cultural and political activity.[7] They insisted that real communism could withstand any ensuing criticisms. These efforts gained the Czech communist government much attention throughout eastern Europe and in the Soviet Union itself, especially in nearby Ukraine. The reforms, however, proved to be too provocative, and on 21 August the Warsaw Pact, in its only collective action, invaded Czechoslovakia and ended the brief period of liberal communism. The invasion force included soldiers from Bulgaria, East Germany, Hungary, Poland, and Soviet Russia. The invasion met mostly passive resistance. Faced with overwhelming force, the Czechs submitted. Dubček, however, did not suffer the same fate as Nagy. Instead, the Soviets gradually erased him from the Czechoslovak political scene. The Soviets justified this intrusion into a Warsaw Pact member country with the so-called Brezhnev Doctrine, which stipulated that when communism appeared to be threatened in a country where it was already established, other communist countries had an obligation to intervene and restore it.[8] The Brezhnev Doctrine was in fact a justification for the use of force to maintain Soviet control over eastern Europe. The Prague Spring was not merely a Czech version of events in Hungary and Poland in 1956. It represented the last chance for the Soviet ideology to find acceptance in eastern Europe. Had the Soviets exercised some restraint in 1968, a moderate eastern European version of communism might have developed. But because of the invasion of August 1968, the eastern Europeans recognized that the only possible model for communism was the Soviet one.

The most consistent opposition to Soviet control of eastern Europe came in Poland. The failure of the Gomułka government to institute meaningful reform eliminated whatever small chance the pro-Soviet regime in Poland might have had. In 1970 discontent over high food prices led to repression from the Polish security forces as well as the ouster of Gomułka and his replacement by the genial Eduard Gierek (1913–2001). Six years later another rise in food prices led to more riots. Although Polish intellectuals and Polish workers made tentative approaches to each other, the momentous election of Karol Wojtyla (1920–2005), the archbishop of Krakow, as Pope John Paul II in 1978 and his visit to his homeland the next year energized and focused Polish national feeling. In the summer of 1980 strikes in the Gdansk shipyards were carried out by Polish workers led by an electrician named Lech Wałęsa (1943–), advised by Polish intellectuals, and under the spiritual guidance of the Roman Catholic pontiff. This movement assumed the name "Solidarity," emphasizing the alliance between Polish workers and intellectuals.[9] Solidarity conducted massive strikes throughout the summer of 1980. These efforts led to concessions by the regime, which gave the Roman Catholic Church greater access to the media and recognized Solidarity as a legal organization. By the fall of 1980 almost one-third of all Poles belonged to Solidarity.

The Soviets counterattacked the next year. First, on 13 May 1981 a Turkish terrorist with shadowy connections to the Bulgarian state security service, Mehmet Ali Ağca (1958–), seriously wounded the pope. Later that same year the Polish army, led by General Wojciech Jaruzelski (1923–), seized control of the country and proclaimed martial law. The Soviets hesitated to act in Poland in 1981, just as they had in Hungary in 1956 and Czechoslovakia in 1968. In 1981 they were bogged down in Afghanistan. They also realized that the Polish army would resist any attempt to implement the Brezhnev Doctrine in Poland. Instead, the Polish army itself overthrew the Polish Communist Party in order to suppress Solidarity. This military coup sent shivers through the other communist regimes of eastern Europe. They all feared this possibility. However, a failed coup in Bulgaria in 1965 was the only other place this even came close to realization. Whether General Jaruzelski acted as a Polish patriot to forestall Soviet intervention or as a Soviet surrogate to curtail the influence of Solidarity remains unclear. Nevertheless, as a result of the December 1981 coup, Poland became, in effect, the first post-communist state in eastern Europe. Jaruzelski's coup also succeeded in containing Solidarity for a while, with most of its leadership either held in detention or forced into hiding.

By this time Soviet-American relations had deteriorated. One problem was the Soviet presence in Afghanistan; another issue was Poland. The U.S. government denounced the suppression of the Solidarity movement and the persecution of its leadership. The Soviets resented American support for Solidarity; they also hated and feared the papal influence in

Poland. Leadership on both sides contributed to the waning of détente. The election of President Ronald Reagan (1911–2004) in 1980 had placed an overt anticommunist in the White House. In Soviet Russia, Leonid Brezhnev had begun to decline physically and mentally during the late 1970s. His main advisers in the Soviet government were also elderly and increasingly infirm. By the early 1980s the era of détente was coming to an end. The Cold War resumed, but never with the intensity of the late 1940s and early 1950s.

The return of the Cold War brought few serious consequences for most of Europe. Relations between the two Germanys remained good. Military planners in NATO focused their attention on the Fulda Gap in southern West Germany as a pressure point where Warsaw Pact forces might aim an invasion of western Europe. Nuclear deterrence remained NATO's main strategy to avert such an attack. There was little danger that the hostility in American-Soviet relations would escalate to a nuclear exchange. Cold War–related issues in Afghanistan and Central America during this time resulted in extensive fighting, including the participation of Soviet but not Warsaw Pact troops in Afghanistan. Soviet authorities evidently calculated correctly that the use of Warsaw Pact forces in an unpopular and difficult war in Afghanistan would only increase anti-Soviet feelings in eastern Europe, and such troops were unlikely to be very useful in Afghanistan anyway. The renewed Cold War in its European context was really little more than an exercise in incivility.

After Stalin's death in 1953 there existed an opportunity to resolve the Cold War in Europe through the efforts of Khrushchev. He took these actions not to end Soviet control of eastern Europe but to stabilize it. The Americans, however, never trusted the Soviet leader, and the Soviet suppression of the Hungarian uprising in 1956 seemed to prove them right. Cold War tensions rose in Europe in the early 1960s after the Americans spurned Khrushchev's attempts to establish a viable postwar order. These tensions centered on Berlin, where the extension of the Iron Curtain to the city's streets stabilized East Germany and removed the most obvious source of Cold War contention in Europe. Although Khrushchev failed to end the Cold War, the period of détente was, to a great degree, his legacy. During this time the Helsinki Accords provided a basis for the settlement of territorial issues emanating from the Second World War. At the same time, *Ostpolitik* signaled the postwar revival of Germany. Real violence from the mid-1950s to the early 1980s was, for the most part, confined to eastern Europe. Citizens of Czechoslovakia, East Germany, Hungary, and Poland rejected Soviet Russian order and paid with their blood in 1956, 1968, 1970, 1976, and 1981. These incidents indicated clearly that the Soviets had failed to establish popular regimes in eastern Europe. Neither communist ideology nor Russian friendship could take hold in that region.

Chapter 14

BALKAN WARS, 1991–2001

As Cold War tensions revived, Soviet leadership deteriorated into a gerontocracy. These two events were not coincidental. The increasingly frail and decrepit Leonid Brezhnev lived until 1982, but in his final years he exercised little control over events around him. Most of his advisers were likewise elderly and ill. Brezhnev's successor, Yuri Andropov (1914–1984), seemed to promise change if not reform. He was, however, already fatally ill at the time of his elevation to Soviet leader. He died in 1984 only to be succeeded by another sick individual, Konstantin Chernenko (1911–1985). Chernenko's illness was so obvious that he became known as the "living corpse." Under these circumstances, the Soviet government was unable to address a number of both foreign and domestic issues that required its attention.

Chief among these problems was the Soviet economy. Strains on the economy were extensive. The Soviet industrial infrastructure dated back to Stalin's time and lacked reinvestment. Soviet collectivist agriculture was grossly underproductive. Maintaining the eastern European empire was extremely costly. Soviet troops stationed in East Germany, Poland, and Czechoslovakia required tremendous economic outlays by Soviet Russia. Although Bulgaria and Romania had no Soviet troops stationed on their territories, they and their Warsaw Pact allies received huge amounts of Soviet economic largess. Raw materials and fossil fuels were especially important for the east Europeans. Eastern European states often sold Soviet oil and gas in Western markets, making handsome profits. In addition, the Cold War obligated the Soviets to engage in military competition with the United States to develop and produce costly weapons systems while maintaining a large military establishment. In the early 1980s the ossified Soviet power structure was unable to address these problems.

After Chernenko's death in 1985 a new kind of leader assumed power in Soviet Russia. Mikhail Gorbachev (1931–), born in the Stavropol region, was the youngest man except for Lenin and the first college graduate since Lenin to lead Soviet Russia. He was also the only postwar Soviet leader who was not a veteran of the Second World War.[1] He had entered politics in the 1950s as a supporter of Khrushchev. When he came to power in 1985 he understood that he needed to address Soviet Russia's huge problems. His initial response came to be called *perestroika*, or restructuring. Another important concept associated with restructuring was *glasnost*, or openness. Gorbachev attempted to stimulate the Soviet economy through a relaxed and honest atmosphere. Formerly forbidden topics such as the Russian civil war, the initial defeats during the Second World War, and natural and man-made disasters became the subjects of historical discussion.

Gorbachev also recognized that he had to follow Khrushchev's policy of Cold War disengagement. He made several overtures to President Ronald Reagan, but with few concrete results. In October 1986 he met with Reagan in the Icelandic capital Reykjavik and proposed the elimination of all nuclear weapons within a decade. Initially, Reagan apparently agreed. The intervention of his aides, horrified that the president had approved the surrender of an American advantage, squelched Reagan's concurrence with this idea. Gorbachev also insisted that the American Strategic Defensive Initiative (SDI) remain confined to the laboratory. Reagan would not accept this. Although this meeting did not end the nuclear danger, it established an atmosphere of good relations that led to agreements to reduce intermediate-range nuclear weapons, thus easing nuclear tensions in Europe. Gorbachev's visit to the United States in 1988, accompanied by his intelligent and sophisticated wife Raisa Maksimovna Gorbachevna (1932–1999), also helped relax Cold War strictures.

Gorbachev strove to eliminate tensions between eastern and western Europe as well. His phase the "common European home" was intended to allay concerns of Soviet aggression in western Europe, and to a considerable degree he succeeded. Western European governments and populations responded positively to him. Upon meeting Gorbachev in 1984, British Prime Minister Margaret Thatcher stated, "We can do business together."[2] His reformist stand also became very popular in eastern Europe. Many people there looked to him to loosen Soviet control.

Finally, in 1989 Gorbachev undertook two bold initiatives. First, he announced the withdrawal of Soviet troops from Afghanistan. At the same time, he indicated that Soviet Russia was no longer prepared to support its eastern European client regimes economically or politically (he had actually signaled a Soviet disinclination to support these regimes as early as 1985). One Soviet spokesman, in a conscious reference to the Brezhnev Doctrine, facetiously dubbed this new policy the "Sinatra Doctrine," indicating that eastern European regimes could pursue their own policies "My Way" (Frank Sinatra's signature song). The result was the rapid disintegration of pro-Soviet regimes in eastern Europe.

Not surprisingly, the first collapses occurred in Poland and Hungary.[3] In the summer of 1989 both these countries officially accepted political plurality and Western-style human rights. Regime change came suddenly but without violence in November 1989 in East Germany, Czechoslovakia, and even Bulgaria, long Soviet Russia's staunchest eastern European ally. So peaceful was the regime change in Czechoslovakia that it became known as the "Velvet Revolution." A dramatic unopposed breach of the Berlin Wall on 9 November 1989 signaled the end of the Iron Curtain. Crowds from East Berlin poured through the breach to visit the western part of the city. Nowhere in any of these countries did supporters of the old governments exist in sufficient numbers to impede their rapid collapse.

Only in Romania did violence accompany the transition away from Soviet-model communism. There, the increasingly egotistical and isolated dictatorship of Nicolae Ceauşescu and his wife Elena (1919–1989) endured until December. Through the 1970s and 1980s the repressive Ceauşescu dictatorship had borrowed money from Western sources to finance industrial enterprises and the Ceauşescus' increasingly extravagant lifestyle. By 1989, through the imposition of severe privations on the Romanian population, the Ceauşescus had almost repaid the loans. Then, in December, a popular outburst in the western Romanian town of Timişoara spread to the capital Bucharest. There, members of the Securitate secret police fired on demonstrators on 21 December. After some initial equivocation, the Romanian army joined the popular uprising and took control. The Ceauşescus' attempt to flee ended in their capture and execution on Christmas Day 1989.[4] With the New Year, Soviet control of eastern Europe was over. Only "independent" communist regimes remained in Albania and Yugoslavia.

The collapse of the Soviet Empire in eastern Europe raised some important questions. Chief among these was the fate of East Germany. The former Allies and occupying powers Britain, France, Soviet Russia, and the United States, as well as representatives of both German states, met in 1990 in a series of conferences to address the future of Germany. Later meetings included representatives from Nazi Germany's chief victim, Poland. The result was the Moscow Treaty of 12 September 1990, sanctioning the reunification of Germany. In return, the expanded Federal Republic promised to accept its borders as final, renounce aggressive war, and provide considerable financial aid to facilitate the Soviet troops' return home. This agreement represented not only the end of the Cold War but also the conclusion of the Second World War. Germany had been restored as the hub of Europe.

The end of the Soviet Empire also made COMECON and the Warsaw Pact obsolete. The Warsaw Pact dissolved in June 1991, as did COMECON. NATO remained the only military alliance in Europe. The Common Market underwent a transformation. With the reunification of Germany, power in Europe flowed back to the center. On 7 February 1992 the eleven nations of the European Community (the old Common Market) signed the Maastricht Treaty, which established the European Union. This treaty added political responsibilities to the largely economic ones of the old organization. It also brought about the adoption of a common currency—the euro—by most member states (Britain and Sweden opted out) and coordinated the implementation of a common foreign and economic policy for the European Union. In this circumstance, the newly unified Germany enjoyed a position of great importance.

The end of the Cold War caused tremendous political changes in eastern Europe. One of the most important was the collapse of the Soviet Union. The Soviets had attempted to contain nationalist sentiment among non-Russian peoples through the establishment of a hierarchy of political constructs, from region to republic. These were managed by the formula "national in form, socialist in content." In some European areas—such as the Baltic republics, with their recent history of independence, and the western area of Ukraine—nationalist ideas had always been strong. In others, such as Byelorussia, nationalism was confined largely to the educated classes. Nationalist agitation grew in the atmosphere of perestroika and glasnost. The peaceful Soviet withdrawal from eastern Europe encouraged the non-Russian peoples' nationalism. In a reversal of its Cold War program, the United States sought to preserve the Soviet Union as a stabilizing force in eastern Europe. In a speech delivered in Kiev on 1 August 1991, President George H. W. Bush (1924–) warned, "freedom is not the same as independence" and stated that the United States would not "aid those who promote a suicidal nationalism based upon hatred."[5] This became known as the "Chicken Kiev" speech.

Later that month a cabal of dissident Soviet military and civilian officials attempted to oust Gorbachev from power. Through ineptitude and bungling, the successors of Lenin utterly failed. However, the failure of the August 1991 coup against Gorbachev convinced the leaders of all the Soviet republics to proclaim independence. The Soviet Union formally dissolved on 31 December 1991.

The end of the Soviet Union engendered some violence, and three locations in particular became the sites of some desperate fighting. Two of these places were in Transcaucasia. Stalin's homeland, Georgia, became the scene of fighting when Abkhazia, the northern region along the Black Sea coast, sought to separate. Much of the Georgian population fled or was expelled by the Abkhazian separatists. South Ossetia in the north-central part of the country and Adjaria in the southern Black Sea region also established separatist regimes, but fighting there was minimal. In 2004 the Tbilisi government restored control over Adjaria. These Georgian separatist movements all found much support among the Russians, who resented the new Georgian government's pro-Western policies and sought to retain their influence in Transcaucasia.

Severe fighting also erupted in Transcaucasia over the mainly Armenian-inhabited Nagorno-Karabakh autonomous region of Azerbaijan. After heavy fighting and with some Russian help, the Armenians managed to take control of Nagorno-Karabakh and expel most of the Azeri population.

The third area of post-Soviet conflict was the former Moldavian republic—after 1991, Moldova. There, a separatist movement developed in the enclave east of the Dniester River. Although most of the population of Moldova is Romanian, Russians and Ukrainians predominate in this eastern enclave. Ironically, this territory took the name Transnistria, evocative of the province in the same area annexed by Romania during the Second World War. This time, the separatist movement received Russian support as a way to pressure neighboring Ukraine, deflect any expectations of a Moldovan union with Romania, and retain a Russian military presence near the Danube delta. The Russian-backed separatists established control after heavy fighting with Moldovan government forces.

One multinational eastern European country managed a peaceful transition to post-Soviet status: Czechoslovakia. The political union of the Czechs and the Slovaks had been the goal of Tomáš Masaryk during the First World War as a way to establish a viable state between Germany and Russia without Habsburg domination. It fell apart under German pressure in 1939. The first Slovak state in history gained some initial nationalist support as a satellite of Nazi Germany, but Czechoslovakia was restored after the Second World War. After the end of the pro-Soviet regime in 1989, nationalist Czech and Slovak politicians established some political advantage by emphasizing one nation at the expense of the other. The Czech areas were more developed and Western leaning, whereas the Slovak areas were less developed and more dependent on the Soviet-era economic infrastructure. Almost inadvertently, and without any popular sanction, the two elected leaders—Czech Václav Klaus (1941–) and Slovak Vladimir Mečiar (1942–)—agreed to separate.[6] The "Velvet Divorce" became official on 1 January 1993. The peaceful separation of the Czechs and Slovaks at the end of the twentieth century recalled the similarly nonviolent disconnection between the Swedes and Norwegians at the beginning of the century.

Tragically, by the time of the Velvet Divorce, attempts to separate in the other large, multinational eastern European state—Yugoslavia—were far from nonviolent. The Long War persisted in an appalling manner in Yugoslavia even after the conclusion of the Cold War, giving rise to the worst fighting in Europe since the Second World War and atrocities directed against civilian populations that, after the Nazi war crimes, seemed unimaginable.

After his victory in 1945, Tito established the Federal Republic of Yugoslavia as a means to avoid the nationalist conflicts that had plagued the state between the world wars. In 1948 Tito severed relations with the Soviet bloc and went on to help found the nonaligned movement. Because of its position between the lines of the Cold War, the new Yugoslavia adopted a policy of national self-defense, locating weapons factories and caches in the mountainous center of the country, especially in Bosnia.

Tito pampered the Yugoslav National Army (JNA), which included all military branches. The state permitted Yugoslav citizens considerable latitude in travel and in economic endeavors. During much of the Cold War, this second Yugoslavia prospered. Tito ruled as a relatively benign dictator, and only overt expressions of nationalism and acts of *lèse-majesté* were strictly forbidden.

In an effort to maintain his regime after his death, Tito erected a complex political structure whereby the presidency rotated on a yearly basis among the heads of the six republics and two autonomous republics. For a decade after Tito's death in 1980, this institution, buttressed by the official communist ideology and the JNA, appeared to function successfully. Two issues, however, increasingly undermined it. The first was economics. During the 1980s the Titoist prosperity waned as foreign loans came due, energy prices rose, and the Yugoslav currency inflated. Attempts to develop exports, notably the Yugo automobile, failed. The second corrosive issue was the reappearance of nationalism. The absence of Tito's commanding figure and the age and venality of the communist leadership allowed nationalists to reemerge. The worsening economic situation further weakened the communist ideology and leadership.

After 1986, Serbian nationalists began to openly demand to be recognized as the leading nationality in Yugoslavia. A particular source of concern for Serbian nationalists was the restive Albanian population of Kosovo. Although Albanians accounted for 90 percent of the population of that autonomous republic, Kosovo retained great symbolic importance in Serbian nationalist mythology: in 1389 a Serbian army had fought an invading Ottoman Turkish army to a standstill there. In 1986 the Serbian Academy of Sciences, concerned about the dwindling Serbian population of Kosovo, published a widely disseminated memorandum that accused the Kosovo Albanians of genocide—an unsubstantiated charge. This highly inflated rhetoric inflamed Serbian nationalist sensibilities. Perceiving a political opportunity, Slobodan Milošević (1941–2006), a junior Communist Party official, placed himself at the head of the Serbian nationalist movement with an April 1987 speech in Kosovo defending Serbian rights.[7]

The collapse of the Soviet Empire in eastern Europe in 1989 and the increasing Soviet problems at home eliminated the last remaining prop for the communist ideology in Yugoslavia. By then nationalism had emerged throughout the country. The strength of Serbian nationalism and the fear that the Serbs would attempt to return Yugoslavia to its pre–World War II status greatly alarmed the non-Serbian nationalities. Milošević's squelching of the autonomy of Vojvodina and Kosovo in 1989 confirmed these concerns, because it represented a direct assault on the federal structure of Yugoslavia. As he became more popular in Serbia, he became more feared elsewhere. Over the next two years, tensions increased throughout Yugoslavia as extremists on all sides began to arm for war.

The first armed conflict began in the northernmost republic of Yugoslavia, Slovenia. Unwilling to allow revenues from their still prosperous economy to fund Serbian nationalist ambitions through the federal tax structure, the Slovenes declared independence on 25 June 1991. The Slovenes feared that the Serbs might attempt to do to them what they had done in Kosovo two years earlier. When the JNA moved to secure the frontiers of the republic, a newly formed Slovene territorial militia opposed it. Well armed and well motivated, the Slovenes stopped the JNA in a series of sharp engagements. Using Partisan tactics, the Slovenes succeeded in gaining a demonstrative victory rather than a decisive one. The Brioni (Italy) Agreement, signed on 7 July 1991 and brokered by representatives of the European Community, provided for the JNA to evacuate Slovenia and, in effect, established the independence of this small republic. The fighting in Slovenia incurred relatively light causalities: the Slovenes lost 12 dead and 144 wounded, and the JNA lost 37 dead and 163 wounded. The JNA itself was the main casualty of the war in Slovenia, falling apart after this failure. Its conscripts melted away, its senior leadership retired, and its junior officers found employment in the nationalist forces forming throughout the country. The majority of such officers were Serbian, and they succeeded in procuring most of the JNA's equipment and supplies for Serbian forces.

Just as the fighting ended in Slovenia, it began in Croatia. In 1990 a former Partisan and JNA officer, Franjo Tudjman (1922–1999), became president of Croatia. He instituted a strongly nationalist regime that soon alienated the Serbian minority by its insistence on Croatian linguistic norms and its revival of Ustaše symbols. Located primarily in the center and east of the country, these Serbs demanded the right to remain in Yugoslavia. If Yugoslavia fell apart along nationalist lines, the Serbs of Croatia wanted to remain with other Serbs. With the help of the JNA, they began to arm themselves, and fighting between Serbian militias and Croatian government forces began in March 1991. A May 1991 referendum supported independence for Croatia, which was declared on 25 June 1991. Nevertheless, the Croatian government in Zagreb failed to prepare for the military consequences of independence. The Croats were so desperate for arms that they raided museums for World War II vintage weapons. Hostilities first occurred in central Croatia (Krajina) and spread to Dalmatia and eastern Croatia (eastern Slavonia). By July heavy combat developed in eastern Slavonia around Vukovar, and Serbian militias, assisted by JNA personnel and equipment, besieged the town. The Serbs took the town from the outgunned Croats after a siege lasting almost ninety days. Upon entering Vukovar, the Serbs massacred some of the surviving Croat soldiers and some civilians.[8] With their bombing of the medieval city of Dubrovnik and the massacres at Vukovar, the Serbs began a series of horrifying atrocities that characterized the wars of Yugoslav disintegration and undermined the validity of the Serbian cause.

The European Community, still undergoing its post–Cold War transformation, tried but failed to end the fighting in Croatia through the use of unarmed observers—called "ice cream men" due to their white clothing. They were unable to maintain a number of truces between Croatian and Serbian forces. This failure led the United Nations to become involved in the fall of 1991. Finally, in November, a UN-sponsored truce took effect, leaving the Serbs in control of one-third of Croatia. Blue-helmeted troops, the United Nations Protection Force (UNPROFOR), arrived in Croatia to enforce the truce and, in effect, protect the Serbian gains. The casualties of the fighting in Croatia were high; perhaps 10,000 died and 30,000 were wounded on both sides.

In January 1992 the European Community, under the leadership of Germany, recognized the independence of Croatia and Slovenia. This forced the two remaining non-Serbian Yugoslav republics, Bosnia-Hercegovina and Macedonia, to either remain in a Serbian-dominated Yugoslavia or declare independence themselves. The situation was complicated in Bosnia-Hercegovina, where about 45 percent of the population were Slavic-speaking Muslims (Bosniaks), 35 percent Serbs, and 20 percent Croats. For the most part, these peoples all lived in nationally mixed areas. Faced with no good choices, the Bosnian government held a referendum on independence at the end of February 1992. The Bosniaks and Croats mainly favored a

break with Yugoslavia, but most Serbs, who boycotted the referendum, wished to remain in Serbian-dominated Yugoslavia. The Serbs of Bosnia, like those of Croatia, did not want to live as a minority in a non-Serbian nationalist state. The complexities of the issue are summed up by this question: Why should I be a minority in your country when you could be a minority in mine? The delimitation of purely Serb areas in Bosnia was virtually impossible owing to the mixture of the population. The Bosnian

Serbs, led by Radovan Karadžić (1944–), declared their independence on 27 March, but the European Community recognized the independence of the Bosnian government on 6 April.

By this time the first phase of fighting in Bosnia had already begun, initiated by Serbian militias that had absorbed large numbers of former JNA personnel and equipment. The Bosnian Muslim leader Alija Izetbegović (1925–2003) attempted to rally Muslims, Croats, and nonnationalist Serbs to the defense of an independent and unified Bosnia. On 22 May the United Nations recognized Izetbegović's government; it condemned Yugoslavia as the aggressor and imposed economic sanctions on it. This first phase of fighting lasted from April 1992 until March 1993. The Serbs soon controlled much of eastern and northern Bosnia, which provided a physical connection between the Serbian-held Krajina in Croatia and Serbia itself. The Bosniak and Croat populations of northern and eastern Bosnia were "ethnically cleansed" as Serbian units terrorized them with murder, rape, and intimidation, forcing the survivors to abandon their homes and flee. At the same time, the Serbs systematically destroyed the monuments of Bosniak and Croat culture: mosques, churches, libraries, and schools. Their intention was to establish an ethnically pure nationalist Serb state extending from Krajina in Croatia to Serbia.

After failing to take the Bosnian capital of Sarajevo by direct assault, the Serbs began a siege. From the commanding heights around the city, they rained down artillery and sniper fire on the ethnically mixed civilian population of the city. Reports of ethnic cleansing and mass rapes, media pictures of skeletal prisoners of war, and the deliberate targeting of civilians by Serb gunners and snipers all produced great sympathy throughout the world for the Bosnian government but brought few tangible benefits. In November 1992 UNPROFOR arrived in Bosnia from Croatia. Its lightly armed soldiers interposed themselves between the warring factions but could do little to stop the fighting. The United Nations designated six Bosnian government-held cities, including several completely surrounded by Serb forces, as safe areas. These cities included the beleaguered Sarajevo, as well as the eastern cities of Goražde, Srebrenica, and Žepa; the northern city of Tuzla; and the northwestern city of Bihać. The United Nations also imposed an arms embargo on all of Bosnia. This had the effect of confirming the Serb superiority in weapons.

In January 1993 Cyrus Vance (1917–2002) of the United States and David Owen (1938–) of the United Kingdom proposed to divide Bosnia into ten cantons, with three for each national group and a common canton in Sarajevo. This Vance-Owen Plan envisioned Bosnia as a Balkan Switzerland. The Croats embraced it, because they would gain territory, but it found little support among the Bosniaks. The Serbs, who were winning the war at this point, rejected it outright.

The failure of the Vance-Owen Plan in March 1993 initiated the second phase of Bosnian fighting, which lasted until March of the next year. The Bosnian government's cause further deteriorated, and the government itself began to fragment. A northern enclave around Bihać became a virtually independent entity ruled by Bosniak warlord Fikret Abdić (1939–). Brutal fighting erupted in central Bosnia between Bosniak and Croat forces. The Croats, anticipating the demise of the Sarajevo government, sought to seize as much territory as possible for direct annexation to Croatia. This betrayal caused the Sarajevo government, up until then somewhat cosmopolitan, with both Croat and Serb participation, to become increasingly Bosniak. The Serbs continued to subject Sarajevo to intense bombardments. In February 1994 a Serbian mortar attack on a Sarajevo marketplace killed sixty-eight people. Pictures of the victims and false Serb allegations that the Sarajevo government had fired on its own people produced outrage around the world.

At this point the U.S. government intervened, evidently driven by the political costs of appearing to do nothing in the face of atrocity. This began the third phase of the Bosnian war. American intervention had a political and a military dimension. Politically, the United States stepped in to broker a peace agreement between the Croat and Sarajevo government forces in Bosnia. A secret agreement signed in Zagreb, Croatia, in March 1994 ended the fighting between these two factions. That same month an agreement signed in Washington, D.C., established a Muslim-Croat federation for Bosnia.

Militarily, the United States began shipping arms and equipment to Croatia and Bosnia. U.S. "contractors" also began to train Croatian and Bosnian troops. This aid served as leverage in getting the Croats and Muslims to agree to stop fighting each other and to cooperate. At the same time, NATO airpower assumed a higher profile in patrolling

Bosnian skies. On 28 February 1994 four NATO F-16s shot down four Serbian super-Galeb light attack aircraft. This was the first time in its history that any NATO force had drawn blood.

The initial Serb response to the American intervention was defiance. On several occasions the Serbs took UNPROFOR troops hostage to deter NATO air attacks. This stance persisted through 1994 and into 1995. In June 1995 the Serbs shot down an American fighter. That same summer, Serb forces from Bosnia and Krajina intensified attacks on the Bosniak enclave of Bihać. In July Serbian troops overran the UN-designated safe city of Srebrenica. After intimidating the protective force of Dutch soldiers, the Serbs, under the command of General Ratko Mladić (1943–), massacred more than 6,000 Bosniak men and boys, perpetrating the largest European atrocity since World War II.[9]

In August 1995 the Croatian army, trained and equipped by the United States, launched a major offensive, Operation Storm, against the Krajina Serbs.[10] The weary Serbs offered little resistance, and 200,000 Serb civilians fled the region that had been Serbian for more than three centuries. The Croatian army forced many of those who did not leave on their own to flee. Bosniak and Croatian forces in Bosnia joined the offensive, overrunning the area around Bihać and taking territory in western and northern Bosnia from the Serbs. Largely because of outrage over the Srebrenica massacre and the continued shelling of Sarajevo, NATO began Operation Deliberate Force, an air attack directed against Bosnian Serb forces. The combination of Deliberate Force and the ground victories by Bosniak and Croatian forces contributed to the collapse of the overextended and exhausted Serbs. At no time did Milošević make any effort to assist the Bosnian Serbs.

With the military situation now favoring the Croats and Muslims, the warring sides in Bosnia agreed to talks in September 1995. Izetbegović, Milošević, and Tudjman journeyed to Dayton, Ohio, in October 1995. The resulting settlement, the Dayton Accords, divided Bosnia-Hercegovina into a Bosniak-Croat federation and a Serbian republic bound together in a federal structure. The Dayton Accords also provided for the return of eastern Slavonia, including Vukovar, to Croatia. The biggest beneficiary of the Dayton Accords was Croatia, which regained control of all its territory. No good figures exist for losses in the Bosnian war, but at least 250,000 people died in the fighting proceeding from the collapse of Yugoslavia. NATO and Russian troops arrived in Bosnia to enforce the accords at the end of the year. Bosniak leader Izetbegović lamented, "My government is taking part in this agreement without any enthusiasm, but as someone taking a bitter yet useful potion or medicine."[11] The Dayton Accords stopped the fighting, and they indicated that despite the end of the Cold War in Europe, American intervention was necessary to achieve a viable end to conflict.

The end of the fighting in Bosnia did not resolve all the problems resulting from the collapse of Yugoslavia. The most serious one remaining was the plight of the Kosovo Albanians. Under the Tito regime, they had received considerable political and educational benefits. Soon after Tito's death, however, the Serbian government in Belgrade began to act against Kosovar autonomy. Attempts in 1981 to rescind some of these benefits led to large-scale rioting and a disputed number of fatalities. In 1989 the Milošević government seized direct control of Kosovo, and Albanian political and educational institutions went underground. The failure of the Dayton Accords to mention them greatly disappointed the Kosovo Albanians. In 1996 an Albanian resistance organization, the Kosovo Liberation Army (KLA), became active. The next year the government of neighboring Albania wavered as a result of a failed pyramid scheme. Rioters looted government arsenals throughout the country, and soon thereafter, large numbers of weapons became available in Kosovo. Beginning in 1998 the well-armed KLA undertook terrorist attacks against Serbs. Serbian security forces responded brutally, murdering civilians. NATO's efforts to achieve a settlement in Kosovo failed in January 1999 when Milošević rejected an accord negotiated at Rambouillet near Paris. This agreement would have granted Kosovo autonomy within Serbia.

That same month, Milošević authorized Operation Horseshoe, which involved a semicircular sweep of Kosovo by Serbian army and paramilitary units to drive the Kosovo Albanians into Albania. He appears to have calculated that since NATO had not acted against the Croatian ethnic cleansing of Krajina Serbs in 1995, the alliance would not act in Kosovo either. However, NATO authorized air strikes if Milošević did not resume talks with Kosovo leaders. When he failed to do so and continued to expel Kosovo Albanians, NATO initiated Operation Allied Force on

24 March 1999. Although Milošević announced a cease-fire on 6 April, NATO continued the air campaign and built up ground forces in Albania and Macedonia in preparation for an invasion. Finally, on 3 June the Serbs agreed to withdraw their troops from Kosovo.[12] NATO forces and a Russian force from Bosnia then entered the province, acting as the Kosovo occupation force (KFOR). The Albanian refugees soon returned to Kosovo. Most of the Serbs left with the Serbian troops. In a foreseeable reversal of events, KFOR forces had to protect the remaining Serbs from vengeance attacks by Albanians. Today, the KLA acts as a destabilizing influence. Kosovo, though still a part of Yugoslavia, remains a NATO protectorate with an uncertain future. Its return to Serbian rule is doubtful.

The Kosovo problem also aroused concerns in neighboring Macedonia. The Macedonians opted for independence in January 1992 but soon ran into problems. They avoided involvement in the Croatian and Bosnian wars, but neighboring Greece adopted a hostile attitude toward the small, weak Macedonian republic. The Greeks feared that use of the name "Macedonia" implied a territorial claim on their northern province of the same name.[13] They closed their borders to the new republic, causing great economic hardship. Finally, a 1995 agreement between Greece and Macedonia secured international recognition for Macedonia. With this recognition came a UN force, including 300 U.S. troops, to enforce an embargo against Serbia. During the Kosovo operations, NATO troops deployed in Macedonia. Their initial purpose was to provide security for European Union monitors in Kosovo, but they have remained in place as a buttress for the Macedonian government. Macedonia has a large Albanian population, amounting to somewhere between one-fourth and one-third of the total. Despite some feeble efforts by the Macedonian government to placate this minority with political and educational concessions, the apparent success of the KLA in Kosovo encouraged the formation of an armed Albanian movement in northwestern Macedonia, where most of the Albanian population lives. Its military branch is known as the National Liberation Army (NLA). This movement claims to be acting to achieve greater rights for Macedonian Albanians. Its real intent, however, like that of the KLA, is to establish a Greater Albania, forming a nationalist Albanian state out of Albania, Kosovo, and northwestern Macedonia. This would damage the viability of the Macedonian state and destabilize the entire region. Serious fighting occurred in 2001 around Tetovo between Macedonian government forces and the NLA. NATO intervention in the summer of 2001 ended the fighting and produced the Ohrid settlement. This agreement accepted the use of Albanian as an official language in northwestern Macedonia, the training of additional Albanian police, and the sending of additional NATO forces to the country. At present, a tenuous peace holds.

The status of the smallest Yugoslav republic remained unresolved until 2006. Formally, Montenegro remained a member of the Yugoslav federation, together with Serbia and Serbian-ruled Vojvodina. Since 1998, however, an advocate of independence, Milo Djukanović (1952–) has led tiny Montenegro. Because he was a political opponent of Milošević, he received some aid and encouragement from western Europe and the United States. Montenegro voted for independence on 21 May 2006 with a plurality of 55.4 percent. An independent Montenegro set a precedent for Kosovo, which proclaimed its independence on 17 February 2008. It is likely that an independent will seek unification with Albania at some point, which might further destabilize Macedonia. An independent Kosovo might also cause the Serbs and Croats of Bosnia to separate from the weak federal structure there. Without Kosovo and Montenegro, Serbia has been reduced to little more than its 1900 borders, plus half of the Sandjak of Novi Pazar and Vojvodina.

The death of Tudjman in 1999 and the electoral defeat of Milošević in 2000 and his subsequent imprisonment in 2001 removed two major participants in the collapse of Yugoslavia from the political scene. With his opportunistic nationalism, Milošević in particular deserves odium as the individual most responsible for the collapse. The election of more moderate nationalists—Stipe Mesić (1935–) in Croatia and Vojislav Kostunica (1944–) in Serbia—is a positive development. Because of this change in leadership, regional economic cooperation and the pursuit of war criminals in both states, as well as in Bosnia, have become more likely.

Nevertheless, nationalist sensibilities remain strong throughout the region. After a decade with at least four wars, hundreds of thousands dead, hundreds of thousands of refugees and displaced persons, and massive destruction of infrastructure, the Yugoslav lands are years away from economic, political, psychological, and social recovery. The promotion of stability and development still depends largely on the continued presence of the NATO-led peacekeeping forces. These forces, in turn, rely on a sustained American interest and effort in the region.

The end of the Cold War and the conclusion of the Long War at the end of the twentieth century were generally peaceful. Germany reunited. The Soviet Union withdrew from eastern Europe and collapsed two years later. Only in Romania did any violence accompany the change of regime. Conflict did result, however, in several areas of the former Soviet Union and especially in Yugoslavia. Death and destruction ensued, reaching World War II levels. The nationalization of southeastern Europe, begun at the beginning of the twentieth century, was largely complete at the end of the century. In the aftermath of the conflicts, Europe was more united politically and economically than ever before.

CONCLUSION

International conflict was pronounced throughout twentieth-century Europe. This conflict in general can be divided into three parts. The first phase began with the Balkan Wars in 1912, extended through the end of the First World War, and lasted until 1921 in Europe. The Paris peace settlement proved to be fragile, and after a brief respite of only eighteen years, the most intense phase of the conflict, the Second World War, exploded in Europe. Many Europeans—including, most importantly, the Germans, but also the Bulgarians, Hungarians, and Italians—were unwilling to support and sustain the peace settlement. As soon as a new generation grew to the age of maturity, the conflict restarted. Although the second phase was the shortest in duration, it cost the most lives and did the most damage by far. The third conflict, the Cold War, segued neatly with the end of the Second World War, given the lack of an effective peace settlement. Although the Cold War was the longest lasting of the conflicts and potentially the most deadly, it was in fact the least damaging in terms of human lives and material losses. The collapse of Soviet Russian power in eastern Europe in 1989 and in the Soviet Union two years later not only ended the Cold War in Europe but also concluded the issues still outstanding from the Second World War. Most notable among these was the reunification of Germany. The end of the Cold War did not finish armed conflict in Europe. The collapse of Yugoslavia was, to some degree, a consequence of the termination of the division of Europe, and it extended European conflict into the twenty-first century. Collectively, all these wars constituted the Long War.

To a degree, the first and second rounds of fighting in Europe replicated each other. In both conflicts major fighting occurred in western and eastern Europe. During the first round, western Europe was the primary arena of conflict. During the second round, eastern Europe was the main battleground. During the prolonged third round, the line of conflict ran through central Europe. After the resolution of the third round, conflict returned to eastern Europe at the end of the twentieth century.

The main arena overall for these conflicts was eastern Europe. The twentieth century began with the nationalist-inspired Balkan Wars in eastern Europe. The Balkan Wars then led to the First World War, which ended with fighting between Russia and Poland and other local clashes in eastern Europe. The German and Russian attack on Poland in 1939 initiated the Second World War. The collapse of Soviet power in eastern Europe in 1989 and in Soviet Russia in 1991 ended the Cold War. Conflict in eastern Europe persisted, however. Yugoslavia, established in the aftermath of the first phase of conflict and restored after its collapse in the second phase, disintegrated again in 1991. By the beginning of the twenty-first century, this conflict had not achieved total resolution.

Ideological issues also caused conflict during much of the century. During the period 1917 to 1989, the major ideological powers were Nazi Germany and Soviet Russia. In the case of Nazi Germany, extreme German nationalism was the ideology. The situation was more complex in Soviet Russia. The Soviet Union was ostensibly a federative, not a national, state. Although ideology sometimes diluted nationalism, it was always a component of Soviet foreign policy. Especially after the Second World War, however, Russian nationalism became a very important factor in the determination of state policy. This was not always apparent to the Soviets' Cold War opponents in the United States and western Europe. They often tended to perceive Soviet actions purely in terms of spreading Marxist Leninism.

Many nationalist agendas were realized during the prolonged conflict. Independent national states arose in Norway and Ireland and throughout eastern Europe. By the end of the twentieth century virtually all significant European nationalities had achieved if not full independence at least considerable autonomy. Some independence movements, such as the Basque separatists in Spain, continued to sputter along at the end of the century. Attempts by Mussolini's Italy, Hitler's Germany, and Milošević's Serbia to achieve maximalist nationalist agendas inevitably ended in disaster.

With the end of the Cold War and the collapse of Yugoslavia, southeastern Europe reverted to a physical condition not unlike that in which it had begun the twentieth century. The Serbs lost all the gains of the Balkan Wars. Macedonia and Kosovo were gone; all that remained were half of the old Sandjak of Novi Pazar and Vojvodina. The other southeastern European countries had seen most of their nationalist dreams vanish. Bulgaria could not retain Macedonia after successive defeats in the Second Balkan War and the First and Second World Wars. Romania was unable to attract Bessarabia (later Moldavia and then Moldova) even after the Soviet collapse. The *Megale Idea* had failed Greece back in 1922 on the plains of Anatolia. More recently, union with Cyprus became impossible after the Turkish occupation of the northern part of the island in 1974. Ironically, at the end of the twentieth century, only the Albanians had any expectation of realizing a nationalist agenda. Kosovo, with its 90 percent Albanian population, was no longer under Serbian control and could gravitate toward the Tirana government and further the establishment of a Greater Albania.

The costs of the twentieth-century conflict defy comprehension. Material costs are incalculable. Few major European cities escaped some destruction. Only those in Portugal, Sweden, and Switzerland entirely avoided damage during the Long War. Paris was bombarded during the First World War. Many important European cities, including Berlin, Beograd, Budapest, Leningrad, London, Minsk, Rotterdam, and Warsaw, suffered significant damage and even annihilation during the Second World War. Taken together, the First World War, the Balkan Wars, and the Russian civil war cost approximately fifteen million military and civilian lives. The Second World War cost more than three times that number in Europe alone. The Cold War cost few lives in Europe. Only during the Hungarian revolt of 1956 and in the various manifestations of Polish discontent in the 1960s and 1970s did significant numbers of people, mainly civilians, lose their lives. However, the possibility of total annihilation that lurked behind the Cold War affected all of Europe. The fighting that accompanied the collapse of the Soviet Union and especially the demise of Yugoslavia resulted in as many as 300,000 deaths. Overall, as many as sixty million Europeans lost their lives as a result of the Long War.

Nevertheless, after all the conflict, death, and destruction, the twentieth century ended hopefully. The European Union has established an infrastructure by which European nationalist and ideological conflicts can be overcome. Its success is not secure, but it has made a positive start. The expectation that the Yugoslav successor states will be admitted to the European Union has assisted in resolving conflict in southeastern Europe. Undoubtedly, the century of conflict, with all its human and material destruction, facilitated the development of greater unity and even the beginning of a European identity.

NOTES

1. Balkan Wars, 1878–1914

1. Spencer C. Tucker, *The Great War 1914–18* (Bloomington: Indiana University Press, 1998), 2.

2. See Luigi Albertini, *The Origins of the War of 1914*, 3 vols. (New York: Enigma, 2005), 1:187–89.

3. On the Bosnian Crisis, see Bernadotte E. Schmitt, *The Annexation of Bosnia 1908–1909* (Cambridge: Cambridge University Press, 1937).

4. Ernst Christian Helmreich, *The Diplomacy of the Balkan Wars 1912–1913* (New York: Russell and Russell, 1969), 323–24.

5. Richard C. Hall, *The Balkan Wars 1912–1913: Prelude to the First World War* (London: Routledge, 2000), 135–36.

6. Helmreich, *Diplomacy of the Balkan Wars*, 249–309.

7. Samuel R. Williamson Jr., *Austria-Hungary and the Origins of the First World War* (New York: St. Martin's, 1991), 153.

8. D. C. B. Lieven, *Russia and the Origins of the First World War* (New York: St. Martin's, 1983), 146.

9. Laurence Lafore, *The Long Fuse: An Interpretation of the Origins of World War I* (Philadelphia: Lippincott, 1971), 241.

2. Western Front

1. For a solid evaluation of the Schlieffen Plan, see Gerard Ritter, *The Schlieffen Plan: Critique of a Myth* (New York: Praeger, 1958).

2. Robert A. Doughty, *Pyrrhic Victory: French Strategy and Operations in the Great War* (Cambridge, MA: Harvard University Press, 2005), 92–93.

3. John Ellis, *Eye-Deep in Hell: Trench Warfare in World War I* (Baltimore: Johns Hopkins University Press, 1976).

4. On the German crimes against the Belgian and French civilian popula-

tion, see John Horne and Alan Kramer, *German Atrocities, 1914: A History of Denial* (New Haven, CT: Yale University Press, 2001).

5. Michael S. Neiberg, *Fighting the Great War: A Global History* (Cambridge, MA: Harvard University Press, 2005), 80.

6. Doughty, *Pyrrhic Victory*, 251.

7. Holger H. Herwig, *The First World War: Germany and Austria-Hungary 1914–1918* (London: Arnold, 1997), 179–83.

8. Alistair Horne, *The Price of Glory: Verdun 1916* (London: St. Martin's, 1962), 145–54.

9. Pyrrhus (318–272 BCE) was a king of Epirus whose victories against the Romans were more costly to him than to his adversaries.

10. John Keegan, *The Face of Battle: A Study of Agincourt, Waterloo and the Somme* (London: Penguin, 1976), 242–69.

3. Eastern Fronts

1. Dennis E. Showalter, *Tannenberg: Clash of Empires* (Garden City, NY: Archon, 1991), 213–319.

2. Norman Stone, *The Eastern Front 1914–1917* (New York: Scribner, 1975), 136–43.

3. See Timothy C. Dowling, *The Brusilov Offensive* (Bloomington: Indiana University Press, 2008).

4. Gunther Rothenburg, *The Army of Francis Joseph* (West Lafayette, IN: Purdue University Press, 1976), 195–96.

5. See Alan Moorehead, *Gallipoli* (New York: Hamilton, 1956).

6. Andrej Mitrović, *Serbia's Great War 1914–1918* (West Lafayette, IN: Purdue University Press, 2007), 71–73.

7. On the Serbian anabasis, see John Clinton Adams, *Flight in Winter* (Princeton, NJ: Princeton University Press, 1942).

8. Alan Palmer, *The Gardeners of Salonika* (London: Simon and Schuster, 1965), 38–39.

9. Glenn E. Torrey, *Romania and World War I* (Iaşi, Romania: Center for Romanian Studies, 1998), 137–53.

4. American Intervention, 1917–1918

1. Richard Hough, *The Great War at Sea 1914–1918* (Oxford: Oxford University Press, 1983), 125–28.

2. Paul G. Halpern, *A Naval History of World War I* (Annapolis, MD: Naval Institute, 1994).

3. Basil Liddell Hart, *The Real War 1914–1918* (Boston: Little, Brown, 1938), 273.

4. Ibid., 279.

5. Orlando Figes, *A People's Tragedy: The Russian Revolution 1891–1924* (New York: Penguin, 1998), 339–53.

6. Holger H. Herwig, *The First World War: Germany and Austria-Hungary 1914–1918* (London: Arnold, 1997), 250–52.

7. On the fighting in northwestern France and Belgium in 1917, see Nigel Steel and Peter Hart, *Passchendaele: The Sacrificial Ground* (London: Cassell, 2000).

8. See Mario A. Morselli, *Caporetto 1917: Victory or Defeat?* (London: Cass, 2001).

9. See John Wheeler-Bennett, *Brest-Litovsk: The Forgotten Peace, March 1918* (London: Macmillan, 1938).

10. Hubert C. Johnson, *Breakthrough! Tactics, Technology and the Search for Victory on the Western Front in World War I* (Novato, CA: Presidio, 1994), 215–39.

11. Alan Palmer, *The Gardeners of Salonika* (London: Simon and Schuster, 1965), 225.

12. Herwig, *The First World War*, 436–37.

5. Peace Settlement

1. Fritz Fischer, *Germany's Aims in the First World War* (New York: Norton, 1967), 103–6.

2. Z. A. B. Zeman, *The Gentlemen Negotiators: A Diplomatic History of World War I* (New York: Macmillan, 1971), 107–8.

3. David Stevenson, *The First World War and International Politics* (Oxford: Oxford University Press, 1988), 193–98.

4. Harold Nicolson, *Peacemaking, 1919* (New York: Harcourt Brace, 1933), 69–73.

5. Stephen Bonsal, *Suitors and Suppliants: The Little Nations at Versailles* (New York: Prentice Hall, 1946), 96–117.

6. Stevenson, *The First World War and International Politics*, 274–81.

7. Geoffrey Swain, *Russia's Civil War* (Charleston, SC: Tempus, 2000), 102–9.

8. Evan Mawdsley, *The Russian Civil War* (Boston: Allen and Unwin, 1987), 132–47.

9. Orlando Figes, *A People's Tragedy: The Russian Revolution 1891–1924* (New York: Penguin, 1998), 662.

10. Norman Davies, *White Eagle, Red Star: The Polish-Soviet War 1919–1920* (London: Orbis, 1983), 188–225.

6. Preserving the Peace, Undermining the Peace

1. On the League of Nations, see Elmer Bendiner, *A Time for Angels: The Tragicomic History of the League of Nations* (New York: Knopf, 1975).

2. On Poland's dilemma, see Josef Korbel, *Poland between East and West: Soviet and German Diplomacy toward Poland 1919–1933* (Princeton, NJ: Princeton University Press, 1963).

3. See Robert Joseph Kerner and Harry Nicholas Howard, *The Balkan Conferences and the Balkan Entente 1930–1935* (Westport, CT: Greenwood, 1970).

4. Georg von Rauch, *The Baltic States: The Years of Independence 1917–1940* (Berkeley: University of California Press, 1974), 109–10.

5. See Annelise Thimme, "Stresemann and Locarno," in *European Diplomacy between Two Wars 1919–1939*, ed. Hans W. Gatzke (Chicago: Quadrangle, 1972), 73–93.

6. John Wheeler-Bennett, *The Nemesis of Power* (New York: Viking, 1967), 91.

7. Ibid., 131–33.

8. Denis Mack Smith, *Mussolini's Roman Empire* (New York: Viking, 1976), 20–21.

9. Dejan Djokić, *Elusive Compromise: A History of Interwar Yugoslavia* (New York: Columbia University Press, 2007), 104.

7. Germany Resurgent

1. P. M. H. Bell, *The Origins of the Second World War in Europe* (London: Longman, 1986), 87–90.

2. Donald Cameron Watt, *Too Serious a Business: European Armed Forces and the Approach to the Second World War* (New York: Norton, 1975), 94–95.

3. An excellent but dated study of the Spanish civil war is Hugh Thomas, *The Spanish Civil War* (New York: Harper, 1961).

4. Klaus Hildebrand, *The Foreign Policy of the Third Reich* (Berkeley: University of California Press, 1973), 60–65.

5. See Telford Taylor, *Munich: The Price of Peace* (New York: Doubleday, 1979).

6. On this point, see Williamson Murray, *The Change in the European Balance of Power 1938–1939* (Princeton, NJ: Princeton University Press, 1984).

7. Denis Mack Smith, *Mussolini's Roman Empire* (New York: Viking, 1976), 159–68.

8. John A. Lukacs, *The Great Powers and Eastern Europe* (New York: American Book, 1953), 241.

9. Geoffrey Roberts, *The Unholy Alliance: Stalin's Pact with Hitler* (Bloomington: Indiana University Press, 1989), 154–55.

10. Bell, *Origins of the Second World War,* 296–97.

11. Klaus Hildebrand, *The Third Reich* (London: Allen and Unwin, 1984), 88.

8. Renewed War

1. Williamson Murray, *Strategy for Defeat: The Luftwaffe 1933–1945* (Maxwell Air Force Base, AL: Air University, 1983), 3–14.

2. On this issue, see Williamson Murray and Allan R. Millett, *A War to Be Won: Fighting the Second World War* (Cambridge, MA: Harvard University Press, 2000), 18–43.

3. Nicholas Bethell, *The War Hitler Won: The Fall of Poland, September 1939* (New York: Holt, Rinehart and Winston, 1972), 133.

4. The best book in English on the Winter War is William R. Trotter, *A Frozen Hell: The Russo-Finnish Winter War of 1939–40* (New York: Algonquin, 1991).

5. François Kersaudy, *Norway 1940* (New York: St. Martin's, 1987), 81–121.

6. Hugh Sebag-Montefiore, *Dunkirk: Fight to the Last Man* (Cambridge, MA: Harvard University Press, 2006), 26–37.

7. Ibid., 395–439.

8. Denis Mack Smith, *Mussolini's Roman Empire* (New York: Viking, 1976), 232–33.

9. MacGregor Knox, *Hitler's Italian Allies: Royal Armed Forces, Fascist Regime and the War of 1940–1943* (Cambridge: Cambridge University Press, 2000), 101.

10. George E. Blau, *Invasion Balkans! The German Campaign in the Balkans, Spring 1941* (Shippensburg, PA: White Mane, 1997), 126–35.

9. German-Russian War

1. John Keegan, *The Second World War* (New York: Viking, 1989), 174.

2. On this point, see David E. Murphy, *What Stalin Knew: The Enigma of Barbarossa* (New Haven, CT: Yale University Press, 2005).

3. Professor Rimvydis (Frank) Sibaljoris, Ohio State University, personal communication.

4. See Mark Axworthy, Cornel Scafeş, and Cristian Craciunoiu, *Third Axis*

Fourth Ally: Romanian Armed Forces in the European War, 1941–1945 (London: Arms and Armour, 1995), 89–112.

5. Antony Beevor, *Stalingrad: The Fateful Siege 1942–1943* (New York: Viking, 1998), 291–310.

6. A riveting account of the destruction of the Italian Eighth Army is found in Eugenio Corti, *Few Returned: Twenty-eight Days on the Russian Front, Winter 1942–1943* (Columbia: University of Missouri Press, 1997).

7. David M. Glantz and Jonathan M. House, *The Battle of Kursk* (Lawrence: University Press of Kansas, 1999), 79–147.

8. On the important but obscure fighting at Cherkassy and Tarnopol in 1944, see Alex Buchner, *Ostfront 1944: The German Defensive Battles on the Russian Front 1944* (Atglen, PA: Schiffer, 1995), 19–95.

9. Paul Adair, *Hitler's Greatest Defeat: The Collapse of Army Group Centre, June 1944* (London: Arms and Armour, 1994), 87–106.

10. On the horrific events in Budapest during the fighting, see Krisztián Ungváry, *The Siege of Budapest: 100 Days in World War II* (New Haven, CT: Yale University Press, 2005).

11. Christopher Duffy, *Red Storm on the Reich: The Soviet March on Germany, 1945* (New York: Da Capo, 1991), 290–91.

12. Anthony Beevor, *The Fall of Berlin 1945* (New York: Viking, 2002).

13. On the number of German and Soviet Russian losses, see David M. Glantz and Jonathan M. House, *When Titans Clashed: How the Red Army Stopped Hitler* (Lawrence: University Press of Kansas, 1995), 291–307.

10. American Intervention, 1940–1945

1. Williamson Murray and Allan R. Millett, *A War to Be Won: Fighting the Second World War* (Cambridge, MA: Harvard University Press, 2000), 248–49.

2. Gerhard L. Weinberg, *Germany, Hitler & World War II* (Cambridge: Cambridge University Press, 1994), 188.

3. See Frederick Taylor, *Dresden: Tuesday, February 13, 1945* (New York: HarperCollins, 2004).

4. Gerhard L. Weinberg, *A World at Arms: A Global History of World War II* (Cambridge: Cambridge University Press, 1994), 445–47.

5. On the Italian campaign, see Richard Lamb, *War in Italy 1943–1945: A Brutal Story* (New York: St. Martin's, 1993).

6. Russell A. Hart, *Clash of Arms: How the Allies Won in Normandy* (Norman: University of Oklahoma Press, 2001), 247–64.

7. See William B. Breuer, *Operation Dragoon: The Allied Invasion of the South of France* (Novato, CA: Presidio, 1987).

8. On the V-1s and V-2s, see Murray and Millett, *A War to Be Won*, 599–600.

9. Charles B. MacDonald, *A Time for Trumpets: The Untold Story of the Battle of the Bulge* (New York: Morrow, 1985), 102–29.

11. Collaboration, Neutrality, Resistance, and Genocide

1. Mark Mazower, *Hitler's Empire: How the Nazis Ruled Europe* (New York: Penguin, 2008), 294–318.

2. The most comprehensive work in English on the collaboration and fighting in Yugoslavia during this period is Jozo Tomasevich, *War and Revolution in Yugoslavia, 1941–1945: Occupation and Collaboration* (Stanford, CA: Stanford University Press, 2001).

3. Richard L. DiNardo, *Germany and the Axis Powers from Coalition to Collapse* (Lawrence: University Press of Kansas, 2005), 92–115.

4. See Catherine Andreyev, *Vlasov and the Russian Liberation Movement* (Cambridge: Cambridge University Press, 1987).

5. Karel C. Berkhoff, *Harvest of Despair: Life and Death in Ukraine under Nazi Rule* (Cambridge, MA: Harvard University Press, 2004), 289–300.

6. On Mihailović and the Četniks, see Jozo Tomasevich, *War and Revolution in Yugoslavia, 1941–1945: The Chetniks* (Stanford, CA: Stanford University Press, 1975).

7. Joachim Fest, *Plotting Hitler's Death: The Story of the German Resistance* (New York: Owl, 1994), 255–91.

8. Lucy S. Dawidowicz, *The War against the Jews, 1933–1945* (New York: Holt, Rinehart and Winston, 1975), 400.

9. Nevertheless, the work of the *Einsatzgruppen* continued. See Christopher R. Browning, *Ordinary Men: Reserve Police Battalion 101 and the Final Solution in Poland* (New York: Harper Perennial, 1992).

10. Henry Friedlander, *The Origins of Nazi Genocide: From Euthanasia to the Final Solution* (Chapel Hill: University of North Carolina Press, 1995), 86–110.

11. Mark Roseman, *The Wannsee Conference and the Final Solution: A Reconsideration* (New York: Metropolitan, 2002), 94–113.

12. See Guenter Lewy, *The Nazi Persecution of the Gypsies* (Oxford: Oxford University Press, 2000).

12. Origins of the Cold War

1. Anna M. Cienciala, ed., *Katyn: A Crime without Punishment* (New Haven, CT: Yale University Press, 2008).

2. On the Warsaw uprising, see Norman Davies, *Rising '44: The Battle for Warsaw* (London: Penguin, 2003), 246–430.

3. John A. Lukacs, *The Great Powers and Eastern Europe* (New York: American Book, 1953), 625–26.

4. On the problem of Poland at the Yalta meeting, see Gregor Dallas, *1945* (New Haven, CT: Yale University Press, 2005), 405–9.

5. Telford Taylor, *The Anatomy of the Nuremberg Trials* (New York: Knopf, 1992), 571–611.

6. Alfred-Maurice de Zayas, *A Terrible Revenge: The Ethnic Cleansing of the East European Germans 1944–1950* (New York: St. Martin's, 1993), 152.

7. Hugh Seton-Watson, *The East European Revolution* (New York: Praeger, 1951), 178–79, 217–18, 222.

8. John Lewis Gaddis, *The Cold War: A New History* (New York: Penguin, 2005), 30–32.

9. On the Anglo-American airlift effort, see Daniel Yergin, *Shattered Peace: The Origins of the Cold War and the National Security State* (Boston: Sentry, 1977), 377–80.

10. Tony Judt, *Postwar: A History of Europe since 1945* (New York: Penguin, 2005), 149–53.

11. On Russian policies in their zone of occupation, see Norman M. Naimark, *The Russians in Germany: A History of the Soviet Zone of Occupation, 1945–1949* (Cambridge, MA: Harvard University Press, 1995).

13. Europe Divided

1. William Taubman, *Khrushchev: The Man and His Era* (New York: Norton, 2003), 277–84.

2. Victor Sebestyen, *Twelve Days: The Story of the 1956 Hungarian Revolution* (New York: Pantheon, 2007).

3. A. W. DePorte, *Europe between the Superpowers: The Enduring Balance*, 2nd ed. (New Haven, CT: Yale University Press, 1986), 185–86.

4. Tony Judt, *Postwar: A History of Europe since 1945* (New York: Penguin, 2005), 501–3.

5. Peter Siani-Davies, *The Romanian Revolution of December 1989* (Ithaca, NY: Cornell University Press, 2005), 9–51.

6. Miranda Vickers, *The Albanians: A Modern History* (London: Tauris, 1997), 193–201.

7. Joseph Rothschild and Nancy M. Wingfield, *Return to Diversity: A Political History of East Central Europe since World War II* (Oxford: Oxford University Press, 2008), 135–38.

8. John W. Young, *Cold War Europe, 1945–89: A Political History* (London: Arnold, 1991), 257.

9. The best source on Solidarity is Timothy Garton Ash, *The Polish Revolution* (New Haven, CT: Yale University Press, 2002).

14. Balkan Wars, 1991–2001

1. On Gorbachev, see Martin McCauley, *Gorbachev* (London: Longman, 1998).

2. www.margaretthatcher.org/speeches.

3. J. F. Brown, *Surge to Freedom: The End of Communist Rule in Eastern Europe* (Durham, NC: Duke University Press, 1991), 71–123.

4. Peter Siani-Davies, *The Romanian Revolution of December 1989* (Ithaca, NY: Cornell University Press, 2005), 53–96.

5. www.en.wikisource.org.

6. J. F. Brown, *Hopes and Shadows: Eastern Europe after Communism* (Durham, NC: Duke University Press, 1994), 56–66.

7. Louis Sell, *Slobodan Milosevic and the Destruction of Yugoslavia* (Durham, NC: Duke University Press, 2002), 1–9.

8. Laura Silber and Allan Little, *Yugoslavia: Death of a Nation*, rev. and updated ed. (New York: Penguin, 1997), 175–83.

9. See Jan Willem Honig and Norbert Both, *Srebrenica: Record of a War Crime* (New York: Penguin, 1997).

10. On Operation Storm (*Oluja* in Serbo-Croatian), see *Balkan Battlegrounds: A Military History of the Yugoslav Conflict, 1990–1995*, 2 vols. (Washington, DC: Central Intelligence Agency, 2002), 1:377–96.

11. Silber and Little, *Yugoslavia*, 377.

12. Tim Judah, *Kosovo: War and Revenge* (New Haven, CT: Yale University Press, 2002), 265–85.

13. John Phillips, *Macedonia: Warlords & Rebels in the Balkans* (New Haven, CT: Yale University Press, 2004), 53–64.

SUGGESTED READINGS

Adair, Paul. *Hitler's Greatest Defeat, The Collapse of Army Group Centre, June 1944.* London: Arms and Armour, 1994.

Adams, John Clinton. *Flight in Winter.* Princeton, NJ: Princeton University Press, 1942.

Albertini, Luigi. *The Origins of the War of 1914.* 3 vols. New York: Enigma, 2005.

Andreyev, Catherine. *Vlasov and the Russian Liberation Movement.* Cambridge: Cambridge University Press, 1987.

Ansel, Walter. *Hitler and the Middle Sea.* Durham, NC: Duke University Press, 1972.

Armstrong, John. *Soviet Partisans in World War II.* Madison: University of Wisconsin Press, 1964.

Ash, Timothy Garton. *The Polish Revolution.* New Haven, CT: Yale University Press, 2002.

Axworthy, Mark, Cornel Scafeş, and Cristian Craciunoiu. *Third Axis Fourth Ally: Romanian Armed Forces in the European War, 1941–1945.* London: Arms and Armour, 1995.

Balkan Battlegrounds: A Military History of the Yugoslav Conflict, 1990–1995. 2 vols. Washington, DC: Central Intelligence Agency, 2002.

Bartov, Omer. *The Eastern Front, 1941–45: German Troops and the Barbarisation of Warfare.* New York: Palgrave, 2001.

———. *Hitler's Army: Soldiers, Nazis and War in the Third Reich.* Oxford: Oxford University Press, 1991.

Beevor, Antony. *The Fall of Berlin 1945.* New York: Viking, 2002.

———. *Stalingrad: The Fateful Siege 1942–1943.* New York: Viking, 1998.

Bell, P. M. H. *The Origins of the Second World War in Europe.* London: Longman, 1986.

Bendiner, Elmer. *A Time for Angels: The Tragicomic History of the League of Nations.* New York: Knopf, 1975.

Berenbaum, Michael, ed. *A Mosaic of Victims: Non-Jews Persecuted and Murdered by the Nazis.* New York: New York University Press, 1990.

Berkhoff, Karel C. *Harvest of Despair: Life and Death in Ukraine under Nazi Rule.* Cambridge, MA: Harvard University Press, 2004.

Bethell, Nicholas. *The War Hitler Won: The Fall of Poland, September 1939.* New York: Holt, Rinehart and Winston, 1972.

Blau, George E. *Invasion Balkans! The German Campaign in the Balkans, Spring 1941.* Shippensburg, PA: White Mane, 1997.

Bonsal, Stephen. *Suitors and Suppliants: The Little Nations at Versailles.* New York: Prentice Hall, 1946.

Bosworth, R. J. B. *Italy and the Approach of the First World War.* New York: St. Martin's, 1983.

Breuer, William B. *Operation Dragoon: The Allied Invasion of the South of France.* Novato, CA: Presidio, 1987.

Brown, J. F. *The Grooves of Change: Eastern Europe at the Turn of the Millennium.* Durham, NC: Duke University Press, 2001.

———. *Hopes and Shadows: Eastern Europe after Communism.* Durham, NC: Duke University Press, 1994.

———. *Surge to Freedom: The End of Communist Rule in Eastern Europe.* Durham, NC: Duke University Press, 1991.

Browning, Christopher R. *Ordinary Men: Reserve Police Battalion 101 and the Final Solution in Poland.* New York: Harper Perennial, 1992.

Buchner, Alex. *Ostfront 1944: The German Defensive Battles on the Russian Front 1944.* Atglen, PA: Schiffer, 1995.

Burrin, Philippe. *France under the Germans: Collaboration and Compromise.* New York: New Press, 1993.

Cienciala, Anna M., ed. *Katyn: A Crime without Punishment.* New Haven, CT: Yale University Press, 2008.

Clark, Alan. *The Eastern Front 1914–18: The Suicide of the Empires.* Gloucestershire: Windrush, 1999.

Clayton, Anthony. *Paths of Glory: The French Army 1914–18.* London: Cassell Military, 2003.

Corti, Eugenio. *Few Returned: Twenty-eight Days on the Russian Front, Winter 1942–1943.* Columbia: University of Missouri Press, 1997.

Crowe, David M. *The Holocaust: Roots, History, and Aftermath.* Boulder, CO: Westview, 2008.

Dallas, Gregor. *1945.* New Haven, CT: Yale University Press, 2005.

Dallin, Alexander. *German Rule in Russia 1941–1945.* Boulder, CO: Westview, 1981.

Davies, Norman. *Rising '44: The Battle for Warsaw.* London: Penguin, 2003.

————. *White Eagle, Red Star: The Polish-Soviet War 1919–1920*. London: Orbis, 1983.

Dawidowicz, Lucy S. *The War against the Jews, 1933–1945*. New York: Holt, Rinehart and Winston, 1975.

DePorte, A. W. *Europe between the Superpowers: The Enduring Balance*, 2nd ed. New Haven, CT: Yale University Press, 1986.

de Zayas, Alfred-Maurice. *A Terrible Revenge: The Ethnic Cleansing of the East European Germans 1944–1950*. New York: St. Martin's, 1993.

DiNardo, Richard L. *Germany and the Axis Powers from Coalition to Collapse*. Lawrence: University Press of Kansas, 2005.

Djokić, Dejan. *Elusive Compromise: A History of Interwar Yugoslavia*. New York: Columbia University Press, 2007.

Doughty, Robert A. *Pyrrhic Victory: French Strategy and Operations in the Great War*. Cambridge, MA: Harvard University Press, 2005.

Dowling, Timothy C. *The Brusilov Offensive*. Bloomington: Indiana University Press, 2008.

Duffy, Christopher. *Red Storm on the Reich: The Soviet March on Germany, 1945*. New York: Da Capo, 1991.

Ellis, John. *Eye-Deep in Hell: Trench Warfare in World War I*. Baltimore: Johns Hopkins University Press, 1976.

Ellwood, David. *Italy, 1943–1945*. New York: Holmes and Meier, 1985.

Ferguson, Niall. *The Pity of War: Explaining World War I*. New York: Basic, 1999.

Fest, Joachim. *Plotting Hitler's Death: The Story of the German Resistance*. New York: Owl, 1994.

Figes, Orlando. *A People's Tragedy: The Russian Revolution 1891–1924*. New York: Penguin, 1998.

Fischer, Fritz. *Germany's Aims in the First World War*. New York: Norton, 1967.

————. *War of Illusions: German Policies from 1911 to 1914*. New York: Norton, 1975.

Friedlander, Henry. *The Origins of Nazi Genocide: From Euthanasia to the Final Solution*. Chapel Hill: University of North Carolina Press, 1995.

Friedman, Norman. *The Fifty Year War: Conflict and Strategy in the Cold War*. Annapolis, MD: Naval Institute, 2000.

Gaddis, John Lewis. *The Cold War: A New History*. New York: Penguin, 2005.

Garliński, Józef. *Poland in the Second World War*. New York: Hippocrene, 1985.

Gatzke, Hans W., ed. *European Diplomacy between Two Wars 1919–1939*. Chicago: Quadrangle, 1972.

Glantz, David M., and Jonathan M. House. *The Battle of Kursk*. Lawrence: University Press of Kansas, 1999.

———. *When Titans Clashed: How the Red Army Stopped Hitler.* Lawrence: University Press of Kansas, 1995.

Glenny, Misha. *The Fall of Yugoslavia: The Third Balkan War,* 3rd ed. New York: Penguin, 1993.

Hall, Richard C. *The Balkan Wars 1912–1913: Prelude to the First World War.* London: Routledge, 2000.

Halpern, Paul G. *A Naval History of World War I.* Annapolis, MD: Naval Institute, 1994.

Hamilton, Richard F., and Holger H. Herwig, eds. *The Origins of World War I.* Cambridge: Cambridge University Press, 2003.

Hart, Russell A. *Clash of Arms: How the Allies Won in Normandy.* Norman: University of Oklahoma Press, 2001.

Hastings, Max. *Overlord: D-day and the Battle for Normandy.* New York: Simon and Schuster, 1984.

Helmreich, Ernst Christian. *The Diplomacy of the Balkan Wars 1912–1913.* New York: Russell and Russell, 1969.

Herwig, Holger H. *The First World War: Germany and Austria-Hungary 1914–1918.* London: Arnold, 1997.

Hewitson, Mark. *Germany and the Causes of the First World War.* New York: Berg, 2004.

Hildebrand, Klaus. *The Foreign Policy of the Third Reich.* Berkeley: University of California Press, 1973.

———. *The Third Reich.* London: Allen and Unwin, 1984.

Honig, Jan Willem, and Norbert Both. *Srebrenica: Record of a War Crime.* New York: Penguin, 1997.

Horne, Alistair. *The Price of Glory: Verdun 1916.* London: St. Martin's, 1962.

Horne, John, and Alan Kramer. *German Atrocities, 1914: A History of Denial.* New Haven, CT: Yale University Press, 2001.

Hough, Richard. *The Great War at Sea 1914–1918.* Oxford: Oxford University Press, 1983.

Jacobson, Jon. *Locarno Diplomacy: Germany and the West, 1925–1929.* Princeton, NJ: Princeton University Press, 1972.

Johnson, Hubert C. *Breakthrough! Tactics, Technology and the Search for Victory on the Western Front in World War I.* Novato, CA: Presidio, 1994.

Joll, James. *The Origins of the First World War.* London: Longman, 1984.

Judah, Tim. *Kosovo: War and Revenge.* New Haven, CT: Yale University Press, 2002.

Judt, Tony. *Postwar: A History of Europe since 1945.* New York: Penguin, 2005.

Keegan, John. *The Face of Battle: A Study of Agincourt, Waterloo and the Somme.* London: Penguin, 1976.

———. *The Second World War.* New York: Viking, 1989.

Keiger, John F. V. *France and the Origins of the First World War.* New York: St. Martin's, 1983.

Kerner, Robert Joseph, and Harry Nicholas Howard. *The Balkan Conferences and the Balkan Entente 1930–1935.* Westport, CT: Greenwood, 1970.

Kersaudy, François. *Norway 1940.* New York: St. Martin's, 1987.

Knox, MacGregor. *Common Destiny: Dictatorship, Foreign Policy and War in Fascist Italy and Nazi Germany.* Cambridge: Cambridge University Press, 2000.

———. *Hitler's Italian Allies: Royal Armed Forces, Fascist Regime, and the War of 1940–1943.* Cambridge: Cambridge University Press, 2000.

Korbel, Josef. *Poland between East and West: Soviet and German Diplomacy toward Poland 1919–1933.* Princeton, NJ: Princeton University Press, 1963.

Kramer, Alan. *Dynamic of Destruction: Culture and Mass Killing in the First World War.* Oxford: Oxford University Press, 2007.

Lafore, Laurence. *The Long Fuse: An Interpretation of the Origins of World War I.* Philadelphia: Lippincott, 1971.

Lamb, Richard. *War in Italy 1943–1945: A Brutal Story.* New York: St. Martin's, 1993.

Lewy, Guenter. *The Nazi Persecution of the Gypsies.* Oxford: Oxford University Press, 2000.

Liddell Hart, Basil. *The Real War 1914–1918.* Boston: Little, Brown, 1938.

Lieven, D. C. B. *Russia and the Origins of the First World War.* New York: St. Martin's, 1983.

Littlejohn, David. *The Patriotic Traitors.* Garden City, NY: Doubleday, 1972.

Lukacs, John A. *The Great Powers and Eastern Europe.* New York: American Book, 1953.

MacDonald, Charles B. *A Time for Trumpets: The Untold Story of the Battle of the Bulge.* New York: Morrow, 1985.

Magaš, Branka, and Ivo Žanić, eds. *The War in Croatia and Bosnia-Herzegovina 1991–1995.* London: Cass, 2001.

Mawdsley, Evan. *The Russian Civil War.* Boston: Allen and Unwin, 1987.

Mazower, Mark. *Hitler's Empire: How the Nazis Ruled Europe.* New York: Penguin, 2008.

McCauley, Martin. *Gorbachev.* London: Longman, 1998.

Merridale, Catherine. *Ivan's War: Life and Death in the Red Army, 1939–1945.* New York: Metropolitan, 2006.

Middlebrook, Martin. *The First Day on the Somme: 1 July 1916.* London: Allen Lane, 1971.

Mitrović, Andrej. *Serbia's Great War 1914–1918.* West Lafayette, IN: Purdue University Press, 2007.

Moorehead, Alan. *Gallipoli*. New York: Hamilton, 1956.

Morselli, Mario A. *Caporetto 1917: Victory or Defeat?* London: Cass, 2001.

Murphy, David E. *What Stalin Knew: The Enigma of Barbarossa*. New Haven, CT: Yale University Press, 2005.

Murray, Williamson. *The Change in the European Balance of Power 1938–1939*. Princeton, NJ: Princeton University Press, 1984.

———. *Strategy for Defeat: The Luftwaffe 1933–1945*. Maxwell Air Force Base, AL: Air University, 1983.

Murray, Williamson, and Allan R. Millett. *A War to Be Won: Fighting the Second World War*. Cambridge, MA: Harvard University Press, 2000.

Naimark, Norman M. *The Russians in Germany: A History of the Soviet Zone of Occupation, 1945–1949*. Cambridge, MA: Harvard University Press, 1995.

Neiberg, Michael S. *Fighting the Great War: A Global History*. Cambridge, MA: Harvard University Press, 2005.

Neillands, Robin. *The Battle of Normandy, 1944*. London: Cassell, 2002.

Newman, William. *The Balance of Power in the Interwar Years, 1919–1939*. New York: Random House, 1968.

Nicolson, Harold. *Peacemaking, 1919*. New York: Harcourt Brace, 1933.

Palmer, Alan. *The Gardeners of Salonika*. London: Simon and Schuster, 1965.

Petrow, Richard. *The Bitter Years: The Invasion and Occupation of Denmark and Norway April 1940–May 1945*. New York: Morrow, 1974.

Phillips, John. *Macedonia: Warlords & Rebels in the Balkans*. New Haven, CT: Yale University Press, 2004.

Pitt, Barrie. *1918: The Last Act*. London: Cassell, 1962.

Ramet, Sabrina. *Thinking about Yugoslavia: Scholarly Debates about the Yugoslav Breakup and the Wars in Bosnia and Kosovo*. Cambridge: Cambridge University Press, 2005.

Rauch, Georg von. *The Baltic States: The Years of Independence 1917–1940*. Berkeley: University of California Press, 1974.

Remak, Joachim. *The Origins of World War I, 1871–1914*. New York: Prentice Hall, 1976.

Ritter, Gerhard. *The Schlieffen Plan: Critique of a Myth*. New York: Praeger, 1958.

Roberts, Geoffrey. *The Unholy Alliance: Stalin's Pact with Hitler*. Bloomington: Indiana University Press, 1989.

Rogel, Carole. *The Breakup of Yugoslavia and the War in Bosnia*. Westport, CT: Greenwood, 1998.

Roseman, Mark. *The Wannsee Conference and the Final Solution: A Reconsideration*. New York: Metropolitan, 2002.

Rossino, Alexander B. *Hitler Strikes Poland: Blitzkrieg, Ideology, and Atrocity*. Lawrence: University Press of Kansas, 2003.

Rothenburg, Gunther. *The Army of Francis Joseph.* West Lafayette, IN: Purdue University Press, 1976.

Rothschild, Joseph, and Nancy M. Wingfield. *Return to Diversity: A Political History of East Central Europe since World War II.* Oxford: Oxford University Press, 2008.

Schindler, John R. *Isonzo: The Forgotten Sacrifice of the Great War.* Westport, CT: Praeger, 2001.

Schmitt, Bernadotte E. *The Annexation of Bosnia 1908–1909.* Cambridge: Cambridge University Press, 1937.

Seaton, Albert. *The Russo-German War 1941–45.* New York: Praeger, 1970.

Seton-Watson, Hugh. *The East European Revolution.* New York: Praeger, 1951.

Sebag-Montefiore, Hugh. *Dunkirk: Fight to the Last Man.* Cambridge, MA: Harvard University Press, 2006.

Sebestyen, Victor. *Twelve Days: The Story of the 1956 Hungarian Revolution.* New York: Pantheon, 2007.

Sedlear, Jean W. *The Axis Empire in Southeast Europe.* Booklocker.com, 2007.

———. *Hitler's Central European Empire.* Booklocker.com, 2007.

Sell, Louis. *Slobodan Milosevic and the Destruction of Yugoslavia.* Durham, NC: Duke University Press, 2002.

Showalter, Dennis E. *Tannenberg: Clash of Empires.* Garden City, NY: Archon, 1991.

Siani-Davies, Peter. *The Romanian Revolution of December 1989.* Ithaca, NY: Cornell University Press, 2005.

Silber, Laura, and Allan Little. *Yugoslavia: Death of a Nation.* Rev. and updated ed. New York: Penguin, 1997.

Smith, Denis Mack. *Mussolini's Roman Empire.* New York: Viking, 1976.

Steel, Nigel, and Peter Hart. *Passchendaele: The Sacrificial Ground.* London: Cassell, 2000.

Steiner, Zara S. *Britain and the Origins of the First World War.* London: St. Martin's, 1977.

Stevenson, David. *Cataclysm: The First World War as Political Tragedy.* New York: Basic, 2004.

———. *The First World War and International Politics.* Oxford: Oxford University Press, 1988.

Stokes, Gale. *The Walls Came Tumbling Down: The Collapse of Communism in Eastern Europe.* Oxford: Oxford University Press, 1993.

Stone, Norman. *The Eastern Front 1914–1917.* New York: Scribner, 1975.

Swain, Geoffrey. *Russia's Civil War.* Charleston, SC: Tempus, 2000.

Taubman, William. *Khrushchev: The Man and His Era.* New York: Norton, 2003.

Taylor, Frederick. *Dresden: Tuesday, February 13, 1945*. New York: HarperCollins, 2004.

Taylor, Telford. *The Anatomy of the Nuremberg Trials*. New York: Knopf, 1992.

———. *Munich: The Price of Peace*. New York: Doubleday, 1979.

Terraine, John. *To Win a War: 1918, the Year of Victory*. New York: Doubleday, 1981.

Thomas, Hugh. *The Spanish Civil War*. New York: Harper, 1961.

Tomasevich, Jozo. *War and Revolution in Yugoslavia, 1941–1945: The Chetniks*. Stanford, CA: Stanford University Press, 1975.

———. *War and Revolution in Yugoslavia, 1941–1945: Occupation and Collaboration*. Stanford, CA: Stanford University Press, 2001.

Torrey, Glenn E. *Romania and World War I*. Iaşi, Romania: Center for Romanian Studies, 1998.

Trotter, William R. *A Frozen Hell: The Russo-Finnish Winter War of 1939–40*. New York: Algonquin, 1991.

Tucker, Spencer. *The Great War 1914–18*. Bloomington: Indiana University Press, 1998.

Ungváry, Krisztián. *The Siege of Budapest: 100 Days in World War II*. New Haven, CT: Yale University Press, 2005.

Van Dyke, Carl. *The Soviet Invasion of Finland 1939–40*. London: Cass, 1997.

Van Oudenaren, John. *Détente in Europe: The Soviet Union and the West since 1953*. Durham, NC: Duke University Press, 1991.

Vickers, Miranda. *The Albanians: A Modern History*. London: Tauris, 1997.

Watt, Donald Cameron. *Too Serious a Business: European Armed Forces and the Approach to the Second World War*. New York: Norton, 1975.

Weinberg, Gerhard L. *Germany, Hitler & World War II*. Cambridge: Cambridge University Press, 1994.

———. *A World at Arms: A Global History of World War II*. Cambridge: Cambridge University Press, 1994.

Werth, Alexander. *Russia at War 1941–1945*. New York: Dutton, 1964.

Wette, Wolfram. *The Wehrmacht: History, Myth, Reality*. Cambridge, MA: Harvard University Press, 2006.

Wheeler-Bennett, John. *Brest-Litovsk: The Forgotten Peace, March 1918*. London: Macmillan, 1938.

———. *The Nemesis of Power*. New York: Viking, 1967.

Williamson, Samuel R. Jr. *Austria-Hungary and the Origins of the First World War*. New York: St. Martin's, 1991.

Yates, Keith. *Flawed Victory: Jutland, 1916*. Annapolis, MD: Naval Institute, 2000.

Yergin, Daniel. *Shattered Peace: The Origins of the Cold War and the National Security State.* Boston: Sentry, 1977.

Yockelson, Mitchell A. *Borrowed Soldiers: Americans under British Command, 1918.* Norman: University of Oklahoma Press, 2008.

Young, John W. *Cold War Europe, 1945–89: A Political History.* London: Arnold, 1991.

Zaloga, Steven, and Victory Madej. *The Polish Campaign 1939.* New York: Hippocrene, 1991.

Zeman, Z. A. B. *The Gentlemen Negotiators: A Diplomatic History of World War I.* New York: Macmillan, 1971.

INDEX